Fields of change among the Iteso of Kenya

International Library of Anthropology

Editor: Adam Kuper, University of Leiden

Arbor Scientiae
Arbor Vitae

A catalogue of other Social Science books published by Routledge and Kegan Paul will be found at the end of this volume.

Fields of change among the Iteso of Kenya

Ivan Karp

Department of Anthropology
University of Indiana

Routledge & Kegan Paul

London, Henley and Boston

First published in 1978
by Routledge & Kegan Paul.Ltd
39 Store Street,
London WC1E 7DD,
Broadway House,
Newtown Road,
Henley-on-Thames,
Oxon RG9 1EN and
9 Park Street,
Boston, Mass. 02108, USA
Printed in Great Britain by
Weatherby Woolnough,
Wellingborough, Northants
Copyright Ivan Karp 1978

British Library Cataloguing in Publication Data

Karp, Ivan
Fields of change among the Iteso of
Kenya. – (International library of
anthropology).
1. Teso tribe – Social life and customs
I. Title   II. Series
301.29'676'27   DT433.542   78-40170

ISBN 0 7100 8863 9

Contents

Illustrations

Figures

Maps

Tables

Preface

Fieldwork among the Iteso was carried out from July 1969 to July 1971. The research was financed by a fellowship and research grant from the US National Institute of Mental Health. During this period I spent 22 months among the Iteso, the remaining 2 months were spent in consultations with colleagues at the Institute of African Studies in Nairobi, Kenya, and the Makerere Institute of Social Research in Kampala, Uganda. I was affiliated as a research associate at both institutes. I am grateful to the staff of both of these institutions for the time and facilities that they afforded me. Professor Peter Rigby of Makerere University College was especially generous in the time and effort that he devoted to easing the problems of research and discussing the implications of the study. Both his personal attention and his published work on the Gogo have aided in the completion of this study.

The first 6 months of field research were devoted to a general survey of Iteso social organization and to language study. The next 14 months were devoted to an intensive participant-oriented study of one neighbourhood. The final 4 months were spent in conducting a statistical survey of 200 households and in examining selected neighbourhoods in different parts of the Iteso locations. I was able to dispense with a translator after about 13 months of fieldwork - except for public occasions and court cases, where I was unable to keep up with the flow of speech. In addition to participant-observation and the household survey, I had three literate informants keep diaries for a period of a year. I also collected a number of texts on ritual. The spelling of vernacular words corresponds to that established by Father Kiggen in his Ateso dictionaries. The language of the people is called *Ateso*. They call themselves the *Iteso*. One of them is an *Etesot* (male) or *Atesot* (female).

Anthropological research is a corporate effort and I imagine that every anthropologist thinks that the virtues of his work are due more to the efforts of others than to himself. Certainly this is true in my case. Professor Daniel Scheans introduced me to the field of anthropology and provided me with a model of how an anthropologist ought to behave. I owe a great deal to my teachers in social anthropology: Charles Kaut, William Watson and E.H. Winter. Professor Kaut carefully read and provided helpful comments on an early draft. I have also benefited from discussions with William Arens, Randall Packard, Arnold Sio, Jack Alexander, Dan F. Bauer, David Rheubottom and Anthony Stellato. In the field I was aided by the comments of Dr David Parkin, Professor Peter Rigby and Professor P.H. Gulliver. Professor E.H. Winter provided the training and supervision that made this study possible.

My greatest debt is to the Iteso people. They put up with a great deal of questioning and always returned kindness. Albert Otiti, Chief Raphael Okisai, Gastory Opetoi, Paul Aura, Cornel Ijaja, Mark Odera, Rosemary Imodoi, Michael Okapulu, Salome Atyang, Africanus Etyang, Cornel Edewa, Elunga'at Odiit and my assistant Ernest Aura are only a few of the many who should be mentioned. Finally, this book would probably not exist except for two women who made strenuous efforts on my behalf. The first is my Iteso 'mother', Fulgaria Toto, who took an overly inquisitive stranger in hand and tried her best to teach him to behave like a proper Etesot. The other is my wife, Patty, a better field anthropologist than myself, who shared all of the disadvantages of fieldwork and few of the benefits. To both of them this book is gratefully dedicated.

Ivan Karp

NOTE

The following symbols are used to denote genealogical connections throughout the book:

B	= Brother	S	= Son
Z	= Sister	D	= Daughter
F	= Father	H	= Husband
M	= Mother	W	= Wife
C	= Child	A	= Affine

1 Introduction

I

I shall attempt to describe and analyse changing patterns
of social organization among the Southern Iteso, a relatively small ethnic group of Eastern Nilotic-speaking cul-
tivators living in a predominantly Bantu-speaking area of
Kenya and Uganda. They are virtually all avowed Christians of one denomination or another, but certain traditional pagan ceremonies are practised enthusiastically by
the entire population. They practice a form of sedentary
cultivation. However, until fifteen years ago they had a
very high rate of household mobility. They were the last
ethnic group to enter the Eastern Uganda-Western Kenya
region and, in the course of pushing all tribes before
them, instituted a reign of terror that has influenced
the history and cultural geography of the entire area.
Virtually nothing remains of the political organization
on which their military successes were based. The Northern Iteso and the Southern group separated over one hundred years ago. The political organization of the Northern and Southern Iteso now differ markedly.(1) The Southern Iteso have developed a system of neighbourhood organization that has not been reported for any of the
surrounding societies.

Given the impressions recorded above, it would seem a
description of social change among the Southern Iteso is
not a difficult task. In fact, the description of patterns of change is one of the most difficult tasks in
social anthropology because on comparison it appears sub-
jective in nature. One observer may describe a given
society as changing and another as not changing at all if
they focus on different aspects of that society. In other
words the location of the social facts we call 'change'
are not the same in different societies or even in the

same society - unlike social facts anthropologists call
'politics' or 'economics'. An anecdote from my fieldwork
illustrates this problem very well. The Iteso live on
both sides of the Kenya-Uganda border. There is an immigration and customs post at the border in Malaba. One
day, while I was at the post, the chief immigration officer asked what I was doing so far in the 'bush'. I
explained that I was an anthropologist studying the
surrounding people, the Iteso. The immigration officer
was a young man who had completed a degree in sociology at
the University of Nairobi only six months previously. He
regarded his immigration work as only temporary and hoped
to obtain a grant to do graduate work. He perceived himself as a sophisticated observer and was keen to impress
me with his sophistication. We discussed our experiences
among the Iteso and finally he asked me what dimensions of
their society I was investigating. 'Social change', I
replied. He stared rather fixedly at a mud hut about
thirty yards away. 'That ought to be easy,' he said,
'these people haven't changed since the Europeans came to
Kenya.'

Clearly the immigration officer's impression and the
one I give above are at considerable odds. The Iteso have
a reputation as one of the most 'backward' agricultural
societies in Kenya today. This is certainly the way in
which they are regarded by the surrounding Bantu-speaking
ethnic groups. It is not difficult to understand that
what the immigration officer means by 'social change' is
really economic development. When the Catholic priest at
a local mission told me that the Iteso were very backward,
he meant that they did not come to church very often. I
would guess that an anthropologist with a different set of
interests than myself could perceive Iteso society as
relatively unchanged.

It can be seen that unless one is concerned with analysing the great historical transformations that societies
have undergone, such as the transition from feudal to
industrial society, the problems of describing the locus
and direction of social change have often been insurmount-
able. I would suggest that one of the difficulties has
been that many anthropologists have taken social change
per se as something that merits analysis and description.
(2) Their studies are based on the indisputable assumption that change is an aspect of all social life. (One
of the chapters of Moore's excellent text on social
change is entitled The Normality of Change (1963).) To
say only that a society is changing is to make the most
banal of statements. It is sociologically more interesting to assume that different aspects of given societies

are changing at different rates. Then it will follow that
any specific discussion of change in a society will be an
attempt to explain differential rates of change in different societal sub-systems. As a consequence, any explanation of change can be directly related to an analysis of
the relationship between the various sub-systems.

Cohen (1968) sums up very nicely both the problems of
studying social change and the direction in which any analysis ought to proceed:

> The idea that sociology can provide a single theory of
> change is a myth. Social systems provide many sources
> of change. To attempt to reduce these to a single fac-
> tor is to believe that social change is a specific phe-
> nomenon which must have very specific causes. (p.204)

Given the above he states: 'there are two broad problem
areas in the theoretical study of social change. The
first is concerned with the factors or mechanisms which
produce change. The second is concerned with general
characteristics of the course of change.' (p. 178).
This monograph will proceed exactly along these lines.
First, I shall specify those aspects of Iteso society that
have changed most rapidly, and then I shall examine the
influences on the direction of change among the Iteso.

In chapters 2 and 3, I describe the changing political
system of the Iteso. The primary political changes have
been in the scale and content of leadership patterns, and
these changes are due primarily to the British colonial
penetration and political domination. These external
influences did not determine the direction of political
change, however. Given the limitations placed on the size
and composition of political groups by colonialism, the
form of political organization that developed, the neighbourhood, was an adaptation to patterns of kinship and
processes occurring within domestic groups. Chapters 4
and 6 are concerned to describe areas of conservatism and
change in the Iteso kinship system. In them I distinguish between two aspects of kinship. The first aspect,
the political and social control aspect of relations among
kinsmen and affines, has been subject to change because of
its association with the political dimension of Iteso
society. The second aspect, kinship as a set of ideas
that define social identities, has remained more constant.
In chapter 7, I describe these patterns of persistence and
change in a single Iteso locality. Finally, in chapter 8,
I conclude by relating these changes to Fortes's (1969)
scheme for analysing kinship-based societies.

II

The Iteso live in one of the more linguistically and
ethnically complicated areas of East Africa. Historical
evidence indicates that the region has been an area of
complex ethnic interaction and mixing for at least one
millennium (Sutton, 1970). There is no particular name
for the region since as the result of an historical acci-
dent it was divided between the Uganda Protectorate and
the East Africa Protectorate (later Kenya Colony) in 1902.
Packard (MS) refers to the area as the Eastern Uganda-
Western Kenya border area (see Map 1). Elgon-Nyanza is a
better term since the region does lie between Mt Elgon on
the north and Lake Victoria-Nyanza on the south. But this
was the name of a district in Colonial Kenya and would
make for even more confusion, since I am concerned with an
area bordered by the Western Highlands of the Great Rift
Valley which shade into the Uasin Gishu Plateau on the
east and the Interlacustrine kingdoms of Busoga on the
west.
     There is an ecological boundary on the east and a poli-
tical boundary on the west. On the north the region is
bounded by Mt Elgon and the northern deserts and on the
south by Lake Victoria (see Maps 1 and 2).
     There are four different language groups represented
in the region. These are: (a) Eastern Bantu; (b) Eastern
Nilotes; (c) Northern Nilotes; and (d) Southern Nilotes.
There are probably well over fifty different ethnic groups
represented in the area. The groups with whom the Southern Iteso have had the most contact are the Northern
Nilotic speaking Padhola and Luo, the Southern Nilotic
Kony and various of the Eastern Bantu-speaking Abaluyia
ethnic groups. During the pre-colonial period the
Abaluyia societies were all politically independent and
frequently at war with each other. At present there are
seventeen distinct Abaluyia 'subtribes' of heterogeneous
origins (see Were, 1967a). The most important as far as
the Iteso were concerned are the following: Babukusu -
closely related to the Bagishu of Uganda. They occupied
the territory of the Iteso on the Kenya side of the border and were driven out by the Iteso. Bakhayo - live to
the south of the Iteso. They are traditional allies of
the Iteso and there is considerable intermarriage between
the two tribes even at present. Wanga - the only Baluyia
kingdom. The Wanga kings used Iteso mercenaries to fight
their enemies - particular the Luo. The Iteso were conquered by a Wanga-British alliance.
     By about 1830 the ethnic composition of the Western
Kenya-Eastern Uganda border area was essentially the same

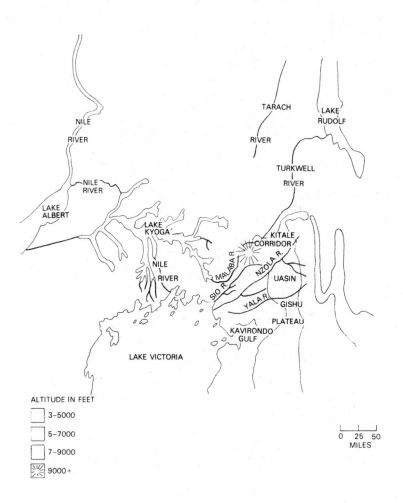

MAP 1   Eastern Uganda - Western Kenya border area

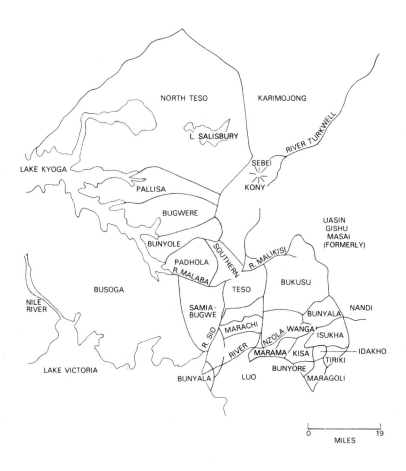

MAP 2   Ethnic map of Eastern Uganda – Western Kenya border area

as at present, except for the Iteso intrusions. By 1902
the areas occupied by the different ethnic groups had been
stabilized under the 'Pax Britanica'. On the whole the
Iteso were the biggest losers in terms of territory, but
this may have been partially the result of Iteso reverses
prior to the coming of the British.

Colonial influence on the area was exerted from two
directions: first, from Jinja in Busoga and second, from
Mumias in Wanga (see Map 2). The territorial transfer of
Western Kenya to the East African Protectorate from the
Uganda Protectorate legitimized this situation. . The Iteso
were partitioned by the established border. The Kenya
part of the region had been conquered by Wanga who were
acting on behalf of the Colonial officials at Mumias
around 1895-1900. The area tended to be administered by
the Wanga until the East African Railway went through in
1920. At that point administrative interest in the border
area increased, although it has never been very intense.

After the transfer, the Kenya side of the region was
split into a number of districts. Until 1909 the area,
which was controlled from Mumias, was called the Elgon
district. In 1909 its name was changed to the North Kavirondo district but it still remained under Wanga influence. In 1948 the name of the district was changed to
North Nyanza. In 1956 North Nyanza district was split in
two - North Nyanza and Elgon Nyanza. The Iteso were
joined together administratively with their traditional
enemies, the Babukusu, into a new district, called Elgon-
Nyanza. In 1963, largely as a result of Iteso-Babukusu
animosity, the Iteso were separated from Elgon-Nyanza
(which was then renamed Bungoma District) and placed with
their Southern Abaluyia neighbours to form Busia District
of the new Western Province of Kenya. In addition some
alteration of boundaries were made to conform with the
actual ethnic make-up of the populations.

Kenya today is divided into six provinces. The Iteso
live in Western Province, Busia District. There are three
districts in the province. Busia is the smallest in both
population and size. Economically it is also the poorest.
Busia District is divided into three Divisions. The
Northern Division is occupied primarily by Iteso and the
Central and Southern Divisions primarily by Abaluyia with
some Iteso and Luo speakers intermixed. The Northern Division is administered from the District Headquarters in
Busia Township. The highest administrative official, the
District Officer for the Northern Division, is under the
authority of the District Commissioner. The District
Officer is always selected from an area outside the pro-
vince and often is a trained administrator. The Division

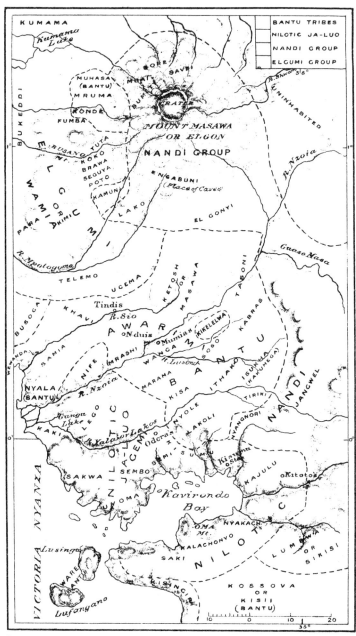

(by courtesy of the Royal Anthropological Institute)

MAP 3   Map of Kavirondo, British East Africa, showing racial distribution. Taken from Hobley, 'Eastern Uganda', plate 1

is divided into two locations. The location is the primary administrative unit for local populations in Kenya.
Almost all services (except for some District Health services) are administered through the location administration. The location is headed by an official chosen from
the local population and called a 'chief'. Northern Division of Busia has two locations called North and South
Teso. Each has its own chief. Each chief has under him
six sub-chiefs, each of whom is in charge of a sub-location. The sub-chief again is a locally chosen, paid, but
untrained, government official. Each sub-chief has from
five to twelve unpaid headmen called either a *lok'alipo*
(Ateso word) or *luguru* (Baluyia word). The headmen tend
to be experienced elders. They receive income from fees
for adjudicating cases and hearing complaints. All officials are responsible for the dissemination of information
about government directives, compliance from local populations, referral of conflicts to the judicial system,
enforcements of laws, and, finally, the collection of
taxes. In form, the administrative system is little different than in the colonial period. It has simply grown
as social services have increased. There is an elected
District Council, but their powers have decreased rather
than increased in independent Kenya. The important element to note is that authority remains externally imposed
since local officials are responsible to their superiors
rather than to the local population, who have no choice in
the selection of officials.

III

The term 'Southern Iteso' distinguishes the Iteso of Busia
District, Kenya, and Bukedi District, Uganda, from the
Northern Iteso who live in Teso District of Eastern Province, Uganda. Linguistically, they belong to the Teso-
Karimojong branch of Eastern Nilotic languages. The other
branch of Eastern Nilotes is the Maasai-speaking language
family.(3) The languages of the 'Teso-Karimojong cluster'
are Karimojong, Jie, Turkana, Dodoth, Didinga, Toposa, and
Northern and Southern Iteso. All languages are mutually
intelligible.
  Most societies of the Teso-Karimojong cluster have a
myth of common origin (see Gulliver, 1952). Historical
evidence clearly indicates, however, that each group is an
amalgam of elements of the different ethnic groups with
whom they have been in contact at various times (Nagashima, 1968/9). The Southern Iteso were until the late
nineteenth Century part of a continuous Iteso belt

stretching from the Northern Teso-Karimojong area to the
west and north of Mt Elgon through Pallisa, Bugwere and so
on to half of present-day Bukusu territory (see Map 2).
Now the Iteso are spatially separated from the Northern
Iteso.   In any case they differ significantly from the
Northern Iteso in many respects.   Linguistically, they are
probably closer to the Karimojong since their language has
not been influenced by Baganda conquest.   The same can be
said for other aspects of Iteso culture.   This also
appears to be true for the Southern Iteso living on the
Uganda side of the Border but contiguous to the Kenya members of the group.   In any case I doubt whether any general description could encompass the variety of social
structures found among the Northern Iteso.

In the remainder of this book I shall treat the Southern Iteso as a separate entity.   Therefore, when I refer
to the Iteso I mean the Southern Iteso only.   The only
really reliable data I have for the Southern Iteso on the
Uganda side of the border is historical and even that is
limited in depth.(4)

According to the 1969 census there are a total of
85,800 Iteso in Kenya.   If we add to that the probable
65,000 Southern Iteso in Uganda, this gives an approximate
total of 150,000 Iteso in all.   There are some 600,000
Northern Iteso - all of whom live in Uganda.   In Kenya
the Iteso are to be found primarily in Busia District of
Kenya where the 1969 census found 61,044 Iteso.   There are
13,433 Iteso in Bungoma District, almost all of whom live
in areas contiguous to Northern Division, Busia.   There
are another 5,364 in the Trans-Nzoia District of Rift
Valley Province.   The remaining 5,000 or so are scattered
throughout Kenya.   Most of these Iteso live in settlement
schemes in the Kimilili Forest.

There is in the Northern Division of Busia District a
population of about 55,348.   About 97 per cent of these
are Iteso.   The others are primarily Babukusu and Bakhayo
Luyia speakers.   Intermixed among the Iteso are a few
descendants of the Uasin Gishu Maasai who were driven from
the Western Rift Highlands by other Maasai-speaking
groups.(5)

The Iteso have experienced considerable population
increase since colonial times.   As all but the most recent
estimates of the total population of the Iteso are probably unreliable I shall refrain from comparing the total
numbers of Iteso at different times.   Instead I will deal
with the population density of Northern Division Busia.
The Northern Division is an area of some 217 square miles
(557 sq. kilometres).   The 1969 census gives a population
density of about 245 persons per square mile.   The 1962

census gives a density of 217 and the figure for 1949 is
155. Between 1948 and 1962 the population grew by 40 per
cent and between 1962 and 1969 it increased by 13 per
cent. No matter what questions are raised about the reliability of the census data there can be no question that
the Iteso are experiencing severe and rapid population
growth. If there has been a pattern of sustained population growth since the early colonial period, this would
verify the very earliest estimates of population at well
under 50 per sq. mile. Presently the Iteso areas have the
lowest population densities for Western Kenya. There is
evidence that this was also true for the pre-contact
periods.

IV

The Northern Division of Busia is a series of hills running north and south. The altitude varies between 3,500
and 4,000 feet. The Iteso have occupied these central
hills and flatlands surrounding them. Geologically the
area consists of a granite base with volcanic overlays.
Granite outcroppings are to be found in all parts of the
Teso hills. Soils vary from sandy to clayey loams which
are generally well drained but only moderately fertile.
The depth of the topsoil is shallow (Scott, 1969).
     The technical term for the type of land occupied by the
Iteso is high-rainfall savannah and the average rainfalls
do vary from 50 to 65 inches per year throughout the Division. This does not mean, however, that there is a
regular and even distribution of rain either within the
same year or from year to year. Rainfall presents serious problems for the Iteso for two reasons. First, rainfall is extremely localized. It travels across areas in
very narrow belts that do not affect any large part of
the Division. Second, rain varies considerably from year
to year so that there is a very low level of predictability as to what will be the amount to fall in any given
month. Table 1 sets out rainfall figures for the month of
May over the course of five years at two different stations in the Northern Division.
     During the two years I was among the Iteso, one year of
mild drought was followed by a year of severe flooding.
This makes Teso agriculture a very precarious occupation
for so well watered an area. Cassava was introduced during the late 1920s as a famine relief crop and has been
taken up with enthusiasm. This has eased some of the difficulties caused by climatic vagaries. Iteso informants
say in the past a bad year in one area would increase the

TABLE 1   Rainfall in two localities*

Year	Kolanya	Angu'rom
1966	3.59	4.48
1967	13.32	bad gauge
1968	7.10	9.29
1969	1.53	8.01
1970	34.31	6.13

*Measured in inches

already high rate of residential mobility as people moved
to live with their more fortunate relatives.

Precolonial Iteso agriculture was based on the cultivation of eleusine. Even at present it is still the major
food crop in many areas. Now it is eaten mixed with cassava, and large portions of the crop go into making a form
of beer which graces almost every social occasion. Varieties of sorghum are sometimes grown and a few groves of
green bananas are found in some homes. Women grow green
leafy vegetables in gardens close to their houses. Except
for the plowing or preparation of land, the growing and
preparing of food crops is almost entirely in the hands of
women. Each woman is in charge of the crops that will be
used at her hearth. In the past but not at present men
often grew and kept separate large amounts of eleusine
which they used for making beer to entertain visitors.

There are two main cash crops which are grown in different seasons - maize and cotton. Both are purchased at
controlled prices by the government Maize Produce Board.
A large portion of the crop was smuggled across the border
to Uganda before currency restrictions were imposed and
Uganda money became worthless in Kenya. The Northern Division of Busia produces more cotton than any other area of
Kenya. Every household has at least some small cotton
fields.

Each adolescent and adult usually has his or her own
fields. Men grow considerably more cash crops than women.
A husband is not required to prepare fields for his wife's
cash crops, but a woman often uses a fallowed field of her
husband's. Nowadays most fields are dug up by means of an
ox plow instead of the traditional hoe. About one quarter
of all households own their own oxen and plough, or share
the ownership of them with another household. Otherwise
they rent. Because of climatic uncertainty and the kinds
of crops that Iteso grow (particularly cotton) an important
scarce resource for Iteso is time. Much of the labour
input into farming is communal. This is done through the

institution of the neighbourhood beer party. Large labour
input for short periods is needed. By maximizing the
horizontal and egalitarian ties of neighbourhood organization the Iteso have devised a means of finding the required labour. The Iteso are only beginning to practice any
system of crop rotation. Most households use fields for
four to five years until they are exhausted and then let
them lie fallow. There is no particular pattern of planting except that cassava, which does well in poor soil, is
planted last.

The Iteso must be characterized as a subsistence plus
cash economy (see Winter, n.d.). In 1969 a survey of 112
households produced a mean household income of approximately ₤ 47.00 and a median income of approximately ₤27.00.
Income varied between nothing and ₤ 245.00 per year. The
area of the survey, however, was unusual in that a large
portion of income was derived from jobs at a secondary
school and government offices. If household income based
only on money received from sale of crops is calculated
the figure drops to a mean household income of ₤ 12.00.
This figure is low even for Busia District. It is difficult to see how income will increase so long as the major
cash crop is cotton, which requires a very high labour
input, except, of course, for rises in the price of cotton
and maize on the world market.

Cattle are an important nexus of value for the Iteso.
A sample of forty households kept a total of 109 cows.
This yields a mean of 4.15 per household and a mean 0.72
per capita. Cattle are sources of bridewealth, milk
(including considerable income from milk), oxen for plowing, and prestige. It is always said of a heavy man that
he has grown fat 'because he has milk in his home'.
Cattle were the traditional means to political power because they could be exchanged for followers. There is, as
in other Eastern Nilotic cattle-keeping groups, an extensive vocabulary devoted to describing cattle. Cattle circulate through many different hands as a result of marital
exchanges, kinship obligations and stock contracts. In a
stock contract a man negotiates to give a number of cows
to another man to keep for him. The cattle and their offspring may be taken back at any time (less a fee for good
care). The milk of the cows belongs to the household in
which the cows are kept. These stock contracts are a frequent source of litigation. It is not possible to calcu-
late precisely the number of cattle loaned out, as Iteso
are very reticent about this topic, but of the 109 cattle
in the 40 households sampled, at least 43 (or 39 per cent)
were on loan to household heads. Men are in charge of the
care of cows outside the home. There are no rights in

grazing and a person may graze his cows on whatever land
he wishes. As land is becoming an increasingly scarce
commodity, unrestricted grazing is a source of considerably conflict. The only way an Etesot can prevent other
people from grazing on his land is to enclose it with
sisal or barbed wire fencing. Fencing is a capital outlay
that few Iteso can afford.

The Iteso do not live in any form of nucleated villages. Their houses are spread out in a seemingly random
fashion across the landscape, but people do tend to build
near the boundaries of their land and near to their
neighbours' homes. The major unit of social organization
is a vaguely bounded neighbourhood. Any higher level of
political organization has been imposed from outside by
the colonial government and the national administration
(see chapter 3). Until the mid-1950s, the neighbourhood
system was maintained by a high rate of residential mobility. With the increasing scarcity of land and the introduction of individual land tenure, this rate of residential mobility is now virtually nil. The Iteso are patrilineal, but all forms of descent groups are dispersed.
Residence after marriage is patrilocal with a tendency
toward neolocality associated with a pattern of mild
ritual avoidance between fathers and sons. Households,
ideally, should be occupied by a polygynous family and
about half do achieve this ideal. Generationally extended families are not encountered. Women occupy separate
sleeping houses and have their own hearths, but they have
no status or authority in the political-jural domain and,
consequently, cannot be 'de jure' household heads. Very
few households have 'de facto' female heads.

Except for a few of the oldest people, almost all
Iteso are nominal Christians. This means that most of
them have been baptized, but very few attend church.
The majority are Catholics. There are three Catholic
Missions in the Division and one Salvation Army centre.
There are a few Anglicans, but Islam has never made any
inroads among the Iteso. This may be the result of the
Iteso's lack of involvement with traders from the Coast.
The only Moslems are the few men who claim the religion in
order to get a fee for slaughtering at a public market.

It is difficult to determine what it means to be a
Christian for the Iteso. They are largely unaware of
religious dogmas. They have a mundane attitude toward
their own religious ceremonies, hence it is not surprising
that they take a pragmatic attitude toward their Christ-
ianity.

The Iteso have retained those parts of their traditional religious practices that are socially relevant and
discarded those which no longer apply.

2 The precolonial political system

I

The evolution and development of Iteso forms of social
organization cannot be understood without first examining
the historical context in which they have occurred. While
this is a valid principle for any kind of sociological
analysis, it is particularly relevant to the Iteso material because the area which is both the present Western
Province of Kenya and Bukedi District of Uganda is one of
the most ethnically heterogeneous regions in all of
Africa. In addition, it has been the scene of a bewilder-
ing variety of tribal migrations, religious influences,
and patterns of domination.(1)

I can only quote with approval Wright's (1958) comments on Lawrance's general monograph on the Northern
Iteso:

> The important migration of the Iteso through Bukedea
> and Pallisa into Bugwere and Budama and over the
> border into Kenya (Elgon Nyanza) forms an essential
> piece of tribal history, which could advantageously be
> included in a book of this title.... Teso political
> relationships with the Sebei and Bagishu tribes along
> the foothills of Masaba (Mt. Elgon), with the Bagwere
> and Jo pa Dhola in the plains of Mbale and Tororo dis-
> tricts and with the Jo Pa Owiny and Baluhya, as they
> spread over what is now the Kenya border, are of
> importance.

Much research, especially on the Uganda side of the
border, is still to be undertaken.(2) The best that I
can hope to do here, in the absence of a great deal of
this information, is to present a brief account of the
political environment of the Iteso institutions that I
shall describe later in the chapter.

Iteso are aware of their affinity to the other tribes

of the Karimojong cluster. They state that they were originally members of the Karimojong tribe which migrated
south. The Karimojong who remained behind told the younger men who were pushing on that they were going to their
graves, *atesin* - hence, the Iteso. The people who stayed
in Karimoja were called the 'tired old men' - *Ikarimojong*.
This story, along with an account of the Southern Sudanic
origins of the Iteso, may also be found in Lawrance (1957,
pp. 7-9).(3)

Migration is the central theme of the few historical
tales that the Iteso relate. A recent novel concerned
with the nineteenth century history of the Iteso, 'Restless Feet' (Erapu, 1969), is concerned with the obsess-
ional search by generations of Iteso for a promised land
to the South. In the genealogies that I collected it was
unusual for both a father and son to have died and been
buried in the same place. Frequently their graves were
said to be at important stopping places along a migration
route. A typical progression could be Bukedea - Kacum-
bala - Tororo - Malaba - Amukura. Men were usually said
to have died fighting the enemy and driving him from the
land the Iteso were to occupy. There can be no question
that Iteso penetration once reached as far as Sang'alo
hill in Bungoma District but they were driven back from
there toward the end of the nineteenth century (see
chapter 3).

The Iteso entry into Bukedi seems to have been peace-
ful at first. Ogot (1967) speaks of Iteso pioneers as
coming in 'drips and drabs'. It is only after warfare
became endemic in the area that he refers to the 'Iteso
hordes'. The Iteso were occupied in continuous warfare
with the Babukusu, part of whose territory they occupied.
They also describe battles with the Samia and later the
Jo Padhola, all people with whom they competed for territory.

Earlier there was considerable intermarriage with some
Jo Padhola groups (Ogot, 1967). According to Iteso oral
tradition, Shiundu, the King of the Wanga, allied himself
with the Iteso (probably about 1860) to drive the Luo of
Gem further to the south; an alliance which provides us
with two interesting and improbable stories. Iteso say
that, in gratitude for Iteso help, Shiundu called his son
Mumia after the Iteso (also known as the Wamia). Many
Wanga deny this story. The Iteso also claim that the Luo
gave them the name Bakidi or Bakedi because of their
fierceness in fighting. *Kidi* is the Luo word for stone.
Iteso say the Luo saw the Iteso fighting so hard that they
said 'these people must be made of stone'. Some Luo informants have confirmed this story, but it should also be

noted that *kedi* is a Luganda word for 'nakedness' and
Bakedi was the Baganda word for peoples of Western Kenya
and Eastern and Northern Uganda, a sort of Baganda equivalent of the Greek 'barbarian'. Bishop Hannington, the
Anglican martyr killed by the Baganda, is reputed to have
said that the peoples of Western Kenya were the 'most
naked and the most moral' that he had ever seen.

The most important Iteso alliance on the Kenya side of
the border was with the Bakhayo Luhia. Frequent intermarriage has occurred between Bakhayo and Iteso as well as
considerable trade, with the Iteso exchanging cows for
Bakhayo pots and Marachi spears. Even the Iteso-Bakhayo
alliance was often broken by mutual raids. Peters (1891,
pp. 306-7) was present at an Iteso raid on the Bakhayo.

Iteso patterns of warfare were regarded by the surrounding peoples as particularly brutal and terrifying. The
surprise raid at night seems to have been their major
tactic. Continuous raiding and an exceptional amount of
slaughter went on until the local inhabitants fled and
then the area was pioneered by Iteso.(4)

Peters (1891) and Thomson (1885) are the only two European travellers to give any account of the Iteso. Their
perspectives and attitudes were derived from the surrounding societies, and this gives us some insight into the
terror that the Iteso caused. Thomson describes travelling through areas totally devastated by the Iteso; he
saw ruined villages largely deserted except for a few
terrified inhabitants. As far as he is concerned the
Iteso lived up to their reputation. Peters was approached
by Sakwa, the chief of lower Wanga, who apparently offered
Peters his chiefdom in exchange for protection from the
Iteso. I quote from Peters's account in which he describes a conversation that occurred after he sent some of
his men with guns to beat off an Iteso attack.

'Two hours to the north of this place', said he [The
'Sultan Sakwa'], 'dwells the robber tribe of the
Mangati [another Iteso name], in a land which we call
Ngoro. These people are continually making inroads
into my territory, threatening my herds, and burning
down my villages. They have laid waste the whole west,
from the Nsoia River. I have begged the English re-
peatedly to beat back these Mangati, and offered, if
they would do this, to accept their flag for Kawirondo.
But the English are people of fear; they have shut
themselves up in their stations, and are afraid of
strife with the Mangati. Now you Germans are come,
you who have beaten the Maassai themselves, I will give
you all my Askaries. You shall then beat the Mangatti
and I will accept your flag, and give you half the

cattle that shall be taken from the Mangati'....
'Well, we will come under your protection. You shall
be our lord if you beat the Mangati for us'. (1891,
pp. 306-7) (5)

This account gives some idea of just how successful the
Iteso were as a warrior people. I also hope that I have
indicated the complexity of ethnic interaction that is
found in the general area. I turn now to Iteso political
institutions and their relationship to this historical
context.

II

This section of the chapter attempts to describe a political system which no longer exists and which may never have
existed. By that I mean I am attempting to construct an
organizational pattern solely from information gathered
from informants who have never participated as adults in
the system they were trying to describe to me. Thus, the
material that is to be analysed, and this point must be
emphasized, is an incomplete and idealized account of a
political system whose operation was never seen by informants. Since I am attempting historical sociology rather
than history, the validity of this effort at an analysis
could be called into question. It is a truism that verbal
accounts of the operation of organizations tend toward the
ideal. One way to get at the actual patterns as opposed
to their idealized versions is to collect case material,
particularly of instances of conflict, and to question
informants about the discrepancy between the idealized
description and the actual instances that they have given
you. This was impossible in the present instance because
my informants simply had no repertoire of cases to give
me. They were only able to pass on their accounts of what
their fathers had told them.

My research strategy was to visit as many different
sub-locations on the Kenya side of the Iteso area as
possible and question knowledgeable elders about precolonial political organization. I concentrated on the political organization because it was clearly in that domain
that change had been most extensive. The complete absence
of even a residual form of the age system or of corporate
territorial organization was something that I found very
puzzling from the beginning of my research. It was only
after about eight or nine months of sporadic questioning
that I was able to elicit an indigenous term for the traditional age organizations. On the basis of the interviews in the various areas I constructed a composite and,

I hoped, coherent description of the traditional political
organization. Then, in interviews with my better informants, I tested this description and rejected disputed
elements that could not be accounted for by regional variation. There was no significant regional variation that I
could find, not even in the pattern of names for the various age groups. One of the major difficulties of the research was that I had to proceed by asking about the
social significance of the various terms for the traditional territorial and age groups. These terms, like
other important Iteso social concepts, referred to a variety of levels of organization and I found that a question
about one level of organization often elicited an answer
referring to another level.

As I proceeded with the questioning of informants I
recognized my original insight to be correct; the functions of the traditional institutions that no longer
existed were primarily political in nature. My informants' explanation of the operation of these institutions
related to the problem of maintaining order. Therefore, I
will analyse these institutions from a political rather
than from a religious or kinship-based perspective. It
will be seen that the age organization in particular has
implications for an understanding of Iteso religion, but
I have chosen to concentrate on the political implications of the religious aspects of Iteso age organization
rather than on a detailed exposition of the ritual and
symbolism involved.

Since I am dealing with an ideal system and attempting
to describe political structures rather than political
processes, I have found Schapera's (1956) approach to be
the most useful. For him the political domain is concerned with the question of the maintenance of order and
a 'tribal political organization' is 'that aspect of the
total organization which is concerned with the establishment and maintenance of internal cooperation and external
independence' (p. 218). This approach is also utilized
by Fortes in his distinction between the domestic domain
of social life and the political-jural domain (1969, p. 95
passim.). In what follows below I discuss the contribu-
tion of territorial-, age- and kinship-based groups to
the 'maintenance of internal cooperation and external
independence'. I follow the indigenous model implicit in
informants' descriptions because the analysis is oriented
to their terms for groups based on the three principles
of territoriality, agnation, and stratification by age,
which I describe below. It is analytically necessary to
give priority to territorial groups because it is within
the framework of the territorial system that the political

significance of agnatic and age-based groups becomes clear.

Territoriality

The basic Iteso territorial group is what, following con-
ventional Africanist usage, I call a section.(6)   The
Iteso word for section is *etem*.   An etem is also a type of
fireplace that stands outside the main entrance to a house
or homestead.   The etem was also a place at which meat
from cattle killed at some public ceremonials was roasted,
marriage contracts between two families arranged, and conflicts adjudicated.
    A fireplace, etem, always stood in front of the section
leader's home and the adult men of that section gathered
here for discussion, war-councils, decision-making and the
adjudication of cases.   Young men were said to keep watch
by this fireplace at night for enemy attacks.   Through an
extension of its meaning, the word etem was applied first
to the fireplace, second to the people who gather at that
fireplace, and finally to the territory occupied by those
people.
    Unlike other ethnic groups of the Karimojong cluster,
these sections were unnamed.   Instead, they were called
after the name of the section leader whose title was
lok'etem; literally 'the one of the section'.   Thus, if
the section leader was called Palinyang, the section
would be known as Palinyang's section (etem loka Palinyang).   The section leader was said to 'own' or control
the section.   Occasionally, the exogamous clan of the
section leader was said to 'own' the section.   The section leader was primarily a war-leader.   He had overall
direction of war-parties.   He sounded a horn to call all
the people of the section to defend themselves or to go
to war.   He was in charge of dividing the spoils of
battle.   Often his home was located on an elevated place
in order to discover enemy raids and attacks.   He was
empowered to adjudicate disputes between the different
segments of the sections and he could pass a death sen-
tence on wizards.   His most important power not directly
related to warfare was the authority to appoint the
heads of the various sub-sections that composed the
section.
    The sub-section was also, rather confusingly, called an
etem by the Iteso.   The authority of the sub-section
leader vis-à-vis his sub-section was similar to that of
the section leader except that he was subordinate to, and
derived his legitimacy from, the section leader.   The
section leader was subordinate to no other person.

I could discover no formal mechanism for the selection
of a section leader. Informants' accounts suggested to me
that a section leader was chosen by general consent and on
the basis of force of personality, wealth, and prowess in
raiding and warfare. The genealogies that I collected
(see chapter 7) indicate that section and sub-section
leaders aided in the establishment of viable households
for their followers in return for political support. The
sub-section leaders, who often had affinal ties to the
section leaders, exchanged the support of their followers
for the office of sub-section head. Even though the
offices of section and sub-section leaders were articulated in terms of specific rights and duties, continued
incumbency must have depended upon the maintenance of a
fragile coalition. Systems of authority such as this,
which depend on charisma and consent, are liable to change,
either through breakdown, as in the Iteso case, or in the
further institutionalization of the office, which may
become hereditary.

The sub-section was organized around an agnatic core
composed of members of the same exogamous sub-clan. One
exogamous sub-clan would provide agnatic cores for a
number of sub-sections within different sections. This
pattern of dispersal can be associated with Iteso migrations. In practice, members of several sub-clans could
and did reside in one sub-section. Leadership positions
tended to remain within the founding exogamous sub-clan
but I suspect that numbers of non-agnatic followers
played an important part in competition for those positions. In times of warfare, which for the Iteso was an
almost perpetual condition, residents of one sub-section
formed their own war party which was under the ultimate
direction of the section leader. Raiding, as opposed to
organized warfare, was a matter for individual initiative.

Relations between sections were between individuals who
were kin or affines. Iteso assert that it was dangerous
for a person to travel to a section where he did not have
relatives to protect him.

From the above it can be seen that territorial sections
were, above all, political units. Within themselves, they
provided the arena where political competition and the
adjudication of dispute could occur. Relations between
sections and other ethnic groups were the realm of foreign
affairs. The section acted as a solidary unit vis-à-vis
any other section or ethnic group.

Sections themselves were reproduced through a process
of structural replication (Dyson-Hudson, 1966, p. 255).
New areas were settled by pioneers from a number of sub-
sections who followed an enterprising leader who became

a section head. If a prospective leader was able to
induce a sufficient number of followers to settle in an
area so that it became defensible, the success of the
settlement was ensured. These pioneers were usually
composed of three or more different groups of agnates
from different sub-sections within the same section.
Often they were later joined by non-agnatic kin from different sections. These non-agnatic kinsmen tended to be
younger brothers who had been short-changed in their inheritance in their natal sections. A group of these pioneers was called an *ekelai* (pl. *ikelai*), 'tooth'. The term
was also applied to a raiding party which was described as
always being composed of the members of the sub-section.
A war-party, which was always under the charge of a section leader, was called *ajore*, which is also the term for
'battle' or perhaps 'war'.

It is quite clear that during most of the precolonial
period the Iteso were a rapidly expanding people. Their
war tactics and fearsome reputation were enough to enable
them to terrorize a border area and cause the inhabitants
to flee. There was little need for any kind of large-
scale military organization, especially since the victims
of Iteso warfare were not given to large-scale defence or
retaliatory attacks. Rapid expansion, however, did produce the need for a form of small-scale organization which
was capable of immediate replication upon division. The
section system with its particular combination of agnation
and territoriality served very well the needs of the situation. Ideally the sub-sections were solidary groups
which were capable of combining with a number of like
groups into a larger scale war-making and adjudicative
unit. This meant that the components of the section could
(and often did) have different territorial origins. Yet
because the sections themselves were conceived of as being
composed of a number of localized agnatic groups, there
was no discrepancy between the actuality of differential
origins and the indigenous theory of section composition.

I am tempted to adapt Sahlin's (1967) terminology and
call the Iteso political organization a 'segmentary section system'. The section was a social institution that
allowed small solidary raiding groups from different areas
to come together to exploit a new territory and was also
capable of expansion by reproducing itself. An unanswered
question regarding this interpretation is that there
should be some form of prior relationship between the sub-
section heads - perhaps of an affinal kind. The limited
information available indicates that this was the case. I
must say that I am dubious as to whether (given the shal-
lowness of Iteso genealogical memory) further inquiries

would elicit any more information. There can be no doubt,
however, that the Iteso conceived of the founding members
of a sub-section as a number of agnates of one part of a
localized sub-clan who would later bring in followers who
were sisters' children and wives' brothers as well as
younger brothers.

Agnation

Ekitekere (pl. *itekeriok*) translates as the Iteso word for
tribe, clan, exogamous sub-clan, and even minimal patrilineage depending upon the context. On the other hand,
the word *ekek,* whose primary meaning is 'door', may be
used for the minimal patrilineage, exogamous sub-clan,
and, occasionally, even the clan itself. The only way to
distinguish among these groups when discussing them with
the Iteso is on the basis of function. Thus, the clan
becomes 'those who share the same name'; the exogamous
sub-clan, 'those who may not marry each other'; and the
minimal patrilineage, 'those who share meat at a funeral'.
The most inclusive agnatic unit found among the Iteso is a
name-sharing unit which I call a nominal clan. This nominal clan is divided into various exogamous sub-units which
I call sub-clans. The people of any sub-clan share a
number of taboos which they believe are exclusive to their
clan, and those residing in a given locality participate
in domestic ceremonies together. The minimal patrilineage
is the group within which efforts are made to trace bonds
of common kinship. This group emerges during funeral
ritual. It is a group of shallow genealogical depth,
going back one or two generations from the senior adult
living members.
  The sub-clan was the vengeance-sharing group among the
Iteso. Cattle extracted for the death of a member were
shared among the members of the clan who were resident in
any one area. Here, as in many other aspects of their
social life, Iteso practice differed from ideology. A
homicide against a co-resident of a sub-section obliged a
person to participate in a vengeance group whether he belonged to a different clan or not. Members of one sub-
clan who were resident in different sections also participated in the vengeance group. The consequence of this
rule was to unite members of a residentially dispersed
sub-clan into one unit.
  During the precolonial period that I am discussing in
this chapter, the Iteso ideology of agnation was rather
more explicit. In addition to the terms which are generally applied to nominal clan and lineage, ekitekere and

ekek, there was another term in use which was most often
applied to the exogamous sub-clan. This was the word
erute, which translates as 'gate'. The model that the
Iteso used for their agnatic terminology is that of the
traditional plan of the Iteso homestead. The words for
the various agnatic groups are derived from increasingly
more comprehensive parts of the traditional homestead.
The word *etogo* (house) is used to describe a matrisegment
composed of a woman and her children in a polygynous
household. An ekek (door) is the exit through which one
passes from the house into a larger world, while an
erute (gate) is the exit from the homestead to the bush.
Domestic ceremonies among the Iteso were and are concerned
with the symbolic incorporation of women into agnatic
groups. Ritual action in these ceremonies is often oriented to the distinction between the home and the bush, to
which one passes by going through a gate, and also between
the inside of a house and the outside, to which one passes
by going through a door.

Initially, I was confused by the answer to the question 'What is an etem?' Informants began their answer
with the statement - 'Each clan has its own etem!'   The
etem of the sub-section functions in much the same way as
the larger etem except that negotiations for marriage took
place around the etem and the funeral of a sub-section
member was conducted at the etem and involved all the
people of the sub-section.

The people of a sub-section all lived in one compound
for protection. Their cattle were pastured at night in a
kraal in the centre of the compound for protection. A
thorn fence or hedge of euphorbia was planted around the
compound. There was only one gate, erute. The symbolism
of Iteso terminology for agnatic groupings was clearly
derived from this residential grouping. In some areas
which were particularly prone to attack, high mud walls of
ten feet and more were built around the compound. The
Babukusu also built such walls for their 'villages', and
a picture of one is to be found in Johnston's 'The Uganda
Protectorate' (1902). I walked around the ruins of one
such walled compound and I would guess it to be about one-
quarter of a mile in circumference.

Although clans were residentially dispersed, sub-
sections were organized around sub-clans in the sense that
members of these sub-clans formed the residential core
through which membership in a sub-section could be achieved. The result of obtaining membership in a sub-section
was, ipso facto, membership in a section. When a new section was formed, its sub-sections often came from different sections. The agnatic principle was directly related

to the process of territorial group formation and maintenance at the sub-section level in addition to playing an
important role in defining positions of authority and in
enforcing means of social control during this period.

Authority, as will be seen in the section on stratification by age (below), is based on two principles. The
first is the jural authority of elders who have not
retired. The second is the control by those elders of the
most important forms of property. Inheritance among the
Iteso is patrilineal and the most significant heritable
objects were cattle and rights in women. Until elders
went through the retirement ceremony, they were able to
reinforce their jural authority through control of these
scarce resources. Hence, it is not surprising that the
younger Iteso who were willing to move away from the
authority of their elders were younger brothers (particularly of junior houses), as, in any case, they remained
a relatively disinherited group. Since sub-sections were
formed around agnatic cores composed of members of a
single sub-clan, the combination of jural authority based
on relative age and control of the distribution of women
and cattle gave senior agnates considerable power over the
junior co-residents of their sub-clan.

Stratification by age

The Iteso variant of the Karimojong-type Age system was
somewhat unusual and needs careful elucidation. As far
as I am aware, the late age at which members entered the
system and the extreme emphasis on religious function-
aries have no parallel in Africa, although some aspects of
the Kuria age system as described by Ruel bear some re-
semblance (n.d.).

The Iteso use the word *aturi* (pl. *aturin*) to stand for
a group based on relative age. Like most other Ateso
words which are terms for important elements of their
social structure, the word aturi is used in a number of
different but related senses. There is a common element
of meaning in all the contexts in which this word is used.
I would suggest that the word aturi stands for a group of
coevals of similar age who are distinguished from other
such groups whose age is relatively different. The key
phrase here is 'of similar age'. I have kept it deliberately vague. In examining the various uses of the word I
shall show that the age span of the kinds of groups cov-
ered by the word aturi could be as little as one year or
as much as fifty years.

The first and most inclusive use of the word aturi is

one which many English-speaking Iteso translate as 'generation'. At any given time during the precolonial period I am discussing, there existed only two aturin in the 'generation' sense of the word. These were called the aturi nak'itelepai (generation of the boys) and the aturi nak'imojong (generation of the elders). The former were the active men of the society and, by definition, of any particular territorial section. These were the people who fought in wars, went on raids, farmed, herded cattle, had children, etc. The latter group remained at home, led prayers to the High God (especially supplication for rain), and participated primarily in the public rituals of the people.

Another use of the word aturi is a group of men who were born about the same time. These men often take a nickname from some significant event that occurred during the years of their birth. Men born during the 1939-45 period which the Iteso know as ejie ka Mussolini ka Hitler (Mussolini and Hitler's war) are known by the name *Panyako*. This is an Ateso corruption of 'Pioneer Corps', a Kenyan African unit for which recruitment was very active at that time. *Etenge* (hunger) is another popular name and may commemorate a famine which occurred during the years when the people named etenge were born. When Iteso describe their own aturi, in the sense of a group of coevals born around the same time, it is always with a great deal of nostalgia. They speak of herding cows together as children with their age mates and playing in meadows and always of friendships which developed with age mates during these childhood years which they try and maintain evey today.

I should note that the word aturi is never, as far as I could tell, applied to a group of women. This may be related to the general lack of status ascribed to women in the political-jural domain. The primary status positions that women occupy are those of sister, wife and mother, and all of these involve roles whose primary relevance is within the domestic domain. While men also have domestic roles such as father, brother and husband, they also relate to other men as household heads, neighbours, office holders, and followers. This failure to stratify women into age groups indicates a relationship between the principle of stratification by age (as encoded in the use of the word aturi) and status within the political-jural domain of society.

The third and perhaps primary use of the term aturi in the precolonial period was to describe a series of named groups of coevals of advanced age who have participated together in a ceremony also called aturi. This ceremony

was believed to have been held at fairly lengthy inter-
vals: most informants suggest anywhere between ten and
twenty years. The word aturi is closely associated with
the ceremony. All those who had at one time or another
completed this ceremony were known as the aturi nak'
ekiworone. *Ekiworone* is a difficult word to translate.
Presently it has fallen out of use. Discussions with
Iteso elders who remember the use of the word indicate
that there are a number of English terms that might serve.
These include 'bless', 'beseech', and 'rejoice'. I think
that the most suitable term would be 'to celebrate' in
the sense that a Mass in the Roman Catholic Church is
celebrated. Thus, I translate the phrase aturi nak'
ekiworone as the 'age group of those who celebrate'. This
indicates that the Iteso conception of the social role of
the men who had performed this ceremony was primarily that
of religious officiants.

My informants told me that participation in this ceremony could only occur at a fairly advanced age. Most
older informants claimed they were still too much in their
prime to be allowed to engage in the ceremony. One old
man, who was clearly more than ninety, allowed that he
might be eligible for entry into these age groups. Many
informants suggested that once a man passed the age of
seventy he could participate in the ceremony.

The ceremony itself was a rite de passage. Performance of the ceremony transferred the performer from the
occupation of one status to another which was defined by
a different set of rights and obligations. In addition
the ceremony itself was characterized by a liminal period
in which the characteristic suspension of normal, daily
activities was said to have occurred.

Before performing the ceremony a man was said to belong
to the aturi nak'itelepai and, assuming he was a household
head, was allowed to participate fully in the activities
of the political-jural domain. He could succeed to the
office of lok'etem, participate in raiding and warfare,
engage in the adjudication of cases, and marry. Someone
who had performed the aturi ceremony could not be a section leader.

After a man had participated in the aturi ceremony he
could no longer engage in any of the above activities. He
was deemed to have entered into a special relationship
with the High God and was 'closer' to God than the men who
had not performed the aturi ceremony. The collectivity of
all the men who had performed the aturi ceremony was known
as the aturi nak'imojong. This collectivity (also known
as aturi nak'ekiworone) engaged in certain activities for
which they were uniquely suited because of their relation-

ship to the High God. They were the leaders at all public
rituals, particularly supplication for rain. They consumed all fines of livestock that were levied by the section leader, and, if a person refused to accept a decision
made by a section leader and forfeit a fine, the aturi
nak'ekiworone could meet and perform a ceremony which
would bring a curse upon the recalcitrant man.

Participation in the aturi ceremony was not always a
voluntary act. Many men were said to have been physically
dragged to the ceremony. This is not surprising in view
of the rights that a man was obliged to forego. The
examples given above demonstrate that a man was no longer
allowed to participate in the political processes of
social life. Because of this and because of the alleged
unwillingness of many men to undergo the ceremony, I think
that 'retirement sets' is an apt term for describing the
named groups which performed the aturi ceremony.

This retirement dimension of the age system may throw
some light on a rather surprising custom which many Iteso
say occurred during this period. It was frequently told
that before a son was allowed to marry he had to physically fight and defeat his father. My first reaction was
to think that this was a ritual enactment of the structural antagonism between fathers and sons that occurs in
patrilineal societies. Yet Iteso informants were themselves rather appalled by this custom. They would often
speculate on how such a thing could occur, since, in view
of the fact that ritual avoidance between fathers and
sons is a basic principle of Iteso social relations, this
is a very immoral act. (In chapter 5 I discuss what I
regard as an axiomatic principle of social relations, the
separation of adjacent generations.) This separation is
particularly severe when it occurs between actual fathers
and sons. The father-son relationship is characteristic-
ally distant, reserved, and formal. For violent conflict
to happen within the context of this relationship is un-
thinkable to most Iteso, and I doubt whether such conflict
ever did occur. Rather I think that statements about the
required defeat of a father before a son could marry are
a symbolic expression of a man's reluctance to proceed
towards retirement. A man's marriage establishes him as
a participant in the political-jural domain. The implication of a son's marriage for his father is that the father
has proceeded a very long way toward retirement. This
must be especially true, if like other societies of the
Karimojong cluster, the average marriage age of a man was
his mid-30s. This would mean that when a man was ready to
marry, his father was in his early 60s at least. Thus,
retirement from an active role in the field of political

relations to an active role in the field of religious relationships aided in the enactment of another Iteso ideal
of father-son relations - that they should not compete in
the same arena or for the same scarce resources (women and
cattle). I note here that a traditional and now neglected
Iteso rule of exogamy is that a man may not marry the
sister of his son's age mate.

There is evidence of two different naming systems for
the groups that performed the aturi ceremony. They were
all called ekiworone after the ceremony, but they were
also stratified into the named groups of coevals who had
performed the ceremony together. One naming system consists of the names of three birds - *ewatutu* (ground hornbill), *esiele* (secretary bird), and *ekulu* (ostrich).
These names, according to some informants, were repeated
in an undetermined order, the only rule being that name
could not succeed itself. Thus, esiele could not be followed by a group called esiele. These birds are among the
three largest found in East Africa and, according to my
Iteso informants, the fastest. They say that it is their
speed that made them ideal emblems for a retiring group
of successful warriers.(7)

Other informants give a list of animal names which they
say were the names of some retirement sets. The most frequently mentioned name was *erisa* (leopard); others were
itome (elephant) and *eputera* (warthog). According to informants who described this system, any name could be
chosen but usually not that of a bird. There was no re-
peating order.

There was no regional variation or any other kind of
pattern to informants' answers to questions about the two
naming systems. My own suggestion, which unfortunately
developed after leaving the field, is that the retirement
sets may have had more than one emblematic name. Informants stated that they wore the feathers of the bird that
they were named after. This is a custom common in all of
the tribes of the Karimojong cluster. Kiggen's Ateso
dictionary gives one translation of the word aturi as
'plumage, feather-ornament' (1953a, p. 417). I also note
that his translation of a verb formed from the -*tur* root
of the word aturi is 'to praise, glorify, exult, extol,
applaude' (p. 417). Thus, I suggest that there were two
systems of nomenclature, one cyclical and one linear, and
both were operating at the same time.(8).

Some of the details of the retirement ceremony are uncertain, but a few are clear and relevant to the analysis
being undertaken here. The ceremony united the members of
a few neighbouring sections. It was under the direction
of a 'prophet' (*lokadwaran* - one who can see ahead) who

also blessed warriors who were about to go to battle. The liminal portion of the ceremony took place during the dry season in a type of land known as *akapian*, a seasonal swamp. Bulls (or oxen) contributed by the participants were ritually slaughtered and consumed by the participants over a period of weeks while they remained in akapian. Any woman, child, or younger man who happened to pass by the ceremony was said to be killed. The women were tortured by squeezing their breasts between two pieces of a freshly split wooden wand.

After the completion of the ceremony the men returned to their homes for a round of feasting, dancing, and beer-drinking. While the old men who had completed the ceremony drank beer, the young men danced. Occasionally the old men would emerge from the house where they were drinking beer and dance in a line opposite the young men and upbraid them and urge them to perform valorously on the field of battle as they had. Then the old men would resume drinking. This celebration went on for some weeks in different homes where the hosts were the men of the retirement set that was undergoing the ceremony.

There are a number of elements in the aturi ceremony that are interesting for our analysis here. There is the association during the liminal period of the ceremony with seasonal swamps. Seasonal swamps are where the aturi nak'ekiworone led prayers for rain. Prayers for rain were extremely important because of the uncertainty of rainfall for the whole of Eastern Uganda and Western Kenya. Also, there is the segregated status accorded the men who had performed the aturi ceremony. Interlopers were dealt with violently and when participants returned to their homes it was as a part of an exclusive beer-drinking group which admonished those who remained in their previous status to perform their duties properly. From all this we can see that the men who performed the aturi were separated and segregated in a context that associated them with the ritual activities of their future status.

IV

The most important organizing element in Nilo-Hamitic societies is the territorial section system. Except for Gulliver's 'The Family Herds' (1955) and Dyson-Hudson's 'Karimojong Politics' (1966), scholars who have been concerned with these societies have concentrated almost exclusively on the more exotic and spectacular age systems (see Bernardi, 1951). A general understanding of how the

age and descent systems operate in Iteso society can only
be obtained by examining them in the context of the territorial section system.

Politically the section system corresponds to Schapera's definition of a tribal political organization.
Through the office of the section leader it was concerned
both with the maintenance of internal order and external
independence through organizing for warfare and defence.
Agnation served as an ideology which provided a set of
norms for relations within sub-sections and also, through
the institutions of clanship, cut across territorial sections. In addition, the jural authority of senior agnates, combined with their control of scarce resources,
allowed them considerable control over the junior members
of their sub-clan.

The age system provided a set of categories through
which interaction could take place. This was particularly important where personal relations had not previously been established - as in the process of forming a new
territorial section.

It is more important, however, to consider the activities of age groups within the various sections. It has
been made clear that sections undertook collective action
within the political-jural domain. Sections also acted
collectively within the religious field, and through the
age system the religious field was related to the political-jural domain. The most important group that enacts
public ceremonies is the section. Prayers for rain and
the avoidance of natural disaster as well as the punish-
ment of wizards were all performed by individual sections,
and these prayers were not believed to have any efficacy
for any section except the one that performed them. In
addition, action by a section which was religious in
nature sanctioned action within the political-jural
domain, through the ritual authority of the generations
of retired elders to curse those recalcitrant offenders
who refused to pay their fines.

In Durkheim's sense of the word, a section is a
'ritual congregation', a group of people who come together
to pray and enact rituals. The only public rituals that
involved groups larger than the section were under the
aegis of a prophet. These rituals were not performed
regularly but only on extraordinary occasions. Finally,
and this is a very important point, the roles performed by
the men engaged in public rituals were allocated by position in the age system. Thus, the aturi nak'ekiworone
were the leaders and directors of all public ritual because they were in a special relationship to the High God.
I should add that they also were the main material

beneficiaries of the rituals through their consumption of slaughtered cattle.

The section provided the context in which the political and religious elements of Iteso society came together. It was through the political institution of the section leader and the religious leadership of the aturi nak'eki-worone that the section became a unified corporate group. The religious activity of the ritual elders sanctioned and validated political activity. While one can say that the section was a political organization, it was also a religious organization in which ritual roles were allocated by the age system.

It remains now to discuss the reason why this political and religious organization that I have been describing disappeared so rapidly and so completely after the imposition of colonial rule. It is not difficult to understand why the political organization and age system disappeared together. I have shown that age and political groups were closely integrated in their territorial context and, as a consequence, were mutually dependent upon each other. What I shall suggest is that changing historical conditions made the territorial section as an organization no longer politically viable, and because the age and political systems were so dependent on the section as a context in which action occurred, they also lost their effectiveness.

3 The emergence of neighbourhoods

I

In the preceding chapter I described a political system
that has completely disappeared. This rather extreme
structural change raises considerable problems of explanation. In this chapter I try to answer four questions that
are concerned with the conditions that made these funda-
mental changes in political structure possible. These
are: (a) What are the external forces that impinged on the
members of the territorial sections to predispose them to
change? (b) What elements in the political system
remained relatively continuous during this period?
(c) What kind of political structure replaced the territorial section, and what can account for its particular
form? (d) What are Iteso social ideas about this new
form of political organization?

It must be remembered that Iteso territorial groups
engaged in two kinds of activities: politics and ritual.
Although territorial sections were political corporations,
they were at the same time a set of ritual congregations.
The close relationship between the religious system as
expressed in public ritual and the nature of political
corporations among the Iteso cannot be overestimated as
territorial organization among the Iteso was defined,
partially at least, in terms of ritual activities. It is
necessary to stress the functional interdependence of
these two systems before the nature of political changes
can be understood.

The traditional system as described above no longer
exists in any form. By 1905, at the very latest, the
territorial sections, the position of section and sub-
section leaders, and the retirement sets had completely
disappeared. There are two sets of factors which contributed to these changes. The first relate to the political

position of the Iteso vis-à-vis the surrounding ethnic
groups at the period just prior to British intervention.
The second were the conditions under which political order
was established by colonial officials.

The most significant element affecting this pattern of
radical political change was the administrative policies
of the British colonial officials. I suggest that there
were two other elements that predisposed the Iteso to
adjust easily to radical changes that were, in a certain
sense, thrust upon them. These were, first, military reverses suffered by the traditional political groups; and
second, activities relating to crucial political processes
such as recruitment of followers, were able to be maintained in the structural context of colonialism.

Iteso military successes were based on highly co-ordinated groups of men under the authority of a section
leader, or a notable aspiring to office. The replicate
nature of Iteso territorial organization allowed for rapid
duplication of social units capable of adequate defence.
The victims of the Iteso were ethnic groups of heterogeneous origin who were organized on a segmental rather
than a segmentary basis.(1) These were primarily the
Bantu Abaluyia with the notable exception of the Wanga
Kingdom which was, in any case, allied with the Iteso.
The Nilotic Luo appear to have been better organized militarily than the Abaluyia groups (Southall, 1952) but they
did not utilize the flexible tactics of the Iteso, nor
were their administrative and leadership roles institutionalized in the person of one man, such as the Iteso
section leader.

In the late nineteenth century the military situation
changed to the disadvantage of the Iteso. New military
powers and techniques entered the scene. To the northwest of the Iteso, the Bagishu became better organized
militarily and were able to cut off the Iteso from their
northern brothers.

Directly to the west, the Jo Padhola were becoming more
centralized under the leadership of Majanga and Oguti, an
Iteso renegade. As a result of the 'wars of Oguti', many
Iteso fled across the Malaba River to Kenya and those who
remained were absorbed by the Jo Padhola. It was only
after an Iteso county was recognized in Bukedi District in
1949 that many of those absorbed began to claim Iteso
identity again. Paradoxically in Iteso-Padhola areas of
Bukedi such as Iolwa, men in their 60s claim to be Jo
Padhola and their sons claim an Iteso identity (Southall,
1957). This example of ethnic flexibility is remarkable
only if 'tribes' are conceived of as right- and duty-
bearing corporate groups. Clearly this was not the

situation in the late nineteenth century and the Iteso, at least, exhibited a high degree of personal flexibility as regards residence choices.

Finally, to the east there was the emergence of the Nandi as a military power after the dispersal of the Uasin Gishu Maasai. Except for occasional raids, the Nandi pressure on the Iteso was indirect. Iteso expansion to the east had been primarily at the expense of the Babukusu. Nandi raids on the eastern edge of Babukusu territory forced the latter to unite against the weaker of their foes, and they drove the Iteso out of a considerable part of their original territory (Were, 1967a, pp. 156-84).

A particularly severe blow to the Iteso was the acquisition of firearms by their enemies, from Arab traders. The Iteso have no history of Arab trade at a time (circa 1890) when other groups were involved in this kind of exchange. Ogot (1967) cites Samia-Bagwe traditions to the effect that the Iteso were defeated only after the Samia-Bagwe acquired guns from Arab traders operating out of Buganda (pp. 118-19). He refers to the effects of the Iteso defeat as a 'reverse migration' (p. 119).

Although these events were not simultaneous, the Iteso experienced a succession of severe military setbacks. I suggested in chapter 2 that the section was an organization fitted for 'predatory expansion' (Sahlins, 1969) and not really suitable for defence. The interethnic climate in which the section as an organization thrived changed radically during the period just prior to colonial rule. It is possible that the emergence and increasing significance of prophets among the Iteso at this time was a response to the changing military situation, but the sacred and eternal nature of the office of prophet makes it difficult to evaluate Iteso oral tradition on this score. It is reasonable to assume, however, that the position of the prophet as a ritual leader of a number of otherwise discrete territorial sections made him a natural focal point of common organization (see Evans-Pritchard (1940) for a similar discussion, pp. 187-8).

The Iteso were subjugated and pacified by the British in 1894-5.(2) Murunga, the half brother of the Wanga King Mumia, was sent by agents of the British East Africa Company with a command of Swahili soldiers to the Iteso area. He rounded up a number of the section leaders and had them shot. There is also evidence that some Iteso were guilty of complicity in this pacification. Omerikwa, a very famous warrior and section leader was among those killed by Murunga. Omerikwa's son, Obure, was still living in 1970, and he told me that Murunga captured and

killed Omerikwa with the aid of Omerikwa's own father.
He said that the Iteso aided Murunga in their own defeat
because Omerikwa refused to desist in organizing raids
which brought severe retaliation on the Iteso.   The Iteso
on the Uganda side of the border were said to have been
the victims of a number of raids led by William Grant, the
sub-administrator for Busoga.

This evidence suggests that the Iteso were becoming
aware that the section and its organizational pivot, the
section leader, were no longer politically viable, since
independent action brought severe retribution.   The death
of a large number of section leaders was surely a severe
blow, and it would appear that succession to the position
of section leader would not have been thought desirable.
Without a leader, the section could not be an effective
political or jural unit and thus it readily disappeared.
Since the age system, through its rituals, was tied to the
section system, without the section system, the performance of rituals (which were the major age system activity)
became meaningless and structurally irrelevant.

A few Iteso also assert that the colonial administration forbade the performance of the rituals of the age
system.   If this is true, it was probably because the
colonial image of age organization was derived from the
Maasai, where age and military organization are interrelated.   This repression of ceremonies would certainly
have helped expedite the loss of the age and territorial
organization.

II

The pacification of the Iteso did not result in the immediate establishment of an externally imposed local administration.   Instead the most important consequence of
pacification was the suppression of all large-scale Iteso
political and military activities by the colonial officials responsible for the North Kavirondo area.

Early attempts at local administration of the Iteso
failed completely. There were a number of reasons for
this failure.   The most important was that the Iteso were
the society most distant from any administrator.   The two
officials with authority over the Iteso were Hobley in
Mumias and Grant at Jinja.   Both were more conerned with
the Wanga and Basoga of their immediate area.   Administration in the peripheral areas (and the Iteso were the most
peripheral) was virtually non-existent.   The main concern
of C.W. Hobley at Mumias was to ensure the safety of cara-
vans along the road to Uganda (Mungeam, 1966, p. 88).

He did not appear to be interested in bringing the out-
lying areas under his control - even if that were possible.
Mungeam (1966, p. 90) describes this early administration
as 'a limited control developed by a few isolated individuals in strategic places'. In no sense was the area
occupied by the Iteso regarded as 'a strategic place'.
As Ogot (1963) points out, even where administrative
centres were finally established, there was often a considerable hiatus between pacification and administration.
The attitude of early administrators toward the Iteso,
and, apparently, the sum total of administrative knowledge about the Iteso is given in the following confiden-
tial report written either in 1908 or 1909, fifteen years
after the Iteso were pacified.
>   (a)
>   Lugumi
> Chief unknown.
>
> A large and obstreperous people on the boundary of ...
> B.E.A. and Uganda.
>
> Have been fought but will have again to be punished.
> Have a playful way of killing people on road between
> Uganda and B.E.A. In December, 1906 fought the Ketosh
> and tried to hold up a government safari under A.D.
> Supt.of Police.
>
> Rayne.
> Country well watered.
> Food plentiful also potatoes.
> Cattle not supposed to be very pletiful.
> These people supposed to possess many rifles.
>   (KNA DC/NN/.S/1) (3)

It was only in 1914 when the Uganda railroad was being
built through the Iteso area that any kind of administrative control began to be exercised and even that was
tenuous.(4)
     Between 1895 and 1910 a number of attempts were made to
administer the Iteso directly through African agents, none
of whom were Iteso. No effort was made to utilize Iteso
leaders as administrators. Of the first three chiefs
appointed over the Iteso, one was killed by the Iteso,
another fled from office, and the third was removed for
gross corruption and is said to have died in jail.
Finally in 1910 adminstration was officially turned over
to the capable hands of Murunga, the man who had originally pacified the Iteso. Iteso informants clearly indicate that Murunga had, in any case, been the dominant
figure in the area for some time.

Murunga's base was in Kimilili on the eastern edge of
Iteso territory, but among the Babukusu whom he also
administered. Although Murunga appointed official Iteso
headmen, both archival and oral evidence indicate that he
virtually ignored them. Instead he 'administered' through
bands of personal retainers whom he kept about his camp.
Murunga appears to have carried out two policies. First,
he violently suppressed any large-scale (that is, visible)
political and military activity; and second, he extracted,
on an ad hoc basis, hut tax, labour corvee to build roads,
or 'volunteers' for mission training as his superiors
required of him. The instruments of his policy were
bands of retainers. As a large number of his retainers
were Iteso, he was probably well informed about Iteso
activites. None of this information, however, appears to
have filtered through to the European officials.
Murunga's activities, while successful, were viewed by the
District Administration as temporary. However, he
remained in this 'temporary' capacity for twenty years.
By then, the Iteso had developed leaders who had enough
administrative credibility to enable them to make effective protests against the actions of Murunga and his
followers.

The major colonial agent to the west of the Malaba
River was Oguti Ipaade. Oguti was a remarkable man in a
number of ways. He died in harness and managed to escape
being removed by colonial officials despite his reputation as a corrupt predator. Oguti was able to remain a
government official until long after Murunga and the
Baganda general, Semei Kakungulu, had been removed. As
an indication of his remarkable authority and tenacity,
he is supposed to have been poisoned by his sons who felt
that they had been kept from their patrimony for far too
long. He is also said to have owned over 50,000 head of
cattle, a figure so enormous that I find it difficult to
believe. Oguti's career was also remarkable for the way
in which he shed tribal allegiance at will. He was a
very fearsom figure for the Iteso. They did not imagine
that he was subject to any kind of moral rule or any kind
of restraint. His authority was felt to derive from his
skill as an *ekacudan,* a wizard. His death was said to be
an occasion for rejoicing by all the Iteso. According to
Southall (1957) the precolonial wars of Oguti caused the
entire plain between the Malaba river and the town of
Tororo to become depopulated.

The Iteso remember this period as one of anarchy and
uncertainty. In addition to such traditional difficulties as liability to vengeance because of the feud and
the danger of attacks from traditional enemies, there was

added the very real chance of being victimized by one of
Murunga's or Oguti's well-armed bands of agents. Today
one of the most popular of Iteso songs is 'The Stranger
Killed Eroni' which recounts the murder of a number of
tax resisters by one of Murunga's roving bands.

A major result of this political uncertainty was to
increase the high rate of spatial mobility that existed
among the Iteso and thus to change the geographical pattern of household movement. Iteso movement had generally
been in a southeasterly direction toward their expanding
frontier. The first consequence of pacification was to
freeze the existing frontiers. This was an advantage for
the Iteso as the extent of territory they occupied had
begun to shrink. During this period Iteso household
movements began to take on a random character as many
Iteso desperately sought a safe place to live. The only
regularity in this new pattern of household movements was
that they were generally away from an unsafe border area.

The increased rate and arbitrary pattern of household
migrations had a number of interrelated consequences.
Decisions to move were taken on a much more individual-
istic basis so that groups of contemporaries no longer
moved together. This indicates, as also do Iteso accounts
of movement during this period, that the clusters of agnatic kin who formed the residential core of sub-sections
began to break up. This does not mean, however, that
there was complete dispersal of agnatic kin. That has
never been true at any point in the history of the Iteso.
Furthermore, agnates who were already spatially separated
were not prevented from moving together. However, senior
agnates did find it increasingly difficult to control
their juniors by limiting their access to cattle and
women. During this period of political instability,
safety, rather than social advancement, became an important motive for household heads. Hence, the organization
of political power was significantly altered.

Given the number of moves any household head was likely
to make during this period (as many as six or seven), he
probably did attempt at some point to live with agnates.
Finally, a related consequence of this higher mobility
rate was the increased importance and use of non-agnatic
kinship ties by household heads in their search for a
place to live that was safe from marauders, tax collec-
tors, and the feud.

The general political results of the pacification and
early administration of the Iteso can be summed up as
follows: (a) political action that involved relatively
large number of people was ruthlessly and violently suppressed; (b) incumbents of the traditional political

office, the section head, were eliminated; (c) activities
associated with territorial sections were punished; (d) in
a climate of danger and unease, residential patterns became highly unstable and thus leaders could no longer rely
on agnates who would either become the stable core of a
following that they could control through limiting their
access to scarce resources, or, in pioneering a new territory, become the basis for a new residential group.

III

The previous section describes the political environment
which accompanied the disappearnce of the institutionalized political office, the section leader. These factors coupled with the military reversals the Iteso suffered prior to the coming of the Europeans indicate that
the position of section leader was not politically viable
and that the Iteso may have been losing faith in the
institution. Certainly the rapidity with which the Iteso
abandoned ritual activities associated with territorial
sections indicates that this is true. In any case, one
fact is clear; those section leaders shot by Murunga in
1894-5 are described by Iteso as the last of the Lok'-
etem.

It remains now to describe the nature of leadership
during the transitional period and its relationship to
present-day patterns of local-level leadership. In this
section I shall pay particular attention to the continuities that existed between precolonial and colonial
leader-follower relationships.

The word used by Iteso to describe leaders during this
period is *lok'auriaart,* literally 'the one of the cattle-
resting place'. This is the same term as was used to
describe the effective competitors for the office of section leader in the precolonial period. The Iteso describe the person who was called a lok'auriaart as very
much like his precolonial namesake. He was a man of
exceptional achievement - brave in battle and skilled as
a warrior, rich in cows, the possessor of many wives,
forceful in public and judicious in his opinions.

The major effective defining characteristic of a lok'-
auriaart, however, is that he was possessed of a following who would do his bidding in return for protection and
economic support. Iteso were universally agreed that no
matter how excellent and qualified a man might be, if he
did not have a following, he was not a lok'auriaart. For
this reason, I choose to translate the term as 'patron'.

I have chosen the term 'patron' because it implies a

number of outstanding figures who are in competition for
followers. Each patron, in order to obtain a following,
had to attract his clients from some other patron. To do
this he provided the use of his wealth in cows and protection for those followers. Also, he had to be continu-
ously successful as a patron. This meant that his clients
could not be readily harrassed by the government chiefs
or be too vulnerable to attack from other Iteso. In Iteso
political theory, fear of retaliation from the patron
should have prevented other Iteso from attacking his
clients or starting a feud with them. In addition, the
wealth of the patron must have been sufficient to sustain
clients during a period of agricultural famine and also to
be used by new clients during the process of their establishing a household under his supervision.

In return for this, the patron was granted authority,
prestige and the tribute of communal labour on his fields.
But this lasted only so long as he was successful. Failure to provide a relatively safe and comfortable environment for his clients meant that they would move under the
authority of another patron who was better able to provide
those things.

The clientele of a patron was a mixture of different
kinsmen. They included distant agnates and younger full
brothers, sisters' sons, sisters' daughters' husbands,
daughters' husbands, sons and sisters' husbands. Wives'
brothers and half brothers were rarely included. Both
the normative structure of kinship relations and competition over scarce resources precluded the possibility of
some types of kinsmen becoming clients. In addition,
some of these clients were able to attract clients of
their own.

Agricultural activities in the area were under the
general direction of the patron. He told followers when
and where to farm. Their land could be prepared for
sowing only after his land had been prepared. I do not
think it is fair to say that the patron 'owned' the land
that his followers utilized. This implies that he could
transfer it to another patron for a consideration or that
his sons could inherit his rights of transfer in the
land. This was not so for land was a relatively free
commodity. I would say rather that the patron controlled
the distribution of land. He had the right to withdraw
the initial grant of land, but this right was only exercised in the case of suspected wizards. Continued residence, however, transferred the right to grant use of the
land to its occupiers. The death of an adult household
member on the land confirmed that the usufructuary rights
had been transferred into rights of ownership.

The position of patron provides some sharp contrasts
with the position of section leader, and these can be
seen by comparing the connotations of the two indigenous
terms for these leaders, lok'etem, and lok'auriaart. The
term lok'etem is derived from the Iteso word for hearth,
etem, while the term lok'auriaart is derived from the
word *auriaart,* a place where cattle rest during the day.
The auriaart is not an *aujo,* a kraal inside the boundaries of the homestead where cattle are kept during the
night. The group associated with a hearth is a domestic
group in which membership is determined by common residence and acknowledgment of the authority of the household
head. A domestic group is distinctly bounded from other
like groups, and the authority of the household is an
ascribed jural status.

The auriaart is an ad hoc collection of cattle and the
men who happen to be herding that day. Leadership at an
auriaart is based on force of personality rather than any
precisely defined rights. The use of the word etem in
the official's title implies, in its application to the
people of a section, jural authority over a precisely
bounded group of people. The use of auriaart, on the
other hand, suggests something rather different. It implies a voluntary type of association or coming together.
Thus the authority of a patron is symbolized by a group in
which leadership is neither institutionalized nor backed
by specific sanctions. The authority of the section
leader, by contrast, is institutionalized through his
incumbency of an office and backed by ritual sanctions
which could be imposed through the curse of the retirement set. The distinction is between a leader who is an
office holder with specific rights and duties and a
leader whose power is based on the control of scarce
resources. Another contrast which must be noted is that
there may be only one section leader within a section at
any given time while in a patron's area the number of
leaders is limited only by pragmatic considerations.

This change in the pattern of leader-follower relations had important structural consequences. In the preceding section, the consequences of pacification on Iteso
political structure were described. It was demonstrated
that a system of territorial sections and sub-sections
organized around an agnatic core was not able to be
maintained in the face of the pacification policies followed by the British and their agents. There emerged a
flexible pattern of leader-follower relations which were
better adapted to the changing political situation.
Associated with this change in leader-follower relations
was the emergence of a new form of territorial

organization, which I call a neighbourhood.

The neighbourhood differs from the section or sub-section in a number of ways. It is not a corporate group. Its boundaries and membership are not rigidly defined. Members of the neighbourhood are not constrained to inter-act with each other on the basis of laws whose violation will result in the imposition of jural and ritual sanc-tions. Instead, and in accordance with the contractual nature of patron-client relations, relations between neighbours are voluntaristic in nature. The sanctions imposed on persons who violate the norms of neighbourly relations are diffuse rather than specific. Thus, the leadership of the patron and the variety of kinship ties by which followers were linked to him led to the emerg-ence of a local territorial group (a neighbourhood) of mixed agnatic composition in which unilineal descent was irrelevant as an organizing principle.(5)

Despite the changes in the norms of leader-follower relations and the structural consequences of these chan-ges, the Iteso maintained considerably continuity of political action and personnel between 1890 and 1930. A large number of those leaders who set themselves up as patrons in a neighbourhood were either former sub-section leaders or aspirants to that position. In other words, they were the very class of people who had been called lok'auriaart in the precolonial system. Furthermore the actions whereby aspiring leaders became contenders for positions of leadership remained essentially the same. A leader acquired followers through a combination of judicious action, bravery, and the use of cattle wealth. Followers were attracted to leaders on the basis of the protection and economic support which that leader could offer. A leader and his following composed an ego-orien-ted, territorial 'coalition' (Boissevain, 1971) in which political support was given to the leader in return for economic and political benefits.(6) This 'coalition' was recruited by the leader on the basis of a mixture of agnatic and non-agnatic kinship ties. The competitors of the leaders were often closely related agnates. This meant that some potential followers chose between compet-ing leaders and thus maximized their demands by playing one leader off against another. Finally, aspiring lead-ers who were losers in the game of political competition had one of two choices. They could either become the followers of a more successful competitor or attempt to recruit a following and pioneer an unsettled area. This was a pattern continued from the precolonial period.

All of the above constitute a description of the con-tent of political processes relating to competition and

the recruitment of followers which remained constant
during the radical changes in political environment that
occurred between 1890 and 1930. Thus from the perspective
of political actors, the resources in followers, the means
by which followers were obtained and the identity of the
competitors did not change appreciably. The changes that
did occur were not in the 'who' or 'what' of politics, but
in the 'where'. The structural locus of competition and
recruitment changed from the territorial section and sub-
section to a much more ill-defined area made up of a number of neighbourhoods. This means that while the scale of
corporate political action decreased, the scale (perhaps
scope would be a better word) of individual political
action increased in terms of the options available to
people at a lower level.

IV

The real impetus to the establishment of a genuine colonial presence in the Iteso area was the building of the
Uganda railroad through to Malaba on the Kenya-Uganda
border in 1921, when a station was built at Malaba.
Greater official knowledge of events and personalities
among the Iteso meant the end of the period of anarchy
that characterized the early colonial period. Outbreaks
of feud were severely punished as were the few attempts
at intertribal warfare. In addition, the more direct
attempts at exploitation by government chiefs began to
come to the notice of British officials. Ilukoli, one of
the first Iteso sub-chiefs with any genuine authority,
was quickly removed from office when his arbitrary con-
fiscation of cattle came to the notice of colonial officials at Mumias. Also at this time, according to the
archival accounts, Murunga began to lose interest in the
Iteso and although he was to remain as chief over them for
some time his authority was virtually nil (Kenya National
Archives, NN/23). Genuine local authorities began to
emerge. In what were later to become North and South Teso
locations respectively, two chiefly dynasties established
themselves. These were the people of Seme in the South
and Omudek in the North.
    The most significant consequence of the establishment
of an administrative apparatus was the decline in influence of the patron. There were a number of reasons for
this change. The patron was a non-institutionalized competitor with two other types of influential people, who
were able to utilize resources that were not available to
the patron, for his power derived entirely from a local

base, and he had only his personal qualities and wealth in cattle as resources. The first of these influentials was the mission catechist who served as a focal point for the distribution of mission services. The second was the local government official who did not have many resources to distribute (at that time). Instead he was able to reward his followers by not applying government demands as stringently to them as to others. Using his powers, he could also punish his enemies.

Very often a man would combine the identities of mission servant and government official, although not necessarily at the same time. The most successful example of this career history is the ex-government chief of the Iteso, Alexander Papa. When it became clear that his elder brother Enyusat was grooming him for the position of chief, he made a dramatic appearance at the recently established Mill Hill Mission in Amukura in 1937 and converted to Catholicism, renounced all of his four wives and in a Catholic ceremony married a daughter of the government chief of Bukhayo. This was a very clever strategy for a number of reasons. Papa obtained the support of the Europeans most familiar with the Iteso, the missionaries. He established a 'progressive' image for himself which contrasted strikingly with the 'traditional' image of Enyusat, who was then chief, and was regarded by the missionaries as an old beer-drinking, marijuana-smoking reprobate. Finally, he reactivated the precolonial Iteso-Bukhayo alliance and used this tie as a basis for claiming to be the natural successor to Enyusat. After Chief Alexander was forcibly retired at independence in 1963, he married three additional wives. It is interesting to note here that a daughter of Enyusat was married to a son of Omudek, the most powerful sub-chief in what was to become North Teso location. Thus, as political figures began to occupy administrative posts, they solidifed their position by establishing useful marital alliances.

An example that is typical of the Protestant areas of the Iteso locations is the career of Bartholomew Oloo. He was originally trained as a reader for the Anglican Church but switched his allegiance to the Salvation Army Mission that was being established in 1925. Most of the people of his sub-location followed suit. He became the equivalent of what would now be a sub-chief in 1930 and resigned his church position. His younger brother succeeded him in 1935 but died a few years later and Bartholomew re-entered the office, now called *Mlango* (Swahili for 'door'). He retired a wealthy and respected old man in 1960, but continues to serve on church and school committees.

It is important to be specific about the changes in the

leadership pattern that I am describing. Leaders became
part of the extra-Iteso structures and, in fact, were
leaders because of the outside resources that they could
command. These leaders controlled much larger areas than
the patron. The consequence of this was that the scale of
leadership expanded and the content of leader-follower
relations became more specifically political. Thus, the
relationship between leader and follower decreased in intensity. The content of the relationship during the
patron period was in Gluckman's phrase 'multiplex' or
'multipurpose' in that it was kinship-based, economic,
residential, and political (Gluckman, 1965, p. 256). The
new leadership pattern was territorial only in the sense
that leader and follower were very often members of the
same governmentally defined administrative unit. The
relationship was primarily a political one with economic
overtones. Kinship continued to play an important role
in the ideology of politics in that leaders and followers
often used the values of kinship to justify an already
existent political alliance.

During the period I have been discussing, c. 1890-1930,
the nature of leader-follower relationships changed drastically. The primary factor affecting the pattern of
relationships was the changing nature of political resources. During the precolonial and immediate postcolon-
ial periods, political resources were internally based and
patrons exchanged cattle and women with their followers
for support. The establishment of an effective administrative presence brought with it new political resources
which were externally based to the local society. These
resources consist primarily of protection from government demands on labour and household resources (in the
form of taxes, fines, etc.) and, increasingly, access to
social services. The type of leader who is able to provide these resources is different from the patron. He
is, instead, a broker. His power is based on his ability
to operate in two different fields, the field of colonial
and national administration, particularly as it affects
the local level and the field of local politics. Since
1930 the broker has become the dominant type of political
leader. The introduction of cash crops and increasing
national control of local societies has facilitated the
emergence of brokerage as a political institution.

A further examination of leader-follower relations is
not really germain to the problem I am concerned with in
this section, which is the emergence of certain kinds of
territorial organization. I have been attempting to document the decline of the patron as a type of leader. The
contemporary successors to these roles seem to serve as

kind of middlemen between the leaders and the great mass
of Iteso. They are notables without power or authority.
Their importance lies almost entirely in their political
connections and their relative wisdom and experience.
Their followings are ephemeral and difficult to determine,
but they are a focus of networks within and between neighbourhoods.

I have described the decline of the position of patron.
The word lok'auriaart (patron) is another one of those
Ateso words that has disappeared. Modern leaders are
called by Ateso adaptions of their English titles. The
location chief is called *echiefu,* the sub-chief, *esub-
chiefu* and so on. It is important to ask what was the consequence of the decline of the patron for the definition
of neighbourhoods.

Neighbourhoods were originally oriented to individual
patrons and that neighbourhood identity was a function of
political following, in that the followers of a patron
gathered to live around him. Iteso described the original formation of neighbourhoods in just this fashion.
The people who lived over there, they say, were the people
of Omuse (*itunga k'Omuse*), if Omuse was the name of a
patron. Thus the patron's neighbourhood becomes a kind
of residential coalition. This coalition has the structural feature of what Mayer (1966) calls a 'quasi-group'.
These groups are 'ego-centered, in the sense of depending
for their very existence on a specific person as a central organizing focus'. Further, 'the actions of any
member are relevant only in so far as they are interactions between him and ego or ego's intermediary' (1966,
pp. 97-8). The political aspect in the formation of the
patron's neighbourhood is crucial for understanding its
activities and also qualifies it predominantly as a territorial coalition.

The decline of the significance of the patron has
meant, however, that the neighbourhoods were no longer
oriented to one particular person. This is certainly the
situation that exists today. For any household head, a
neighbourhood is a set of co-residents with whom he and
a few other important people interact in more significant
fashion and with greater frequency than with others.

Thus, under modern conditions Iteso neighbourhoods have
become less bounded and there is less agreement on the
exact composition of that neighbourhood. Therefore,
although there is an indigenous term for the neighbourhood, there is rarely any uniform concensus about who are
the members of a neighbourhood or even on its name. There
is, however, pattern and consistency in neighbourhood
organization. If a network of relations between

contiguous household heads were to be drawn, it would be
seen that there were groups of households between whom
social relations were particularly intense and frequent.
It is just such a group that I call the neighbourhood. In
Gulliver's terminology, the present day Iteso neighbourhood should be called a 'cluster' rather than a coalition.
A cluster is a group whose members 'over a period...tended
to cooperate with one another in collective action more
than with other neighbourhoods', and is distinguished from
a quasi-group (coalition) in that interaction is not oriented to a 'focal ego' (1971, pp. 243-4).

V

The preceding sections of this chapter have described
changing patterns of authority relations, particularly as
these affect residence choice, and the changing political
conditions under which these new patterns of authority
have emerged. These changes have resulted in the emergence of a form of territorial organization that I have
called a 'neighbourhood'.

Presently, Iteso neighbourhoods consist of clusters of
households headed by adult males who are related to other
household heads in the 'neighbourhood' in a variety of
ways. Ties among neighbours are neither uniform nor
single stranded. The neighbourhood can be conceived of
as a zone of a territorial network in which the co-
residents tend to choose each other more frequently than
other, sometimes equi-distant, possibilities. Thus the
Iteso neighbourhood can be described as the result of
individual patterns of choice.(7) Two types of relationships predominate among neighbours. Almost all
neighbours are related to each other as kinsmen. Many
kinship relations are asymmetric in content. By this I
mean that the rights and duties that two kinsmen owe to
each other are not the same for each kinsman. Thus,
fathers have a different set of obligations towards their
sons than they have towards their brothers. Kinship becomes significant for social relations among persons who
are neighbours in a variety of circumstances which are
not conceived of by Iteso as normatively appropriate when
persons are interacting as members of a neighbourhood.
Chapter 2 and the earlier sections of this chapter have
indicated kinship relations are appropriate on some ritual
occasions and in terms of recruitment to neighbourhoods.

When neighbours interact as 'neighbours', the normative
and ideological models that are appropriate are not kinship but related to a set of values I call 'neighbourli-

ness'. The remainder of this section will be devoted to
an examination of this second type of relationship among
neighbours. This is a relationship that is, in Barnes's
terms (1972), symmetrical. By this I mean that all persons who call each other 'neighbour' among the Iteso owe
to their 'neighbours' the same set of obligations. In
what follows below I will describe the content and situational relevance of relations among neighbours.

Neighbourhoods are only one of a variety of forms of
territorial units among the Iteso. In order to understand them it is necessary to discuss Iteso ideas and
concepts of territoriality.

In Chapter 1, I discussed the history of the various
forms of administrative organization found among the
Iteso. The smallest administrative unit is under the
responsibility of an unpaid headman called a *lok'alipo*
(also *luguru*). The term most frequently applied by Iteso
to this man's area is *ekitala* (pl. *itela*). An accurate
translation for the primary meaning of this term is 'land
suitable for habitation'.(8) Land which is characterized
as ekitala is contrasted with akapian, swamp or land which
turns swampy during the rainy season and is consequently
unusable for building a house or raising any of the traditional subsistence crops.(9) Ekitala is further sub-
divided into a number of soil types which are characterized by a combination of their relative fertility and
soil composition.

There is an association between ekitala and houses. By
a typical sort of Ateso semantic extension the word becomes 'a place where people live'; in other words, a
locality. Among the Karimojong a locality is a relatively
fixed entity. Although it may vary considerably in size
and population, it remains structurally constant in relation to other kinds of territorial units (Dyson-Hudson,
1966, p. 117). This contrasts sharply with the nature of
the locality among the Iteso. As with many of the terms
for agnatic kin groups, the term ekitala can be applied to
units of different scale and social function. Its meaning
can only be determined by an examination of the context in
which the word is used and in contrast with the other
terms for territorial units.

In most instances an ekitala either contrasts with an
adukete, a smaller scale and more solidary unit, or with
some kind of larger scale and most often administrative
unit. This often means that the term ekitala is applied
to the area ruled by a lok'alipo, or even to two or three
such areas. In theory the term can be used for very
large-scale units. If two Iteso are talking in Nairobi
one may answer the question 'al'ekitala kon?,' ('where is

your ekitala?') by giving the name of a location or sub-
location. On the other hand, when two Iteso who meet at
a market are familiar with a given area the answer to this
question is a unit smaller than that ruled by a lok'alipo.
It is tempting to translate ekitala as 'lok'alipo's area'
but this would not do justice to the functional ambiguity
that is built into Iteso use of these concepts.

One important defining criterion which must be mentioned is that anything to which the term ekitala may be
applied must have a name; an ekitala is a named territory.
The implication of this limitation on the use of the term
is that an ekitala must have a social identity. Statements are frequently made by Iteso about the agnatic composition, morality, politics, wealth, or general culture
of the inhabitants of an ekitala. I have often heard
assertions such as: 'all the people of North Teso want
Oduya to be our MP' (a location). 'The people of Kotur
are all Albert Otiti's followers' (three lok'alipo's areas
around one market). 'The people of Akobwoit are very
primitive' (a lok'alipo's area).

In almost all instances some natural feature is also
used for the name of a locality. Sometimes the natural
feature no longer exists. The lok'alipo's area that is
called Akobwoit is named after the many *akobwoit* trees
that were originally in the place. They have all been cut
down.

When the term ekitala is used to describe an area inhabited by a number of persons, the term simply implies
co-residence and not necessarily significant or intense
social relations. On the other hand, when two co-
residents are said to be living in the same adukete,
rather than ekitala, the speaker is implying that a significant as opposed to casual relationship exists between
those people. The use of the term adukete implies that
this relationship is part of a set of such relationships
among a group of co-residents who are in face-to-face
interaction. For this reason the term adukete is most
frequently applied to the smallest scale co-residential
unit among the Iteso that is not a household, and which I
call a neighbourhood.

The word adukete (pl. aduketa) is derived from the
word *akiduk* which means 'to build' or 'to construct'. The
derivation adukete signifies a group of co-builders. The
term used for all the different levels of territorial
organization was ekitala. Thus, a literal translation of
adukete is 'a group of people who have co-operated in
building together in a place'.

The neighbourhood is the primary unit of non-domestic
face-to-face interaction among the Iteso. Relations among

neighbours are ideally conceived of as being positive,
co-operative, friendly and open, as opposed to social
relations beyond the boundaries of one's neighbourhood
where caution must be exercised in dealing with people
who are relative strangers and not subject to the res-
traints of personal association. It is an ideal that
relations within a neighbourhood are not hierarchical or
ordered in any superordinate-subordinate way and are
essentially communal in nature. The following description
will demonstrate that the amorphous nature of Iteso neighbourhoods is congruent with its communal values.

Although neighbourhoods are conceptualised by the Iteso
as discreet, named, and bounded units, there is a startling lack of consensus between neighbours about just these
issues. The first difficulty I had to overcome in doing
research in any given neighbourhood was the failure of
informants to answer questions about neighbourhoods at the
lowest level of territorial organization. Iteso could not
conceive of a neighbourhood being of interest to anyone
but the people who composed it. Informants described
neighbourhoods which varied from 4 to as many as 50 households. They often could not give the name of their own
neighbourhoods. Whenever I would ask about the name of a
neighbourhood, I would be given the name of a larger scale
unit. This response stemmed partly from a desire to
stress Iteso solidarity to a stranger and partly from an
unwillingness to believe that I could be interested in
anything as small as a neighbourhood. I was also unaware
at the beginning of the research that because there was
such an extreme lack of consensus about neighbourhood composition they had to be circumscribed largely in terms of
both the ideas and values about them and the symbolism
connected with the neighbourhood form of organization.

A relatively simple example of the kind of confusion
that can arise is the neighbourhood where my wife and I
had our home. We lived very close to the administrative
and social centre of South Teso Location, which was about
a mile from a major road along which stretched the location chief's camp, the largest market centre, a government secondary school, a Catholic Mission and the ruins of
a District Officer's camp. All the people for an area of
about three square miles would give the answer 'Amukura'
to the question 'Ngai ekiror k'adukete kon?' ('What is the
name of your neighbourhood?') In answer to further questioning people would answer that Amukura was the only name
they knew, even though they also agreed that someone who
lived three miles away in what he called Amukura could not
possibly live in the same neighbourhood as the first man.
After we began to be absorbed into neighbourhood

activities we discovered names for neighbourhoods that
circumscribed areas smaller than Amukura. Thus houses
around the market were called Osokoni, the school Osukuzi,
the District Officer's camp Okambi, and the various hills
around my home Moru k'aimosing and Moru k'edokolet and,
near the mission, Omissioni. There was never any agreement, however, as to which neighbourhood some of the homes
belonged. My own home, for example, was variously described as being in Okambi, Omissioni and Moru k'edokolet.
Some of the homes I thought should be in Okambi were described as being in Akudiet, another neighbourhood, or
Asinge, still another. Personally, I never thought of my
home .as being in Moru k'edokolet because I had very little
social intercourse with the people who lived in that
direction.

Neighbourhoods have no formal structure. There is no
internal organization into roles that are related to authority, tasks or ritual affairs. Further, there is not
really a precise catalogue of rights and duties that
define relationships between members and the lack of which
define, by omission, relationships with non-members of
neighbourhoods. The very word that I have used to characterize the present development of this type of organization, 'cluster', conveys the impression of a vague and
ill-defined social unit. Because of the vagueness of the
neighbourhood organization one of the most useful analytical procedures in social anthropology - describing an
organization in terms of its internal organization and
external boundaries - becomes useless. There remain two
ways of describing this kind of amorphous organization.
The first is to look at Iteso ideas and values concerning
the proper state of neighbourly relationships, that is,
the Iteso notion of what constitutes a neighbourhood; and
second, to contrast this particular form of Iteso analytical sociology with actually recurring patterns of behaviour that have references to neighbourhood organization.
I have already done a little bit of the second by examining the problem of neighbourhood boundaries and some ideas
about what it is that neighbours do together. In the remainder of the chapter I will complete the picture of
neighbourly social relations by examining ideas and values
about relations between neighbours and activities that
neighbours undertake together.(10).

The neighbourhood is a communal association of households. This is true not only as an analytical description
but as an element of Iteso thought as well. The most
important jural role in Iteso society is that of household
head, and a neighbourhood is an association of household
heads operating in the political-jural domain (see Fortes,

1969). Relations within households are the concern only
of the household heads. Relations and conflicts that cut
across households are ideally the concern of neighbourhoods. In practice, disputes are frequently brought
before the headman in the hope of bringing administrative
sanctions to bear. If a case involves lineage mates it
may be brought before a respected elder of the lineage or
even a real father if the two men are brothers. At present there are no organized sanctions that can be brought
to bear outside recourse to the courts.

The essential characteristic of neighbourly relations
is mutual aid and co-operation. The first obligation of
any neighbour is to help defend the home of his neighbours
from attack or sudden disaster. Institutionalized violence in the forms of feuding, raiding, or warfare is no
longer part of Iteso culture so the most frequent kind of
sudden disaster is a fire. It occasionally happens during
the dry season that the burning of grazing land gets out
of hand and the fire threatens a man's home. The people
of the home make a noise known as *elulu,* which is a sort
of ululation. All neighbours within hearing distance are
required to rush to their neighbour's aid and help beat
back the fire. Another type of fire is one that has been
accidentally or deliberately started in a home. Then
people will rush to that home and try and put out the fire
and save a man's possessions. In this instance failure to
aid a neighbour is such an extreme breach of neighbourly
relations that it is regarded as prima facie evidence that
the person who failed to help was responsible for starting
the fire. Above all, neighbours are conceived of as
people who aid each other in the face of disaster.

Iteso use two contrasting adjectives to describe the
behaviour of good and bad neighbours in order to condemn
or praise them. These words are *epaparone* and *epog.*
Iteso who are literate in English translate the word
epaparone as 'social'. Kiggen's dictionary translates it
as 'friendly' (1953a, p. 320) and Shut's Ateso-English
word list uses 'neighbour, friend') (MS, p. 20). In my
opinion the translation by literate Iteso comes closest to
the core meaning of the word, although Shut's use of
'neighbour' as a translation is interesting. Iteso describe a man characterized by the word epaparone as more
than friendly or jovial. He is a man who is willing to
share his labour and resources with other people, particularly his neighbours. He responds as much as he can to
requests by his neighbours to provide labour for their
farming; he visits his neighbours and invites them to his
home; he requests their aid in his projects and he is
willing, above all, to share his food and beer with them

as well as being willing to share theirs. The picture
of a man described as epaparone is of a person engaged in
mutual aid, co-operation, and commensal sharing with his
neighbours. I find it striking that Iteso translate this
word as 'social', because to listen to them talk about
people who are epaparone and about the word itself is to
be left with the impression that for the Iteso the word
circumscribes the essential normative core of how the
ideal neighbour should behave.

The contrast to epaparone is epog, a word which literate Iteso translate as 'proud'. Kiggen's Ateso-English
dictionary has 'to swagger, strut, be haughty, to be
proud...to flaunt' (1963a, p. 333, an unusually good
translation). In English the opposite of epaparone is
'to be selfish' and Iteso do say that the motive for
being epog is often selfishness or greediness. They use
the phrase 'Emwan'etau keng' ('His heart is hot'). Yet a
man who is selfish may not necessarily be called epog.
He might not have the resources for epog-like behaviour.
Like epaparone, epog is described in terms of behaviour
and not intention. Iteso will describe a person whom
they characterize as epog as someone who does not help
others or ask for their help in return, does not engage
in co-operative activities and belittles the achievements
of his fellows, and finally as a man who does not share
his food and beer with his neighbours. In short, this
describes the behaviour of a man who acts self-suffici-
ently and does not need to engage in the forms of reciprocity that characterize a neighbourhood. The contrast
is between the person who engages fully in relations of
mutual reciprocity and the person who, for whatever
motives, holds himself apart from those relations.

I have discussed the ideal dimensions of proper behaviour for any Iteso household head. Now I should like
to examine briefly the kinds of occasions that are embed-
ded in a neighbourhood context where this behaviour is
particularly appropriate. Of all the occasions when
people might relate to each other as neighbours there are
three occasions when the neighbourhood aspect of their
social personas (Goodenough, 1965, pp. 3-5) overrides or
is as important as other aspects, such as kinship. These
are informal gatherings at people's homes, communal
labour, and what I call commensal sharing of food and
drink. To a large degree these types of occasions overlap with each other, but it is convenient to consider them
separately.

On any afternoon when the daily round of work has been
completed, men will gather informally at one or more of a
few homes to gossip, relax, and play the game called *elee*.

Women's activities are separate from men's.(11)   The
Iteso are avid elee players. Any man who aspires to be
an influential person keeps an elee board at his home
so that potential followers and friends can come and play.
One important man who kept a diary for me had men at his
home playing elee five or six times every week. An examination of these informal gossip and elee playing groups
showed that they were composed of this influential person's circle of friends and did not often contain, interestingly enough, the closely related agnates whose land
bordered on his own. The atmosphere at these occasions is
always one of informality, equality and cheerfulness.

From an economic point of view a neighbourhood could be
defined as a labour co-operative. During the weeding and
harvesting seasons every home except for the very poorest
will utilize their neighbours in a working party in order
to finish work in a short time. When a working party
comes from a different neighbourhood it becomes a matter
of inter-neighbourhood competition where the outsiders
work very hard, Iteso say, in order to uphold the honour
of their neighbourhood. There is no proper name for a
working party but the beer party that is held in the home
where the work is done is called *ajono nuk'ekitai*, 'beer
of a piece of work'. A household head who requires the
labour announces that on such and such a day there will
be beer for weeding, harvesting, or whatever the work is.
Any neighbour who wishes may join the party, which usually
begins at about 8:30 in the morning after personal chores
are done. The people then work for about three hours, or
until the sun becomes too hot, when they break in order to
share a meal provided by the host. After that they go
home and wash and change in order to return to the host's
home for the beer party. Occasionally the beer party is
held some time after the working party. This happens most
often at the end of the dry season when grain is becoming
scarce. The kinds of tasks involved are always those in
which men and women can work together. If the host is a
young man, the men of senior generations will only engage
in light work. A working party for beer is the only way
some old men and women can get their agricultural chores
completed. The importance of communal work and its inclusive egalitarian character cannot be underestimated.
During the rainy seasons in an area of about fifty households I usually found no less than three working parties
every day.

Neighbourhoods are associated with the communal sharing
of meals and beer. This is particularly seen at the home
of influential men.   On informal occasions plates of the
kinds of foods regarded as snacks are brought and shared

by all visitors: roasted maize, groundnuts, and boiled
cassava are very common, as are varieties of bananas.
Eating a meal out of doors is regarded as a disgusting act
by many of the surrounding ethnic groups, yet Iteso say
that a man who eats inside is selfish and 'proud' and does
not wish to share with his neighbours. Very often, especially in an influential person's home, the evening meal
would be brought outside to be shared with whoever was
there (men first, of course). One such informant whose
home I went to at about 5:00 p.m. almost every day invariably shared his meal with me and a group of five or six
other men who happened to be there. The most important
kind of communal sharing both in terms of frequency and
social significance is beer-drinking. Although it is an
activity that can be extra-neighbourhood in scope it is
intimately tied up with neighbourhood organization, and
Iteso conceive of a neighbourhood as a corporation of persons who share beer together.

In this section I have described the results of the
emergence of the neighbourhood form of social organization
among the Iteso. The problems of boundary definition and
the egocentric perspective that Iteso utilize to define
neighbourhood membership have meant that I was unable to
define a neighbourhood entirely in terms of the rights and
duties occurring on the basis of group membership. Instead I have chosen to examine Iteso ideas, values, and
symbols that they associate with the ideal state of neighbourly social relations.

I have been trying to analyse what Lévi-Strauss calls
the 'conscious model' that the Iteso have of their neighbourhood organization (1953, pp. 526-7). A conscious
model is somewhat different from norms and ideals in that
an anthropologist may be able to discover in conscious
models certain principles toward which behaviour is oriented.(12) Because of this they provide standards by
which deviant behaviour may be evaluated and sanctioned,
and also a stable model for the re-emergence of proper
behaviour after some breach of a norm or conflict.

The importance of this analysis for understanding Iteso
social structure lies in the attributes that I have suggested adhere to conscious models in multiplex societies.
Except for the kinship aspect of social identities the
political-jural domain of Iteso society is presently characterized by a lack of positions of authority - except for
those imposed by the national administration. Furthermore, the political processes that are characteristic of
segmentary societies are not found among the Iteso. What
exists instead is an ideology of communal solidarity that
explicitly entails social relations that are egalitarian

in nature despite obvious differences in wealth, prestige,
and political influence. This ideology is found in the
conscious model of neighbourhood organization. In Goffman's (1961) terms the conscious model provides a definition of the situation for co-residents that is like a
'variably permeable membrane' that only allows certain
personal characteristics to become socially relevant.

VI

The transition from a political system based on territorial sections to one whose dominant structural form is the
neighbourhood is the major feature of the social history
of the Iteso during the colonial period. The largest
units of the precolonial political system were defined in
terms of the coincidence of political and ritual activities, and the values expressed through the performance of
public ritual enforced patterns of authority. The decline
of territorial sections was accompanied by the disappearance of public ritual, for there had been a close functional interdependence of politics and ritual within
territorial sections.

   In the place of the section system there emerged a
system of neighbourhoods that were oriented to particular
patrons. As a colonial (i.e., administrative) presence
was established among the Iteso, the social focus of the
neighbourhoods changed, and they became oriented towards
a number of household heads who interact in an egalitarian
manner. This change was the result of a transfer of the
location of political resources from the local level to
externally based structures such as the missions and the
colonial administration.(13)

   In this chapter, I have described the emergence and
characteristic features of neighbourhood organization,
the social relations that are associated with neighbourhoods, and the ideas and values regarding neighbourhoods
and neighbours that are articulated by the Iteso.

4 Changing patterns of kinship and descent

I

Chapters 2 and 3 described changing patterns of social relations and group structure within the political-jural domain of Iteso society. The major change that I have documented has been the emergence of neighbourhood organization as the dominant form of local political structure. In chapter 3, I was concerned with two additional problems. The first was to describe the normative structure and values of social relations that characterize the neighbourhood form of social organization. The second was to discover the most important occasions when these social relations associated with neighbourhoods were situationally relevant, and to show the structural fit of these norms and values with neighbourhoods. I have so far been concerned with groups which were organized on the basis of territorial principles because these groups provided the form for Iteso political structure.

In the next three chapters I shall be concerned with some problems of kinship and descent that are associated with changes within the political-jural domain. This chapter will be concerned with the analysis of cultural and social aspects of the system of kinship and descent that are related to two issues. The first is the changing relationship of the descent system to Iteso politics and political ideology - particularly the manner in which Iteso describe the way their political decisions are influenced by considerations of descent. The second issue to be dealt with here is the influence that the kinship system exerts on patterns of choice and the manner in which individuals utilize values and social relations relating to kinship and descent to resolve personal problems and social conflicts.

In order to deal with these two problems in the

analysis of kinship and descent I have found it necessary
to organize my discussion by distinguishing among three
levels or aspects of kinship and descent conceived of as
a social field. The first level is the cultural or ideological level. A cultural analysis isolates the principles by which categorical distinctions are made within
the system of kinship and descent and focuses upon the
values associated with these principles. The results of
this analysis provide the basis for an understanding of
the ideological significance of kinship and descent in
Iteso society. This is because kinship and descent principles provide a ready-made set of explanations which
Iteso use to describe and analyse behaviour in the political-jural domain.

Conceived of as a cultural system kinship and descent
appear to be relatively unchanged from the immediate precolonial period. The evidence for this statement is
sketchy, since it is very difficult to document changes
of meaning in societies lacking written records and not
given to the erection of works of art that depict ideal
states. However, considered by itself there is no indication that the meaning of the major categories and terms
for kinsmen that the Iteso have show any significant alterations during the period that I am considering in this
analysis. Rules and regulations relating to kinsmen have
undergone some alteration, however. This can be seen
particularly in those jural norms governing relations
among kinsmen that have been affected by changing political conditions. The jural aspect of any situation, as a
number of recent studies have shown, is composed of any
number of cultural elements, and it must be determined in
each particular case to what degree any given system of
meaning is relevant to the rules in terms of which behaviour is organized (see Keesing, 1971; Moore, 1969).
Since the rules themselves can be described as being
determined by a number of social fields, such as kinship
and territoriality in many African cases, they are more
easily affected by changes in one of their components.
This rules and regulations aspect of kinship constitutes
the second level.

The third aspect of the system of kinship and descent
to be considered is the statistical or behavioural level
(Moore, 1969). Any social field generates options among
which actors choose. It will be demonstrated that over
time the Iteso altered the distribution of their choices.
This changing pattern is related to, once again, the
changing political conditions with which Iteso were forced
to cope.

II

Iteso kin types may be divided into three categories with
which differential behaviour is associated. These categories are agnates, maternal kin, and affines. Agnates
are those people who are related by ties of patrifiliation and distinguished through the patrilineal ideology
espoused by the Iteso. Maternal kin are all people related through ties of matrifiliation. Affines are, of
course, related through or by a marriage.

Although it is possible to distinguish between these
three types of kin, they are not fully encoded into the
terms utilized by Iteso to distinguish between kin-types.
The most inclusive distinctions in the Iteso kinship world
divide all kin into either *ipajanatin* or *ikamerak*.
Ipajanatin are related by real or putative ties of filiation. There is no separate word for agnates except the
phrase itunga k'ekitekere epe, 'people of one clan or
patrilineal kin group'. In the conduct of everyday
affairs, as will be shown below, patrilineal categories
are not relevant. In a patrilineal society it is obvious
that a man and his real or classifactory mother's brothers
do not belong to the same unilineal kin group. Therefore,
one must assume that there are some other kind of ipajanatin than itunga k'ekitekere epe, but there is no word or
phrase which can be found in Ateso to describe them. I
have engaged Iteso informants in heated debate by asking
them to decide whether certain maternal kin might or might
not be called ipajanatin. The issue is whether the observer-imposed analytical construct called 'matrifiliation'
is culturally recognized by the Iteso. The solution is
unreservedly ambiguous in that a good Etesot who is knowledgeable about his culture answers 'Yes, sometimes'.

The same kind of problem arises with respect to maternal kin when the issue is whether to classify them as
affines or not. This problem in the classification of
kinsmen is clearly and unambiguously resolved when a
person is related to another person through a marriage in
his own generation. All Iteso agree that a marriage in
one's own generation creates a relationship that is characterized by the use of the self-reciprocal term *ekameran*
(pl. ikamerak), which I translate as affine. They also
assert that all the people who are related to ego through
marriage are to be referred to as ikamerak, whether they
are in ego's generation or not. Ikamerak is also the term
that is used as a contrast for ipajanatin. If most Iteso
are asked if their maternal kin are ikamerak or ipajanatin
they would answer ipajanatin and rather quickly. There
is, however, an ideology of blood that is associated with

affinity. Iteso say that the blood of affines cannot mix
and if one affine does bleed in front of another, especially in the home of the other affine, the act of bleeding
is regarded as an abomination (akicud). The person who
has bled is forced to pay the fine of a ram to the affine
in front of whom he has done the bleeding. If this fine
is not paid, the people of the household of the offended
affine will become ill and die. The ram is ritually
slaughtered to 'cool' the pollution that has occurred.
Because a ram is a 'cold' animal, it is considered appropriate for slaughter whenever ritual pollution, which is
'hot' has occurred. Therefore, affines are defined in
terms of ritual categories as people who can pollute each
other.

Iteso usually view this prohibition on the mixing of
blood as operating entirely between affines. They rarely
mention that two people who are maternal kin to each other
are also forbidden to mix blood and that the offence is as
serious as between affines. When asked why they are forbidden to mix their blood with that of maternal kin, they
reply that it is because maternal kin are affines. When
I would press my informants to define maternal kin as
'real' or 'actual' affines (ikamerak cut), they frequently
answered that they were not real affines, but affines of
their father (ikamerak ka pa'kon). This implies that
maternal kin occupy an ambiguous status between affines
and agnates. Sometimes they are one, and sometimes they
are the other.

The reasons for this conceptual ambiguity do not lie
within Iteso cultural categories relating to kin and
affines. Iteso clearly distinguish between two types of
kin. The first, called ipajanatin, are people who, by
virtue of an act of procreation in the past, share common
substance.(1) The second category, called ikamerak, are
people who do not share a common substance, are united
through a marital bond, symbolized through the enactment
in ritual of an act of sexual intercourse, and who are
polluted in they mix their blood, a substance that they
share only with their relatives. Maternal kin are difficult to classify because they combine attributes of two
clearly separate categories. They are affines because
they are united by a marriage bond and do not share common
substance with one's father and lineage. On the other
hand, as a result of that marriage, a person and his
maternal kin share common substance. Thus from the perspective of ego's lineage, his maternal kin are relatives.
A man's half-brothers' maternal kin, however, remain for-
ever affines. The factor that makes sense of this ambiguous category is time. Over time affines are turned into

maternal kin through the birth of children to the women of
their clan who have married into other clans. Hence,
while they remain affines to some members of a clan, they
are also maternal kin to other members. The group and ego
perspectives are only separable in the abstract. In
actual situations they often affect each other.(2)

This conceptional ambiguity with regard to maternal kin
is resolved situationally. There are some occasions when
persons who are maternal kin to each other act as members
of lineages that are related affinally. On other occasions, maternal kin act as cognatic relatives. These
occasions will be described below when the social dimensions of relations between maternal kin are examined.

In this section I have been concerned to examine the
ideas and symbols associated with the most inclusive kin
categories of the Iteso. In the remaining sections I
shall describe the rules of behaviour associated with and
the situational relevance of the three categories of kin
that are discussed above.

III

Agnation is perhaps the most important kinship relation
in Iteso society. Categories and groups based on the
patrilineal principle are the most stable elements in the
society. Membership in these categories is inflexible
and determined by birth. Every Iteso is born into an
increasingly larger series of named patrilineal groups until
the names of the fifty or so basic patrilineal categories
that compose Iteso society are reached.

The largest of these categories is the one I have
chosen to call a 'nominal clan', because, it is a name-
holding agnatic unit through which common descent is
presumed but cannot be traced (Fortes, 1953).(3) It is
not necessarily, and may never have been, an exogamous
group.

The most important attribute that membership in a nominal clan confers is a shared name. These clans are not by
definition exogamous, although a few are. Iteso say the
reason that some nominal clans are exogamous is that they
are smaller than the other non-exogamous ones. Some are
smaller in numbers. They appear with less frequency in my
census than the largest clans, but then some putatively
larger clans also appear with limited frequency in my
census data. This is not surprising since in a given
locality there is a clustering of members of five or six
clans. Iteso are not aware of all the names of the clans.
In any case, there are not a fixed number, although Iteso

will assert that there are a fixed number of clans until
confronted with contrary evidence. Then they will tell
you that such and such a clan split off from another clan,
but only under exceptional circumstances. Occasionally
there are origin stories about these circumstances. Below
is the text of a story associated with the clan Imara.

In a time of famine very long ago three brothers of the
clan Ikomolo lived together. Only one of them had a
wife to cook for them but they agreed that whatever
food they could obtain they would share between themselves and would not eat alone. One day the youngest
brother returned home after a fruitless day of searching for food in the bush and found that the wife of the
eldest brother had left a pot of lentils (*amaret*, pl.
imare) cooking. He was so hungry he began to eat all
the lentils by himself. While he was eating, he heard
other people of the home approaching. Acting in haste
in order to prevent his actions from being discovered
he hid the lentils in his mud headdress and put it back
on his head. The lentils were so hot that they burned
the head of the greedy young man and all of his hair
and top layer of skin peeled off. He was so ashamed of
his actions and the condition it had brought him to
that he went off to live by himself and never returned
to visit his brothers again. By doing this he started
his own clan which, because of what the young man did,
is known by the name *Imara*, after the lentils (imare).

Members of the Imara clan deny this tale. As the story
would suggest, and Iteso comments regarding clans affirms,
there may be some degree of sentiment that attaches to
nominal clans as social units. There are, however, very
few opportunities in which this sentiment may be manifest-
ed. I have often seen two Iteso who are searching for a
kinship basis on which to establish a relationship reject
ties of or through nominal clanship and search for a
closer kinship-based tie. To be related to a person on
the basis of nominal clanship is rather like saying to the
other man, 'we're in the same category'. Anyone who has
seen joy of recognition that two strangers experience when
they discover a kin basis for their relationship in a
kinship-based society such as the Iteso would see that
nominal clanship, which relates only to a unilineal category, provides a minimal basis for that recognition to
occur. The interesting aspect of the story is that the
origin of the clan Imara lies (as far as the story goes)
in a failure of the reciprocity that characterizes neighbourhood relations, and the indulgence in a type of private and greedy behaviour that is particularly frowned on
among the Iteso.(4)

Very few of the attributes that are associated with unilineal descent groups in African societies can be found in nominal clans among the Iteso, or for that matter, at any of the lower level segmentary units that I shall discuss. Nominal clans are not organized internally by authority roles; membership does not impose a political status on individuals; and unilineality is not used as an ideological or actual basis for the organization of local groups. The structural significance of nominal clans, as with all Iteso unilineal categories, lies primarily in the area of ritual classification and affiliation. At all levels of segmentation, unilineal descent operates primarily on a ritual level. Therefore, the rest of this discussion of nominal clans will concentrate on the relationship between unilineal descent and ritual.

In addition to being named units, nominal clans have ritual attributes attached to them. These attributes often involve some type of ritual power or authority. Examples of some of these attributes are:

Ikomolo - if they eat the first seasonal fruits of certain wild plants, the rest of the plants will turn bitter.

Ikamarinyang - have the ritual ability to curse.

Ikinom - can cure broken bones and sprains by the laying on of hands.

Ikajoro - are able to cure impotence.

Ilogir - the only clan that could officiate at the poison oracle.

Many of these ritual attributes are entirely forgotten or half remembered. A number of clans claimed to have been the only ones able to officiate at the Aturi ceremony.

Another important aspect of ritual relations is the formalized reciprocal relations between clans. Each nominal clan is tied to another clan called its *aoke*. The other clan can cause the infants of its partner to become ill when they are present unless dust taken from the feet of the partner or from where the partner has walked is smeared on the child. I have often seen this happen at beer parties when an infant has started crying and then been smeared with dust. In addition, Iteso say that in the past at least one member of the partner clan was required to be present at the funeral beer party that was given for the clan members of the deceased. The member of the partner clan was the first to dip his straw into the beer and drink. If he was not present or refused to co-operate, the ceremony could not be held. Today the requirement for the other clan to be present is remembered but neglected. The institution of the ritual pairing of

clans sounds much like a weak version of the Central
African custom of funeral friendship (Colson, 1962).
While I am not clear about the significance of the symbolism involved, it is certain that nominal clans are differentiated on the basis of those presumed ritual attributes
and powers. Thus, the social significance of the ritual
aspect of nominal clanship is primarily categorical in
that clans are the basis of differentiated categories of
Iteso society.(5)

IV

The next level of agnatic organization is that of the
'exogamous clan' or 'exogamous sub-clan'. These are
smaller units of 'nominal clans'. Some smaller nominal
clans are not divided into exogamous sub-units. Igara, a
very large nominal clan, is exogamous. The most important
aspect of the exogamous clan lies in the computing of marriage prohibitions. The sub-clan is the basic unit from
which these prohibitions are derived. By looking at exogamous prohibitions in terms of these sub-clans the simple
rule can be derived that when a marriage occurs, the offspring of that marriage cannot marry into that exogamous
sub-clan until the third descending generation. Thus a
man may not marry his father's father's sister's
daughter's daughter because her mother is an 'acen'
(sister's daughter) to his clan. This is one limiting
case.
    The ideology of marriage prohibitions is phrased both
in terms of exogamous clans and complementary filiation.
Violation of an exogamous prohibition is an act which is
classed as an abomination (akicud). Since abominations
are by definition polluting, there are rituals to remove
the pollution. A marriage which offends the rules of exogamy and, in addition, unites persons who are in adjacent
generations is particularly offensive.
    Exogamous clans are not conceived of by the Iteso as
perpetual social units. They can either create new units
or subdivide into separate units themselves. Their names
are composed of the names of the nominal clans followed
by the modifier *luka* meaning 'those who are of' and the
word that stands for the exogamous clan. The word may
have reference to a taboo, a famous man, or the significance of the referent may be obscure. Three of the exogamous clans of Ikomolo are *luk'anyoutiang*, *luk'ederit*,
and *luk'igracole*. Luk'anyoutiang refers to Anyou, the
presumed founder of the clan who speared and killed an
animal (*etyang*) which jumped up and ran away when he

approached it. Luk'ederit refers to the bushbuck, which
the wives of the men of the clan are forbidden to eat. No
informant was able to explain luk'igracole. The following
is a text describing the origin of three exogamous sub-
clans of the nominal clan Ikuruk:

In the beginning there was only one clan (ekitekere)
called Ikuruk. Then after a time the clan (ekitekere)
divided into two groups called Ikuruk Lukolai and
Ikuruk Ikwatat. They divided on their Eastward movement when they came to the Malaba River. Ikuruk Lukolai crossed above (to the north of) present day Malaba
and Ikuruk Ikwatat below (to the south of) present day
Malaba. The people who crossed on the north found many
crows where they went and these crows were all black.
So they called themselves Ikuruk Luk'olai, the clan of
(unmarked) crows. (*Ikuruk* means crow). The people who
crossed below Malaba came across many crows with a
white stripe across their necks. So they called themselves Ikuruk Ikwatat (an *ikwatat* is a string of beads
worn around the waist by a woman or child). Now, after
a long time they can marry each other. Recently
another clan (ekitekere) broke away from Ikuruk
Ikwatat and it is known as Ikuruk Luk'ikileng. This
clan (ekitekere) is still closely related to Ikuruk
Ikwatat and they may not marry.

A man named Ikileng moved away from Ikwatat because
there were so many in the clan (ekek) and Ikileng had
many wives so he found that his share of meat at a
sacrifice was very small for him. This is why he
thought it would be necessary to begin his own clan
(ekek). After starting his own clan (ekek) he moved
to a hill where he found more Ikuruk Ikwatat. They
joined him and his clan became very large and even the
place was called after him Moru k'Ikileng (Ikileng's
hill).

The man called Ikileng died in 1967 at a very advanced age. He left many children and his clan (ekek) has
become very large. Soon they will marry with Ikuruk
Ikwatat.

This text is interesting for the agnatic ideology that
it expresses. (I will return to that later.) It also
indicates that the process of exogamous clan segmentation
is not an immediate and instant phenomenon. There is
often considerable disagreement among members of an exogamous clan as to whether another segment is part of their
exogamous clan or not. For example, the older men of
Ikomolo luk'anyoutiang claim that they are one with
Ikomolo luk'omudek who live primarily in North Teso location. When the younger men are questioned, they say that

they can marry the Ikomolo luk'omudek and, in fact, at
least one marriage has occurred between them. There is
actually an intermediate stage in which the members of two
sub-clans do not marry but the *icenin* (sister's children)
of the clans do. Thus a marriage between two people who
are members of entirely different clans, but whose mothers
were born into Ikomolo luk'anyoutiang and luk'omudek respectively, would be the first step in breaking down the
rules of exogamy. Exogamous clan segmentation proceeds in
three steps. First is the assertion of a separate identity as we see the Ikuruk luk'ikileng beginning to do in
the text cited above. Second is a stage of semi-exogamy
where people united to the clan by ties of matrifiliation
marry each other. Finally there is full exogamy and separation.

These exogamous sub-clans are not internally differentiated with respect to authority or ritual roles; nor are
they corporate with respect to any kind of property or
office. Their primary importance and social significance
lies in the ritual field. There are a number of ritual
prohibitions associated with each exogamous clan. These
prohibitions involve items that may not be eaten and
actions that cannot be undertaken. The prohibitions apply
only to the wives of the men of the clan, and are symbolically associated with the role of women as wives and
mothers. The symbolism is concerned with the continuity
of the exogamous sub-clan. These prohibitions are called
etale (pl. italia). The word is derived from the verb
akitale, 'to be forbidden to eat'. A married woman is
freed of these prohibitions after a ceremony called
egwasit ('sprinkling') is performed. This is the final
ceremony of incorporation into her husband's clan and may
be performed only after the birth of a number of children.

Exogamous clans also play a limited role at funeral
rituals. People feel an obligation to attend the burial
of a fellow clansman, and there is a special mortuary beer
for all members of the clan who wish to attend. In disputes, an elder may be called in to mediate between two
clan members. His mediation is not binding although it
does carry extra moral force because it comes from a common clan member. Also, where there are few members of one
minimal lineage present in a given area, they will align
themselves ritually with another lineage of their exogamous clan in an area. Thus exogamous clanship provides a
potential pool of ritual resources in the event that there
are no available agnates who are more closely related.

When Iteso speak about ties of mutual exogamous clanship in the abstract, they do so in terms of sentiment.
Clansmen feel an obligation to entertain each other; they

travel considerable distances in order to attend and support other clansmen at rituals and when they have to travel to an area where they are strangers they seek out any fellow clansmen who may be resident there for aid, hospitality, and guidance. In uncertain situations fellow clansmen are a known quantity. Thus there is a tendency for fellow clansmen to favour and support each other over strangers with whom no other kinship tie intervenes.

This may account for the unity which Iteso attribute to clans despite the absence of jurally binding ties among exogamous clansmen. I first became aware of this presumed unity when I was listening to cases in the office of the location chief. A madwoman burst into his office and told him that his clan (ikomolo luk'anyoutiang) had stolen the chiefship from her clan (Ikajoro luk'eseme) and that he should give it back. The chiefship is an administrative position whose authority is derived from the national government. It is held by a person and not a group. Yet when I investigated the problem I found that most Iteso believed that the clan of the chief was solidly behind him and would do whatever he told them to do in the political arena. When the parliamentary elections were held in late 1969, people analysed the returns for different sub-locations in terms of members of clans voting for the candidate whom their most politically eminent member supported. In Amukura they said that Ikomolo luk'anyoutiang voted for the loser, Oduya Oprong, because Oduya had paid the location chief to deliver the votes of his clan. My own investigation indicated that this was not true. The older men voted for the incumbent, Oduya, because he emphasized traditional values and tribal fears in his campaign. The younger men voted for the late Lawrance Ojamong because he ran a campaign based on bringing 'economic progress' to the Iteso. This was a pattern that obtained in almost every area of the Iteso constituency, but almost all Iteso, young and old, believed that Ikomolo luk'anyoutiang marched solidly behind the chief, whom they said was in the pay of Oduya.

While these exogamous clans exist primarily as kinship categories, rather than corporations, these categories are the object of both sentiment and opinion. People are proud of their clans and the exploits of eminent clansmen. In marital relations, if a woman wishes to refuse her husband's request, she often will not simply say 'no'. Instead she will refer to her natal clan in the third person and say 'Ikamarinyang will not do that'. Songs praising clans are often sung in beer parties and women will make up chants praising their natal and husband's clans. The highest praise for a woman of proven fertility - one who has mothered many children - is to call her *toto k'ekit-ekere,* mother of the clan. All this suggests that exogam-ous clans retain a symbolic importance that far exceeds their behavioural significance in everyday life. The rea-sons for this are far from clear, nor do I think that it is really possible to ascertain in any certain fashion why clans should loom so large in Iteso conceptual life. It is clear, however, that for Iteso they are the basic cate-gories of their society and the major elements of social differentiation and, because of this, are important for attributing social characteristics to people. This is why people assume that clans are unitary groups as far as certain kinds of action are concerned. Examples include the political behaviour quoted above or attributing char-acter traits such as 'clan so-and-so are all liars' or 'clan such-and-such are poisoners'.

Often one finds the same traits attributed to locali-ties (6) but, upon examination, the trait is believed to exist in a certain area because people of a certain clan are said to predominate in the population. Thus, Chama-siri sub-location in North Teso location is believed to be full of poisoners. It is called 'Katanga' because it is such a dangerous place. I was warned, that if I happened to go there, not to drink from a well or even chew a blade of grass because poison was spread on these in order to kill unsuspecting strangers. Beer-drinking, of course, or eating food was out of the question. One of the rea-sons that Chamasiri is so notorious is that many of the clan Ikamarinyang live there and their power to curse makes them automatically suspect.

The sentiment that exists among clan members when it is combined with the residential clustering that exists in localities makes them a potential pool of human re-source. An astute and influential figure often relies on his fellow clansmen as followers and henchmen. Also, clan sentiment can be put to good use by some individuals. One example will suffice. In 1961 a young man was chosen by Dutch missionaries to go to Holland for further education. He was one of the first two or three Iteso to go beyond the primary school level. In order to obtain more funds to supplement the meagre allowance given him by the Dutch fathers, he relied on his fellow clansmen. A series of beer parties was given in the three separate localities where there were many numbers of his clan living. He went to each party and collected donations. People who were reluctant to give were told that his poverty would shame them because it would be said that their clan was too sel-fish to help him. Since his return from Holland he has become an assistant Education Officer. He has

assiduously avoided all but his closest clansmen. The
other members of his clan say he has become 'proud' and
forgotten them and they say this is one of the reasons the
clan segment in one sub-location will split from the segment in another sub-location, where the Education Officer
comes from, although in fact both sub-clans have members
living elsewhere.

V

The third level of segmentation is the lineage. It is
the smallest in scale and consists of a group of agnates
who can trace their descent back to a founding ancestor
who was the father or grandfather of the senior living
generation of men. The behavioural significance of the
lineage lies primarily within the ritual field. The
lineage conducts funeral rituals and is involved in all
domestic ceremonies. The wives of the men of this group
form a ritual congregation. Their presence is necessary
in order for all domestic ceremonies to be carried out.
Women travel considerable distances so that they can be
present at the most important ceremonies. For ritual
purposes the lineage should be localized, but it rarely
is. Only recently formed lineages are resident in one
locality. The traditionally high rate of Iteso spatial
mobility means that even the minimal lineage is invariably dispersed.
    The ideal pattern of lineage formation is that after
the death of all the members of the senior (and founding)
generation, the offspring of each founder of the lineage
will form their own separate lineages whose names will
memorialize the dead men. As an example, there was a
lineage of which a man called Oteba was a member. It
was called *Nyanganyang*. After the death of Oteba and all
his brothers, with whom he founded the lineage, the six
sons of Oteba formed their own lineage called ekek
k'Oteba (Oteba's lineage) after their dead father. The
ideal pattern is frequently followed. When this pattern
is not followed it is usually because of one of two circumstances. First, the descendants of a man may be so
few that they feel that they are unable to form a viable
lineage. Then they amalgamate with a more numerous set
of siblings. The second cause is the result of Iteso
practice of inheriting widows within lineages. Widow
inheritance does not constitute the true levirate as the
sons born to the successor marriage are not jurally the
children of the dead first husband. The children of the
first marriage usually go to live with their mother at

the home of the second marriage.   The mother-child bond
among the Iteso is very strong.   They say that 'children
always love their mother more than their father'.   The
children of an inherited mother by different fathers often
form a single lineage.   In both of these cases, the genealogies are manipulated after the passage of time so that
the less eminent man is forgotten.   This is not an unusual
process in African societies and has been very well documented (Winter, 1956; Gulliver, 1956).   In this case, however, the manipulation does not occur because of corporate
rights to a common estate but usually because the group is
too small to make effective use of their only common possession, rituals associated with marriage, fertility,
birth and death.

The lineage is centred around life-crisis rituals held
for its members.   One set that is particularly important
are the rituals associated with death.   Because of the
confusing terminology that I discuss below, I was forced
to discuss lineages in terms of ritual function.   In the
course of research, I had to ask about lineages as 'people
who share meat at a funeral', a reference to the recognition of lineage unity at funeral sacrifices.   At the most
culturally elaborated crisis in Iteso society, death, the
lineage emerges as a solidary group.   The failure to participate in funeral rituals is sanctioned through adverse
public opinion, and it is believed that *ipara,* spirits of
the dead, will malevolently attack those who fail in their
funeral duties.   Because of the frequency of rituals involving lineage members, lineage identity plays an important part in the religious life of all Iteso.   Any crisis
that is attributable to supernatural causes may bring lineage members around to consult, mediate, and perform rituals.   Thus, the lineage, although dispersed and not relevant to the regulation of the ownership of property or
politics, still forms an important part of a person's
social identity.

The preceding sections have described the meaning of
kinship and descent categories and the situations in which
rules related to social identities generated by those
categories are relevant.   There remains one very significant situation in which descent has become an irrelevant
category.   This situation is concerned with the regulation
of disputes among members of adjoining territories.   This
changing pattern can be described in the clearest terms
through a brief examination of disappearance of the institution of the feud.   It was mentioned in chapter 2 that
the feud was conceived of by Iteso as an obligation based
on ties of common clanship that devolved upon the members
of a territorial sub-section.   The group that exerted

vengeance for the death of one of its members was the sub-
section. The ideological justification for their acting
as a vengeance group was that they were all members of an
exoganous sub-clan or the clients of one of the members of
that sub-clan. Clearly, membership in the clan itself
constituted a stronger claim than being the client of a
member. This could well have provided incentives for remaining with agnates or even for moving as an agnatic
group. The Iteso do describe precolonial migrations as
the movements of agnates of the same generation.

A feud could be ended by the offending party paying an
indemnity equal to the current rate of bridewealth or by
handing over a woman to be married without bridewealth.
Homicide within an exogamous sub-clan was almost always
ended by the immediate payment of two or three head of
cattle. Within a lineage neither compensation nor a feud
is possible (see the feud described in Case 6). The rules
of a feud indicate that there are relationships among descent, the rules of exogamy, marriage, replacement of personnel and political processes. What is important for
this analysis is the association of political action by a
territorial form of organization with a justification that
is conceived of in descent terms. This indicates that
descent principles formed part of what Moore (1969) calls
the 'political constitution' of precolonial Iteso society.
Some of the organizations that formed Iteso political
structure received their legitimacy from descent principles.

Presently the sub-section no longer exists, the feud
is prohibited, and has not been practised for over forty
years, and Iteso do not regard common descent as a justification for political action. They do, as I described
earlier, regard common descent as a motive for political
behaviour, but these are two different things. Thus,
while some situations are governed by rules of which descent forms a component - in some rituals, the major
component - political action is no longer one such type
of situation.

VI

Until this point in the chapter I have been concerned to
describe the meaning of kinship and descent and the situational relevance of kinship and descent categories. This
has involved me in describing the changing patterns of
regulations associated with the social identities generated by categories of kinship and descent.

In the remainder of the chapter I shall turn my

attention to the third level of description, the statistical or behavioural level. In the succeeding sections I shall be concerned with examining the options presented to Iteso by the field of kinship and descent. In this I shall describe different kinship and descent relationships in terms of the advantages and disadvantages that result from the choice of one over the other. In chapter 3 I described the changing political conditions that have influenced Iteso to pursue a strategy of mixing the type of kinsmen they choose to live with rather than concentrating primarily upon agnates as co-residents. The remaining sections of this chapter describe the consequences of this changing strategy.

The choice of one relationship over another has significant consequences for Iteso. One such consequence is that the choice defines the rights and obligations that one person has vis-à-vis another. Iteso, therefore, often attempt to change the definition of the situation when it suits them. That they have some scope to do so is indicated by flexible use they make of terms for agnatic social relations. There is a pair of terms that, when applied to agnates, indicates relative closeness or distance of social relations. This creates a situation in which these terms become excellent tools for the indirect expression of hostility or solidarity.

I have already described one example of this terminological relativity and flexibility in my discussion of the distinction between locality and neighbourhood (chapter 3). Locality and neighbourhood are observer-imposed categories which are useful for distinguishing between types of verbal behaviour and social interaction found at the local level among Iteso. The indigenous concepts ekitala and adukete only correspond in a very rough sense to the observer categories. Iteso patterns of use for the terms indicate that they can express opinions, ideas, and sometimes even feelings about the relative social distance between co-residents. Thus, although there are patterns in the use of these terms, for an individual their use is conditioned by such personal factors as extent and direction of personal network, economic status, history of conflict and so on.

Iteso terminology for patrilineal groups and categories can be described in the same terms. Two terms are in general use for agnatic groups. They are ekitekere (pl. itekeriok) and ekek (pl. ikekia). The word ekek has 'door' or 'threshold' as its primary referent. The reference is to Iteso domestic ceremonies in which incorporation with a group of agnates is symbolized by the passing of women or children out of a door and over a threshold.

The symbolism implies that the meaning of the term ekek is extended to cover a group of people who are related as agnates through a ceremony of incorporation. The only group that actually passes over the same threshold are the children of one mother, who are brought out of the mother's sleeping house. This group is specifically referred to as *etogo epe* (one house) and the term ekek is never applied to it. The house or matrisegment is, as we shall see below, a corporate group with a specific set of rights attached to it, and the term ekek suggests the very close and solidary relations associated with a matriseg-ment.

The other term, ekitekere, has no other primary referent. It simply refers to a named social group of presumed common origin that can be differentiated from other such groups. When Iteso describe the differences between an ekitekere and an ekek, they invariably describe one by contrasting it with the other. An ekitekere is always made up of a number of ikekia. An ekek is one of a number of similarly constituted parts of an ekitekere. Except that they refer to the operation of the agnatic principle, the definitions of the two terms are circular. Relations within an ekek are always closer than those within an ekitekere. To say something is closer is really to use an impossibly vague term. It implies for the Iteso more sentiment and a greater moral obligation to co-operate with each other, especially on ritual occasions.

The two terms are applied by Iteso to a variety of groups that can be distinguished by both functional (in terms of activities) and morphological criteria. The three agnatic groups that are so distinguished I have called a nominal clan, an exogamous clan, and a lineage. I have also heard the Iteso ethnic group referred to as ekitekere when distinguished from neighbouring ethnic units such as the Baluhya, Luo, and Jo Padhola. This usage is based on the assumption that the Iteso as a whole have a common origin when contrasted to other tribes. I have never heard of any territorial group called an ekitekere. This includes nations because 'they are made up of many itekeriok', i.e., groups of diverse origins. Thus the terms ekitekere and ekek are applied to the same kinds of groups on different occasions depending upon the context and symbolic intent of the user. The term ekitekere is used more frequently for the higher levels of segmentation and ekek for the lower levels of segmentation. The relationship between the terms, fre-quency of use, and levels of segmentation are diagrammed in Figure 1.

To illustrate the use of the terms, I left the original

Ethnoterm	Emergent Groups of Common Origin	Level of Segmentation
Ekitekere	Tribe Nominal Clan Exogamous Clan	Highest
Ekek	Lineage	Lowest

FIGURE 1   Agnatic terminology*
*The arrows point in the direction of lesser frequency of use for the term.

words that I translated as 'clan' in the text on page 66 in parentheses. The informant from whom the text on page 66 was elicited was discussing the division of one group into two and then three groups at the same level of segmentation, exogamous clanship. However, he did not use the same term for all the divisions. When he was discussing divisions that occurred in the timeless past and are completed he used the term ekitekere. By doing this he stressed the point that relations are distant both in the social sense and in the sense that a long time has passed since they were close. In the case of splitting off of Ikuruk luk'ikileng he called both the new and old groups ekek rather than ekitekere. Thus he stressed that the people of Ikileng are still genealogically, socially, and even residentially closely related in spite of their having become an exogamous clan like Ikwatat. Note that he refers to Ikwatat as ekitekere. They are not as closely related as Ikileng.

Another example may prove even more instructive because it involves the deliberate use of terminology to create the impression of distance.

Case 1: Omuse and Ikileng

Omuse and Ikileng both belong to lineage Aine of clan Ikomolo luk'anyoutiang. Omuse and four other household heads of the lineage have long wished to split off from the rest and have stopped going to funeral sacrifices for their dead lineage mates of 'the other side'. There have been a series of disputes and court cases between Ikileng and Omuse. Omuse believes Ikileng has burned down his (Omuse's) house along with the harvested cotton that was in it. One day Omuse was reputed to have suggested to the wife of Ikileng that she leave these people (of Ikileng's home) as she was cooking without any bridewealth having been paid. Osmuru visited Omuse to inquire about these remarks. Omuse told

Omusuru that if he was coming to Omuse's home as an
affine (the F of his 'son' [Ikileng] of lineage's
wife), it was a useless action and he should leave because 'Mam ong k'arai Ekomolot', I am no longer an
Ikomolo. Instead he suggested that Omusuru approach
his home as Omuse's Onac lok'eja (MZA) and be welcomed;
however, they could not talk of this 'business of
Ikomolo'. Eventually Omuse brought Omusuru to court
for defamation of character because he claimed that he
would not have said anything to his 'son's daughter.
A man, Omuse said, 'fears' to do such a thing.

Although this is only a segment of an intricate and
involved case, I present it here for the clear example it
gives of one person's manipulation of the patrilineal
ideology. Omuse had the choice of actualising one of two
possible relationships, affine or maternal kin. As
affines, Omuse and Omusuru are related on the basis of a
marriage between their respective lineages and, by definition, exogamous clans. But the mother of Omuse and the
mother of Omusuru were both sisters of the lineage of a
third clan, Ikajoro. Thus, in Iteso ideology both Omuse
and Omusuru are sister's sons (icenin) of the same clan.
By choosing to define the situation as a relationship between maternal kin Omuse was able to structure the en-
counter so that his membership in Ikomolo clan was irrelevant. This is why his manipulation of terms for agnatic
groups is appropriate and informative - although somewhat
startling. 'Mam ong k'arai ekomolot', 'I am not an
Ikomolo', he said. He did not say 'I am not of the people
of Aine', and thereby imply the term ekek. He said he did
not belong to the nominal clan. Nominal clans are fixed
categories of Iteso society and membership is an ascribed
part of a person's social identity. It is easier, I would
think, to change sex than to change clan identity. The
Iteso cannot imagine a world without clans. The first
question they would ask about my country was the names of
the clans. Omuse is not a stupid man. His behaviour in
the case I recorded above indicates that he is a very
astute judge of the political realities of Iteso life. By
denying his clanship he was avoiding the discussion of a
serious breach of a kinship norm that he had committed.
He also was symbolically making statements about the intensity of the conflicts between himself and the other
side of the lineage. He did not state that relations were
no longer close. To do that he would have disclaimed membership in the minimal lineage and thus implied the word
ekek. By denying membership in the nominal clan, he suggested the word ekitekere and by this meant that the conflict was so intense that even distant social relations

were no longer possible. Thus he used the flexibility of
agnatic terminology to make symbolic statements about the
intensity of social conflict.

In this discussion of patriliny I have concentrated on
the categorical significance of agnation rather than the
corporate nature of the kin groups involved. Mitchell
(1966, pp. 51-6) distinguished between three types of
social relationships, the 'structural', the 'categorical'
and the 'personal'. In my discussion of agnatic social
relationships, I have been concerned with the first two.
Structural relationships according to Mitchell are those
'which have enduring patterns of interaction and which
are structured, i.e., the norms are defined in terms of
the role expectations of others' (p. 51). Structural
relations, for example, characterize the internal organization of unilineal kin groups that have important political functions or, as another example, characterize
political relations between lineages among the Tallensi.

Categorical relations,(7) on the other hand,
arise in situations where, by the nature of things,
contacts must be superficial and perfunctory...(people)
tend to categorize people in terms of some visible
characteristic and to organize their behaviour accord-
ingly....It is essential to categorical relations that
internal divisions within a category be ignored.
Southall...suggests that: 'It is a matter of external
classification rather than of self-identification.'
But this is not quite accurate since if Ego orders
his behaviour vis-à-vis B in terms of a social category it is implied in his behaviour that he identifies
himself with a relevant category vis-à-vis B. (1966,
pp. 52-3)

Mitchell is concerned here with African urban studies,
but his analytic distinctions apply as well to the rural
Iteso. Iteso patrilineal relations should be viewed as
falling on a continuum between the two polar opposites
represented by 'structural' and 'categorical' relationships. The more inclusive the level of organization, the
more categorical the relations become. The lower the
level of organization, the more specific are the rights
and duties attached to membership in the category group.
Thus within the lineage, rights and duties devolve around
funerals and sacrifices and the inheritance of widows.
At the level of nominal clanship, relations are almost
entirely categorical. I have constructed Figure 2 to
illustrate the relationships between the types of relationships and level of patrilineal organization.

Two points emerge from this discussion. First, Mitchell suggests that categorical relations 'arise in

Ideal Type	Level of Organization
Categorical	
	Nominal Clan
	Exogamous sub-clan
	Lineage
	Matrisegment
Structural	

FIGURE 2 Systems of social relations
in the clan and lineage

situations where...contacts must be superficial and perfunctory'. This may be associated among the Iteso with
dispersal of clans and lineages. Ideally, all agnatic
units are dispersed but the higher the level of organization the greater the degree of dispersal and therefore the
more perfunctory the contacts. The text cited above
(p. 66) indicates that there is a tendency towards segmentation when degree of dispersal increases. The second
point is related to the first. The more dispersed and the
more categorical the relationships, the greater degree of
choice that is allowed to an individual over whether to
pursue and maintain a relationship.
    The flexibility of the terminology for agnatic groups
has been discussed at length because it is in this issue
that the relationship between cultural categories and
jural norms relating to the agnatic principle and their
social significance can be discovered. The flexibility
of these categories and the ease with which they can be
manipulated is paralleled by a social system in which
social relations based on agnation are open to choice.
Furthermore, this element of choice is related to absence
of political and economic functions in the clan and lineage system. In chapter 6 I shall discuss the association
of political and economic activities in relation to the
developmental cycle in domestic groups. It is my opinion
that any adequate understanding of the principle of descent in a unilineal society must assess the dual contri-
bution that the unilineal principle makes to the formation
of categories on the one hand, and to the formation of
groups and associated roles on the other hand.

VII

In this section I shall consider all non-agnatic ties

together since the normative context that characterizes
these social relationships cannot be fully understood
without showing that they must be examined over time and
in conjunction with social processes such as the transfer
of property and the developmental cycle in domestic groups.
groups.

Although the term of address between affines, ekameran,
is self-reciprocal, affinal ties are asymmetric in content. Iteso explain that a husband is under an obligation
or has a debt to the relatives of his wife for allowing
him to take the woman, or, if the marriage was by capture,
allowing him to keep her. This debt is represented by the
relatively high bridewealth of ten to twenty head of
cattle. Although this figure is not high when compared to
some pastoral societies, its high cost can be understood
if the cash value of the cows assessed as bridewealth is
computed. The value is between seven and twelve times the
average yearly cash income for an Iteso family. This
figure is even higher when it is considered that the mean
number of cattle per household is 2.6. Bridewealth is
never paid in a lump sum and it may take more than twenty
years for payments to be completed. A consequence of this
process is that a husband is almost always in the position
of fending off the demands of his wife's agnates for
bridewealth. This makes him more amenable to other, less
onerous demands. Bridewealth is returnable under conditions of divorce or desertion by a wife, but if children
have been produced a large portion of the bridewealth is
retained. If the husband dies and the wife is inherited
within the husband's lineage, an additional cow is given
to the wife's natal lineage as an expression of good
faith. Marriage establishes the transfer of sexual, pro-
creative, and productive rights in women from one lineage
to another. The gradual nature of the transfer is symbolized by both the piecemeal transfer of bridewealth and
the ceremonies of incorporation of a woman into her husband's lineage (called *italia*). The ceremonies take place
over a period of ten to twenty or more years. Incorporation can never be completed if the woman fails to produce
children and this is signified by the return of all but
one cow of the bridewealth at her death. Bridewealth is a
source of tension among affines and almost all court cases
between affines (except for land cases) are over differing
claims regarding bridewealth.

A man must avoid his wife's parents. This rule is
especially rigid between a man and his wife's mother. A
man and his wife's mother must not see each other on pain
of blindness striking both of them. I have often been
walking on the road with an informant when he dived head-

long into the bushes in order to avoid his wife's mother. This avoidance is extended to all the women his wife calls 'toto' (mother), but is only strictly adhered to with an actual wife of wife's father. However, even a man and the classificatory mother of his wife are uncomfortable in each other's presence. A man's attitude to his wife's father is one of extreme respect rather than severe avoidance. Again, this relationship is extended to all lineal 'fathers' of wife. The intensity of respect and avoidance lessens with distance between wife and her classificatory parents. This relationship provides a strong contrast with the relationship between a man and his sister's husband's parents. There, the socially enforced attitude is one of relative familiarity.

Within the same generation, relations between affines are more egalitarian. There still remains, however, the implicit superiority of wife-giver over wife-receiver. This superiority is frequently modified by an intense relationship characterized by years of mutual reciprocity. Affines of the same generation very often have very warm and friendly social relations with each other. Their relationship is characterized by continual rounds of visiting and co-operation. During cases of conflict, especially cases of conflict within lineages, a man turns to his affines for support and advice, just as in political contests his opponents often try to implicate his affines in whatever misdeeds he is supposed to have committed. This modification of the hierarchy of relationships has structural limitations, however. Despite all of the many residential moves recorded, I have not one single instance of an individual moving under the authority of his sister's husband, while over 30 per cent of 200 moves that I examined record a man moving under the authority of his wife's brother or father. The normative superiority of a wife-giver over a wife-receiver is simply incompatible with the social relations that would be established if a wife-giver moved to an area to become the follower of a wife-receiver. On the other hand, leader-follower relations are reinforced by the norms of kinship when wife-receiver moves to be a follower of his normatively superior wife-giver. Thus moves to live with a wife's brother or father or even a mother's brother are common.

Two additional points are necessary. First, I have mentioned that the affinal relationship is extended to include all of a spouse's agnates and even on occasion the affines of a spouse's agnates. Thus, a person's wife's brother's wife's brother might call ego ekameran because he is a wife-giver to that person's wife's brother and by extension a wife-giver to ego. Ego self-reciprocally extends the terms as the wife-receiver of a wife-receiver. This is diagrammed in Figure 3 where A and C can call each other ekameran on the basis of their relationship to B. If A and C are agnates, the lineal relationship would, of course, override affinality.

FIGURE 3 Affines

Two men who receive wives from the same agnatic group, that is, who are related to each other as real or classificatory wife's sister's husband, call each other *opatiak*, which is derived from the verb *akitiak*, to share. Their relationship is one of absolute equality and mild joking. Agnates frequently find themselves related as opatiak when, as often happens, two sisters marry into the same lineage. Then the relationship is ignored.

The second point is that affinal relations are theoretically extended to all of a wife's and sister's husband's agnates. In fact, they are frequently maintained only with wife's and sister's husband's full siblings - except for brief contacts with their half and classificatory siblings. Only if a wife of sister's husband has no living full siblings will intense affinal relations be extended beyond the confines of a matrisegment. This is because conflict is endemic within lineages, especially between sets of full siblings, and an affine as a supporter of his wife's or sister's full brothers is drawn into conflict with their lineage mates.(8)

Relations with maternal kin are among the most significant for Iteso. There is not only a formal, customary aspect to these ties but also a warm, affective tone to them. These ties are constantly renewed through continual rounds of mutual visiting and by various types of cooperation. When Iteso discuss their maternal kin, they dwell on the easy intimacy of the relationship and willingness of maternal kin to help in a crisis. In an abstract sense, maternal kin are people to whom one can turn for aid and ungrudging support. From the perspective of any individual, maternal kin of father's generation are

the first and foremost willing elders to whom he turns for
support, aid, and general sympathy in difficult situations. Over and over again I observed the recruitment of
maternal kin by men for support in cases of conflict,
especially when these were cases of interlineage conflict.
   The most important maternal kin for an adult male is
his mother's brother, called *mamai*.(9)   I shall limit my
discussion to relations with the mother's brother. Iteso
automatically assume an intimate connection between a
mother's brother and his sister's son. Fugitives are
thought, for example, to flee to the home of their
mother's brother. A mother's brother and his sister's son
may joke in a very mild fashion with each other by rever-
sing their kinship terms. On the occasion of his marriage
a man goes to the homes of his maternal kin in order to
inform them of the event and collect small contributions
toward the inauguration of his household. The mother's
brother plays a significant ritual role at the funeral of
a sister's child. He is given a brown hen to take home
with him. On the way home he pulls feathers from the hen
to form a trail to his home for the *eparait* (spirit) of
the dead person to follow. While ipara (spirits of the
dead) are very dangerous to their own home, I do not know
of any case where they have attacked their own maternal
kin. The converse of this is that sister's children
bring chickens to the funeral of their mother's brother
which they sacrifice on the morning of the burial.
   Any man who is called onac 'brother' by Ego's mother is
called 'mamai' by ego. Thus, in its extended sense, mamai
may be defined as 'a consanguine of ego and his mother of
the first ascending generation to ego'. Behaviourally
this means very little. Only an actual mother's brother
is a figure of authority. This may be seen in his ritual
authority to curse a sister's son who has failed to recognize the rights of his mother's brother, although his
curse is not as severe, or dangerous, as the curse of a
mother or a father, which Iteso view as a genuinely ter-
rible act that must be done only under conditions of the
most extreme provocation. The mother's brother is a kind
of indulgent authority figure with whom intense relations
are highly valued. When I discussed with Iteso in the abstract which type of kin a man would choose to live with,
maternal kin as embodied by the mother's brother were
invariably a first choice.
   Ideally the maternal kinsman with whom relations are
most intense is a mother's full brother. This also represents a statistical norm. It happens, however, that
for some reason or another a mother's full brother is unavailable or unsuitable for the intense relations that

characterize the role. Then another brother may be chosen
from the same lineage or exogamous clan to act as if he
were a mother's full brother. Since most men regard it as
necessary to maintain a close relationship with his
mother's lineage one rarely finds a younger household head
who does not have some brother of his mother nearby with
whom he interacts intensively. The case I give below
illustrates both the way the relationship may be extended
and the personal usefulness that relations with maternal
kin may serve.

Case 2: Ejakait's Land

Aura (Ikomolo luk'anyoutiang, lineage Palinyang) married four wives. The first, Fulgencia, had four children; the second, Aserena, three; the third, Dolotia,
died in childbirth and left no children; and the
fourth, Veronica, the wife of his old age, had two
children. The first born son was Wasike, the child of
Fulgencia, and the second born son was Panyako Ejakait,
the son of Aserena. Aserena died in childbirth when
Panyako was eleven. Veronica took care of Panyako and
his full brothers and sisters and he says that she is
like a real mother to him. Veronica was born to Ikuruk
clan.
   Wasike was the first son to get married. He received land on the north portion of Aura's holdings,
where his mother Fulgencia had her house and gardens.
The north half is considered the better half of the
holdings as the southern half is part of a seasonal
swamp. Panyako was the second son to get married. He
married at the rather youngish age of twenty-two.
When Aura announced that he was also going to give
Panyako land in the northern half, Fulgencia and her
son Wasike protested. They claimed that the land belonged to their matrisegment by virtue of the fact that
Fulgencia had built her house there and kept her gardens there. Panyako argued that under Iteso traditional law allocation of land is not governed by membership
in a matrisegment. His father and the elders of the
neighbourhood and clan agreed with Panyako.
   When land is transferred to a person, the participants in the transfer walk the boundary with elders of
the neighbourhood and exogamous clan as witnesses along
with whomever the supporters of the transacting parties
choose. The act of a father giving his son a share of
land is not fully completed before the boundaries are
walked. Adjustments are made during the walking. In
order to support his claims, Panyako recruited Odera

and Karani. Odera is a neighbourhood influential of
the same clan as Aura and Panyako. He had recently
lost a land case to Aura in which he claimed the southern half of Aura's land. He kept very quiet during the
walking of the boundaries. Panyako said later that
Odera was still a good choice for a supporter because
his private advice had been excellent, and he had recruited support among the leaders of the neighbourhood
for Panyako by playing on their fear of Aura's success
in bribing court appointed assessors in land cases.

Karani was at the time (1964) a county councillor
and a man of known wisdom and influence. He was also
Panyako's classificatory mother's brother. Panyako's
mother was born in exogamous clan Ikomolo luk'igracole.
All the adult males of her lineage were dead. Thus
Karani was a rather distant brother of the exogamous
clan. He is, however, the most influential member of
the exogamous clan living in the area. After the death
of Panyako's mother he kept an occasional eye on Panyako, and Panyako was a fervent supporter of Karani in
the election campaign of 1962.

During the course of walking the boundaries, Karani
argued eloquently for Panyako's rights and requirements. Out of a total of a nine-acre holding, Panyako
estimates that four acres were the result of Karani's
intervention. Since that time Panyako has visited
Karani's home frequently and has become a very close
friend of Karani's son, who is a university student
and thus a man of obvious potential wealth and influence. Panyako himself says that he feels that he can
refuse Karani very little. One opportunity to help
Karani came when Panyako enlisted me to carry the body
of Karani's sister's daughter to her father's home
after she died of a snake bite while living at the home
of Karani (see Case 4).

The significance of the case is clear. First, it dem-
onstrates the protective role a mother's brother may
assume with respect to his sister's son, especially when
the sister's son is in potential conflict with his own
close agnates. Second, it illustrates how the relationship may be extended in the absence of an actual full
brother of ego's mother. Third, and most importantly, it
illustrates that the relationship viewed as a contract
developed over time by two partners must be distinguished
from the ideal description given by the Iteso. This is a
very important aspect of relations with maternal kin.
While a man has many mother's brothers, he usually has a
special relationship with one or two who are usually
mother's full brothers. This stands in direct contrast

to societies where mother's brothers are part of a unilineal descent group that has significant corporate functions (see especially, Winter, 1956). The Iteso pattern
differs in that agnation is utilized primarily to form
categories rather than corporate lineages. Another point
to be added here is that distant agnates, because of
special knowledge or influence, may be particularly useful
in situations of conflict with closely related agnates.

Thus far I have discussed the normative and contractual nature of relations with maternal kin. These relations are associated with a high degree of positive affect
and a culturally recognized protective relationship between mother's brothers and sister's sons. The relationship is usually most intense between a man and his
mother's full brother. Although their relationship can be
described separately, an analysis of the content of the
relationship cannot be achieved without discussing relations between brothers, sisters and affines as part of a
complex that also includes social relations with maternal
kin.

One of the striking features of Iteso social organization is the very close relationship between full brothers
and sisters, or between a sister and her half or classificatory brothers if there are no full brothers. A full
brother always stands in a protective relationship to his
sister. It is to her brother that she will turn in the
case of marital difficulties and if a woman should run
off with another man, her brother is regarded as jurally
responsible. In the event of a severe illness the sister
may return to her natal home where she is sure (Iteso say)
to receive better and more loving care at the hands of her
brother than she would from her husband. The case of
Gastory and his sister provide a remarkable instance of
this.

Case 3: Gastory and his sister

Gastory is the headman of Akudiet, a man of perhaps
sixty years of age and a very good friend and informant
of mine. During the course of one week he received
messages from neighbours that his older sister who
lived with her hsuband in North Wanga location some
sixty miles away, was critically ill. Finally, on
hearing that her husband of some forty years refused
to do anything for her, Gastory decided to go to Wanga
to bring her home. During the course of the trip it
transpired that Gastory had not seen or visited his
sister for over seventeen years because of a breach
between him and his brother-in-law at which he hinted

darkly. The sister turned out to be suffering from
worms and was slightly demented. During the return
trip Gastory kept admonishing his sister that 'this
nonsense [of seventeen years ago] must be forgotten
now'. Although he was normally a very willing and
eager informant, whatever had happened seventeen years
ago still rankled, and I was never able to find out the
cause of the breach of the relations.

This case is an extreme example of the manner in which
a brother is constrained to protect his sister. It is
extreme because the constraints operated in the face of
the breakdown of relations between affines and maternal
kin. Usually the solidarity of the brother-sister relationship is maintained as part of this complex of relations. It must be remembered that a brother has a superior relationship over his sister's husband. Because of
this he supervises the marriage. Excessive beating and
abuse of a wife will cause her brother to withdraw the
wife's services. A woman, however, is not on equally
close terms with just any brother. The ideal relationship is achieved only between a woman and the full brother who uses the cows of her bridewealth for his own
marriage. The bridewealth cattle in the ideal Iteso model
of marriage circulate from wife's brother to wife's
brother.

This means that a brother has a continuing interest in
the successful maintenance of his sister's marriage. This
success is signified by the sister's production of children, especially male children. The production of these
children creates a corporate unit, the 'house' of matrisegment which has mutual rights in the husband's estate
and the estate of the husband's father if he is still
alive. The matrisegment also has disposal rights over
the bridewealth that accrues to it because of the marriages of the sisters in the matrisegment. This sometimes
sets up a tug of war between the husband-father, who has
the right to control the bovine assets of the house and
the ultimate rights of disposal of the sons of the house.
This tug of war between sons and fathers, and later on
between separate matrisegments, over a father's residual
herd of cows means that the mother and her brother maintain a continual interest in the developing fortunes of
the matrisegment. Thus, the protective relationship of
brother to sister is transferred to her children.

This also accounts for what might seem to be a contradiction, a complex of distant husband-wife relations and
warm brother-sister relations associated with low divorce
rates. If marriages of less than one year's duration are
discounted, after surviving children are produced, the

divorce rate is 17 per cent, according to Barnes' ratio C
(1967).(10)   If marriages in which a woman is transferred
to a different male partner in the same lineage, and cases
of those few women who marry seven or eight times, are
discounted, the rate would probably be something like one
divorce in a hundred.   The standard explanation would be
that the Iteso are characterized by a 'marked father-
right' (Gluckman, 1950) where rights over women are transferred to the husband's lineage (Fallers, 1959).   This is
not wholly true.   First of all, Iteso social structure is
not characterized by the development of corporate unilineal descent groups.   Second, although rights are transferred to a husband's lineage, they are never wholly transferred.   While a women is incorporated into her husband's
lineage through ceremonies performed during the course of
her marriage, she never fully gives up membership in her
natal lineage.   Thus she maintains a dual membership in
one lineage as a wife-mother and in another as a sister.
This is seen clearly in the custom of widow inheritance.
A widow is inherited by a member of her dead husband's
lineage without further payment of bridewealth to her
natal lineage except for a token cow.   Thus rights over
women are transferred to her husband's lineage by the
payment of bridewealth.   The people who choose the man
who will inherit the widow, interestingly enough, are
the sisters of the deceased.   These are the women whose
'cows of bridewealth brought the widow to our lineage in
the first place', as Iteso explains.   Thus even though
they have married out, women retain rights in their natal
lineage through their role as sisters.   Thus their dual
lineage membership is maintained through the complementary sister-wife-mother aspects of their total social
identity.
   I would suggest that high bridewealth and the transfer
of rights over women are epiphenomenal aspects of a more
basic social process which is the establishment of an
economically corporate sub-unit of a household and lineage, the house or matrisegment.   This is the essence of
the 'house-property complex' (Gluckman, 1950).   This group
which is united by a set of common rights in the family
estate is established on the basis of a tie of matrifiliation.   This means that sub-units of a patrilineal group
are differentiated from each other on the basis of extra-
lineage criteria.   It is in the interest of all the parties involved, mother, mother's brother, and mother's
children to maintain and even strengthen the extra-lineage
tie of matrifiliation.   This tie of matrifiliation can
only be effective, however, as long as the marriage bond
is not severed.   Once the marriage is broken the mother

cannot act on behalf of her children and neither can the
mother's brother in his role as the superior affine to
the husband apply pressure on behalf of the sister's children. The mother's brother can serve only as a refuge in
the case of inter-lineage conflict. Therefore, matrifilial ties can only be really effective so long as the
marriage tie has not been severed and affinal ties remain
operative. Even in Case 2, Ejakait's land, Karani, the
classificatory mother's brother of Ejakait, was only able
to act effectively in Ejakait's behalf for one reason.
He was a politically prominent affine to whom deference
was due, especially since no bridewealth at all had been
returned to the lineage of Ejakait's mother on her death.
Even though Aura claimed that all of Aserena's lineage
(ekek) brothers were dead, Karani countered that he was
the senior most living clansman (Karani also used the
term ekek) and some bridewealth ought to have been returned to him.

VIII

To this point, my discussion of kinship patterns has been
concerned primarily with understanding the cultural basis
of the kinship system and the patterns of choice that
prevail among kinsmen. Thus the analytic centre of this
examination has so far been concerned with examining indigenous concepts of kin and the ideas, customs and
values that accrue to these categories. Furthermore, it
was shown that the phenomena under consideration actually
combined both corporate and categorical elements. Therefore, the proper question to ask has not been whether
these phenomena were categories or corporations, but
rather, in what respects are they categorical or corporate and why is it important to regard one aspect as more
significant than the other?
    This is, of course, an observer's problem rather than
an Iteso problem, and, in this case, the observer's
solution has been different from the Iteso solution in
that the Iteso tend to conceive of patrilineal groups as
being far more corporate, in a political sense, than
observations will confirm. The Iteso also have another,
more ego-oriented, way of looking at kin relations which
cuts across their kin categories but is still related to
the way in which they perceive the social nature of these
categories. In any social relation they distinguish between two aspects of the rights and duties that any person
is obliged to perform if he wishes to enter into the relationship. In other words, they describe the role by

which the position is defined (*iboro lubusakit*, 'things that are "proper" or "fitting" and must or ought to be done'). Second, they say that in any relationship there are things a person performs 'out of kindness' (*akingara-kin*, 'to hold out') that he is not required to do on the basis of any kind of sanction, moral or otherwise. These actions once performed must usually be continued if a person wishes to maintain a social relationship.

Some social relations have a more compulsory aspect than others. For Iteso society those kinship relations that are compulsory are centred around rituals concerned with life crises, particularly death. From the discussion of agnation given above, it can be seen that the most important social relations that emerge on mortuary occasions are lineage relations. There is, however, a contradiction involved here. Cases 1 and 2 and the discussion of the developmental cycle given in chapter 6 indicate that a major focus of conflict is between closely related agnates. Thus these non-voluntaristic, prescribed, ritual relations between agnates pose a dilemma for the Iteso. Ritual requires that Iteso maintain social relations between agnates who are frequently in social and economic conflict with each other. Many Iteso are reluctant to engage in social relations with any person with whom there is a serious conflict because of the fear of sorcery. Gossip attributes almost every extra-neighbourhood residential move to the danger of sorcery engendered by conflict between neighbours who are in conflict, often because of intra-lineage competition for scarce resources.

Social relations with distant agnates, affines, and maternal kin are characterized by mutual reciprocity and amiability. This is not to deny, of course, that there is not an ideology of amity between closely related agnates. I have demonstrated that there is. The reality, however, is often at variance with the ideology, and Iteso are aware of the discrepancy. It would seem sensible, then, for every Iteso household head who does not want to be completely subservient to his lineage mates to maximize as much as possible his non-agnatic social relations. There is, however, another contradiction implied in non-agnatic relations. Non-agnatic relations are characterized by mutual reciprocity. At moments of crisis, whether economic or ritual, when a person requires extraordinary support from people with whom he has entered into social relations, non-agnates exhibit a tendency to disappear. They rarely refuse outright support. Instead they are unavailable or missing at the required moments. Unless a man is completely estranged from his closely related agnates, they are ritually constrained to provide a

minimum of help. Thus the Iteso are caught in what seems
to be an unresolvable dilemma. They have a choice of maximizing one of two patterns of social relations - either
with closely related agnates with whom one is likely to be
in conflict and who may be dangerous, but who will help on
occasions of conflict, or with amiable, helpful, non-
agnates who are simply not reliable on occasions of crisis.
The following case, because it is an extreme example, shows
the danger of maximizing only one type of social relation,
the voluntaristic rather than the prescriptive.

Case 4: The death of Nakesa

Karani (see Case 2) had living at his home the two
daughters of his dead sister, Margaret and Nakesa. He
brought them there in 1958 after the death of their
mother, his full sister. His stated reason was that
there was no person in their natal home to take care of
them. The father of the children, Daudi, had moved to
live with his maternal kin in Igara many years before.
Living with him was his mother, wife and children.
There were no agnates nearby at all. The father, Daudi,
claimed that his mother was available to take care of
the children. Karani countered that he would take care
of the children until Daudi had put his house in order
and was able to raise them again.

In the meantime Karani was educating the girls.
Margaret, the eldest, reached standard III level,
dropped out and married in early 1971. Karani will
receive at least three cows of the bridewealth for
feeding the children. Nakesa at this time (May 1971)
was attending standard V.

In 1969 Daudi remarried and asked to be given back
his daughters. Three times he brewed beer in his home
and came to fetch them. Each time Karani refused to
let them go. The girls were said, according to local
gossip, to do all the domestic work in Karani's home,
and he was very reluctant to be deprived of their
labour. Shortly before Margaret eloped, Karani had
refused her permission to return to her father's home.

On 3 May, 1971, Nakesa was walking across a field
with Deseranda, Karani's wife's brother's daughter, who
was visiting at Karani's home, when a snake bit Nakesa.
She died within a few hours. Karani summoned Ejakait
to persuade me to bring Nakesa's body to her father's
home for the burial. When we arrived at Igara, the
area of the home, the father, who was travelling with
us, went to ask his neighbours for help in carrying and
preparing the body for burial. Everyone refused to

help him and his new wife refused to allow the girl to
be buried in her courtyard. So I drove across a rock-
strewn field to the courtyard of Daudi's mother. Mean-
while, it appeared as if no one of the man's lineage
was going to come for the funeral. He was completely
isolated from the people of his lineage who, in any
case, lived at some distance.

The reason for the reluctance of the neighbours to
deal with Nakesa's body soon became clear. They
thought that she had been 'bewitched' (*akisub*) by one
of Karani's neighbours. The snake was said to have be-
haved in a very peculiar fashion. First it wrapped
itself around the girl's leg and then it bit her. Many
people blamed Karani for forcing the girls to remain at
his home. Daudi was regarded as a very unfortunate
man. Not only had a person of his home died, but no-
one was there to help during this crisis.

The reaction of Ejakait was typical of the Iteso with
whom I discussed the case. For him it illustrated the
danger and disadvantages of living away from one's closer
agnates. The situation of death is a highly emotional
occasion for the Iteso. It brings out many latent fears
and anxieties and is always treated circumspectly in
conversation. It is also the predominant occasion for
clan and lineage solidarity. Thus Daudi's dilemma was
regarded as a kind of cautionary tale by other Iteso. In
maximizing his non-agnatic relations, he had left himself
open to a lack of support in this crisis.

I pointed out to Ejakait that his attitude was contradictory since only a few days before he had told me of his
fear that his half-brother Wasike might try to poison him
as a result of his victory in their dispute (see Case 1).
At that time he had been talking of selling his land and
moving somewhere else. Ejakait was unable to resolve this
paradox. Nor is any Etesot really able to resolve it at
the empirical level. He can only try to achieve a good
mix of prescriptive and voluntaristic relations. The
solution, however, can never be wholly satisfactory.

This dilemma that Iteso are faced with is not primarily
a result of their ideas about kinship. Instead it is
related to the optative nature of kinship relations. This
does not imply, however, that Iteso notions of kinship are
entirely removed from the transactional element in kinship. In many cases there is a prescribed set of attitudes that channels the direction of choice. Thus, on the
basis of the discussion of ideas about maternal kinship,
we can easily understand why Iteso turn to their maternal
kin in times of crisis. Yet there is nothing about the
cultural values surrounding maternal kin relationships

that require them to aid each other. Instead there is a
set of values which provides incentives for maternal kin
to aid each other. On the other hand, closely related
agnates are required to aid each other on certain crisis
occasions because of the ideas that Iteso hold about
death, procreation and fertility. The relationship between culture and social organization in the realm of kinship is indirect. That, however, does not make it any
less crucial for understanding patterns of choice among
kinsmen. Only historical analysis of the type undertaken
in chapters 3 and 7 can explain under what circumstances
one type of kinsman will be chosen over another.

IX

This chapter has tried to distinguish between changes and
continuities in the field of kinship and descent. It has
done this by separating different levels of kinship and
descent and describing changes and continuities in each.
As a system of meaning or cultural system, kinship and
descent have been found to have changed very little at
all. The social identities generated by kinship and descent principles remain unchanged from the precolonial
period. In certain contexts, however, membership in a
descent group is no longer relevant. Descent, as I have
shown, does not provide any longer the metaphor for the
description of political rules - even though it provides
for Iteso a means of explaining the motives of political
actions. Thus while descent has the same meaning, it is
no longer part of the make up of political norms.
Finally, I have shown in this and the preceding chapter
that there has been a change in the frequency with which
Iteso have chosen to live with agnates over affines and
maternal kin, and that that change has had consequences
both for the way in which Iteso resolve personal dilemmas
and for the organization of social control.

5 Kinship terms and norms

In the preceding chapter I described the outlines of the
field of kinship and descent and examined continuities and
changes in the system. Since this study focuses upon
social change, and the most significant changes have
occurred in the political-jural domain of Iteso society,
chapter 4 was concerned to describe those aspects of kinship and descent that were related to political structures
and to political processes such as recruitment to coalitions and the marshalling of support in disputes. There
are, however, many other situations in which social identities defined by the field of kinship are relevant for
social relations.. These might be described as situations
of everyday life. In these situations political interests
are not necessarily dominant (although they are never forgotten). During circumstances such as visiting, beer-
drinking, gardening, trading and the simple passing of the
time of day, identities derived from the kinship system
play an important part of the Iteso definition of the
situation. Certain kinship identities are relevant to
every situation. When two kinsmen meet they always interact in terms of kinship, among other things. Hence, kinship provides a system of meaning and a system of roles
which give significance to almost all situations in which
Iteso find themselves.

In everyday social relations descent categories are
largely irrelevant. Instead Iteso use other principles to
distinguish among other kinds of relatives. Kinship, in
the sense that it is an ego-oriented system of social
relations, governs the etiquette of everyday activities.
(1) This is not meant to imply that the etiquette of
everyday social relations is without political significance. As I show below the kinship system defines social

identities the incumbents of which have a relationship of
authority over other social identities. Where interests
and the Iteso definition of the situation coincide, kinship authority and political power often go hand in hand.

In the remainder of this chapter I shall concentrate on
two aspects of Iteso kinship terminology. The first is a
formal analysis of the patterns of kinship terms. The
purpose of such an exercise is to discover some of the
components in terms of which Iteso define social interaction. The second aspect of this analysis of the terminology describes the normative behaviour that Iteso expect
of social persons defined by the system. Thus my primary
purpose is to discover the moral significance for Iteso of
defining persons in terms of their kinship identities.

II

My procedure will be first to list in tabular form (table
2) and then to diagram the consanguineal terms of address
from a male ego's point of view. Then I shall describe
the behaviour expected between terminological reciprocals.

Three major components can be discovered in this simple
system. First, the terminology is largely generational.
All consanguines in grandparental generation and above are
called *papaa* or *tata*. The term papaa is an abbreviation
of *papa'akan* 'father of my father'. In grandchild's
generation all consanguines are called *etatait*, 'grandchild', as are any consanguines below grandchild's generation. Very often a very old person is called *lokapolon*,
literally 'the very big one', as a mark of respect. A
person may be called lokapolon if he is the eldest living
member of a lineage or an elderly retired household head.
In ego's own generation consanguines are only distinguished according to sex. Only in the first ascending and
descending generations do criteria other than generation
and sex become important.

Second, kinsmen are distinguished on the basis of their
sex. This is the only important distinction in ego's own
generation and is also encoded in all the ascending generations and the first descending generation.(2)

In the first descending generation, only sister's children are distinguished on the basis of sex; ego's own and
brother's children are all called ikoku.

The third principle that is recognized is lineality.
MB as a kin-type is distinguished from FB. MZ and FZ are
combined in one term. FZ and MZ are both relations to
whom respect is accorded. Their significance can be seen
in ego's generation. FZC is an *ocen* (ZC) to ego's

TABLE 2   Consanguineal terms of address - male speaker

A The terminological system			B List of kin terms		
	Sex				
	M	F	Term	Plural	Kin type
+2	Papaa	Tata	onac	ikinacan	B
			kinac	ikinacan	Z
+1	Mamai	Eja	papa	keskapapa	F
	Papa	Toto	toto	nukatoto	M
			mamai	keskamamai	MB
Ego	Onac	Kinac	eja	nukija	Z of parent
			papaa	keskapapaa	FF, MF
-1	Ocen	Acen	tata	nukatata	FM, MM
	Ikoku	Ikoku	ikoku	idwe	C
			etatait	itatai	SS, DS
-2	Etatait	Etatait	ocen	icenin	ZS
			acen	icenin	ZD

The rules for understanding the terms of address shown in Table 2 are simple. For a male ego:

1 All consanguines of ego's generation are called onac or kinac, depending upon their sex.
2 All persons called onac by 'mother' are called mamai.
3 Both 'father' and all the persons that 'father' calls onac are called papa.
4 All persons whom either 'parent' calls kinac are called eja.
5 Any woman whom ego's 'father' calls *aberu* ('woman' or 'wife') or *amui* (co-wife or brother's wife) is called toto.
6 All consanguines in the second ascending generation are called papaa or tata, depending upon their sex.
7 All the children of a kinac are called either ocen or acen, depending upon their sex.
8 All of his own children and the children of the persons he calls onac are called ikoku.
9 All the consanguines in the second descending generations are called etatait.

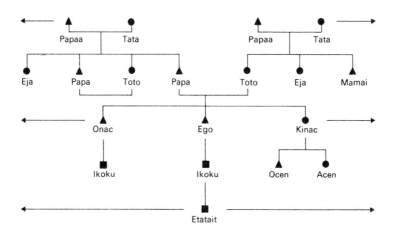

FIGURE 4   Genealogical specification of consanguineal kin
terms

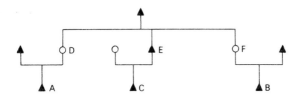

FIGURE 5   Relations between icenin

exogamous clan, and ego and MZC are both icenin to
mother's exogamous clan. Because of the rules of exogamy,
they are forbidden to marry. In terms of the bridewealth
arrangements a MZ, MB and FZ can all claim a cow at some
time from the husband of their ZD, ZD and BD respectively.
This obligation can be inherited by sons of a MZ, MB or a
FZ. In fact, a significant number of court cases occur
over these customary claims. MZH's lineage and FZH's
lineage as well as MB's lineage all qualify as maternal
kin, although MZH lineage and FZH lineage are not as important as MB's lineage. The relationship is diagrammed
in Figure 5.

In figure 5, both A and B bear the same relationship to
E; they are both actual or classificatory sister's children to E and his lineage or clan. C is related to A and B
in the same way. They are both the children of his *eja*.
Both A and B are related to each other in the same way
that C is related to them; that is, they are both the
children of their eja to each other. Thus there are two
kinds of maternal kin relationships. The first is the
mamai-icenin relationship which is between a wife-giver
and the child of his wife-receiver. The second is the
eja-idwe relationship, which is either between a child of a
wife-receiver and a wife-giver or between the two children
whose fathers have received wives from the same lineage or
clan. In the first instance, the relationship is asymmetric and in the second, it is symmetric. I must conclude that the only way in which to understand the combining of the MZ kin-type and the FZ kin-type into one terminological entity is by viewing it as an encoding of the
progression from an alliance relationship (wife-receiving)
to a cognatic relationship (maternal kin).

I now proceed to an analysis of the affinal terminology.

The major difference between the affinal terms and the
consanguineal terms is that the principle of affinity is
recognized only in ego's generation. Thus a woman to
whom an etesot is related affinally is either toto, *kamoru*
or *aberu-amui*. Toto will produce children for the classificatory and real brothers of ego's father and thus for
ego's own exogamous clan. Her children will be siblings
of ego. A kamoru will produce children for the real and
classificatory male siblings of ego's MB. Children of
aberu-amui, who are women ego might have married, will all
be called 'children' (idwe). Generation becomes important
again in the first ascending and descending generations
where affines are assimilated to the terms of father and
mother, and their reciprocal, the term for child. Thus
FZH becomes F. Note, however, that the matrifilial link
is also recognized and FWB becomes mamai, MB. The term is
not often extended to the siblings of a classificatory
mother but usually only to a real mother's male siblings.
More often ego calls FWB papa, 'father', because, as Iteso
explain it, ego's mother calls ego's FWB *omui* or *okileng,*
'father'.

In the referential system of kinship terms siblings are
further distinguished on the basis of degree of agnation
and maternal link.(3) Thus male siblings are referred to
as shown in Table 4.

Lineality and maternal links which are overridden in
the vocative system of kinship terminology are recognized

TABLE 3   Affinal terms - male speaker

	M	F
+2	Papaa	Tata
+1	Papa Mamai	Kamoru Toto Mamai
Ego	Opatiak Ekameran Ejamu	Aberu Amui Ajamu Eja
-1	Ikoku	Ikoku
-2	Etatait	Etatait

The rules for affinal terms are also simple. For a male
ego:
1 All affines can be called ekameran. Male affines of
   ego's generation are called ekameran except as in
   rule 3.
2 All affines of a 'father' in the first ascending
   generation to ego can be called either papa or mamai.
3 All of wife's consanguines are called by the same term
   that wife calls them.
4 Affines with whom ego is united in an alliance con-
   tracted in a descending generation and who are in
   ego's generation are called ejamu or ajamu, according
   to sex. The word ejamu means 'hide'. A hide serves
   as a bed and is the symbol of sexual intercourse in
   Iteso ceremonies. Sexual intercourse is a symbol for
   a marital alliance.
5 Wife's real or classificatory sister's husband is
   called opatiak. The word is derived from akitiak, 'to
   share'.
6 All wives and 'brother's' wives are called aberu or
   amui.
7 All wives of a mamai are called kamoru.
8 All wives of a papa are called toto.

TABLE 4   Referential terminology

Term of address	Referential modifier	Translation label
Onac	Loka toto	Full male subling
Onac	Loka papa	Half male sibling
Onac	Lok'ekek	Closely related male agnate of ego's generation
Onac	Lok'ekitekere	Distantly related male agnate of ego's generation
Onac	Loka'mamai	Child of real or classificatory 'B' of mother
Onac	Lok'eja	Child of real or classificatory 'Z' of M or F
Onac	Lok'aturi	Male age mate of ego - rarely used

in the referential system. The referential terminology is an elaboration of the vocative terminology. It does not conflict with, but only elaborates upon, many of the distinctions described in this section. The primary significance of terms of reference is that they allow Iteso to distinguish among consanguines who are agnates.

III

A major aspect of the system of kinship terminology is that it is capable of vast extension through the expansion of sibling terms to cover all consanguines of ego's generation. This allows wide scope for the element of choice. Simply because the terminology is capable of wide extension does not mean, however, that the extension of a term will always be practised. As I indicated in the preceding chapter, the recognition of a distant relationship very often depends on factors that are extraneous to the kinship system itself. When a relationship is recognized, then the principles that are expressed through the system of kinship terminology provide a normative structure through which the relationship can be carried on. I have already discussed some of the norms of kinship in my analysis of relations between the three major categories of kin - agnates, maternal kin and affines. There are other norms that can be discovered through an analysis of the terminological system.

The two most important of these normative principles are closely related. They are the unity of ego's generation and the separation of adjacent generations. One sibling term with markers to distinguish sex is used by ego for all consanguines of his generation. Relations between ego and members of his own genealogical generation are easy and free. Words that refer to sexual actions and organs can be used between members of the same generation. A male ego can joke about sexual matters with a female of his own generation and, in fact, much of the social intercourse between young coevals of different sexes consists of light sexual bantering. Men often threaten to marry girls by force and girls in return playfully put off a man's advances. Because it suggests adultery, this kind of sexual bantering tapers off after a woman marries, but there is not expected to be any reserve between a man and woman of the same generation. Within the same generation, social relations are supposed to be highly egalitarian and are epitomized by the full sibling relationship, which is one of co-operation and mutual confidence. The kinship system allows for mutually egalitarian relations, if the two parties wish it. Iteso say that there is no innate reason for two members of the same generation to 'fear' each other. This egalitarianism is modified, however, with respect to elder full or sometimes half brothers (see chapter 6).

The next important principle of normative behaviour is the ritual avoidance of adjacent generations. People in adjacent generations address each other by the terms for parent and child. Iteso say that the parent-child relationship is characterized by mutual 'fear' and 'respect'. Although authority resides in the members of the parental generations, the fear and respect of the relationship are enjoined upon both the senior and the junior adjacent generations.(4)   Iteso use one word for the relationship between adjacent generations, *akerit*. It can be translated into both 'fear' and 'respect' in English. Its primary meaning is 'to run away' in the sense of 'to avoid'. This avoidance, however, is customarily enjoined avoidance. When avoidance is voluntary (as when two people no longer wish to have anything to do with each other) the verb *akinyekin* is used.

Thus, for Iteso the major normative characteristic of the parent-child relationship of adjacent generations is one of some kind of avoidance. This avoidance takes the form of complete prohibition whereby the avoiding parties are not allowed to be in each other's presence in only one instance - between a man and his wife's mother. Avoidance is modified in other relationships. Examples of the

prohibition relating to avoidance are: a parent and child
cannot wear each other's clothes; it is very rude for them
to discuss sexual matters in front of each other; at beer
parties closely related members of adjacent generations
are expected to sit on opposite sides of the hut and are
not allowed to dance at the same time as each other, a
'father' may dance but not a 'son', and vice versa. Some
sons claim that a father cannot even enter the hut of his
married son. Furthermore, closely related members of
adjacent generations are required to affect a studied lack
of interest in the affairs of the membership of the adjacent generation. As an example, Ijaja, the father's
brother of Ejakait, wanted to sell part of his land in
order to provide a cow for a domestic ceremony for his
wife. Ejakait went to his home to dissuade him from giving up his only capital resource. Ijaja said to Ejakait,
'I am going to do this thing and I don't want you to
advise me against it.' As Ijaja was in the senior adjacent
generation, Ejakait was effectively prevented from trying
to remonstrate with Ijaja.

Although avoidance is enjoined upon both parties,
members of the senior generation are entitled to 'respect' and service from the junior generation. Thus at a
working party the fathers engage only in light work.
'Fathers' can send their 'sons' on errands or beg small
amounts of money, labour or goods from their 'sons'. The
only way to get out of these requirements is to evade the
issue. It is regarded as very rude to refuse outright.
Thus, the kin-types we distinguished as 'father' and
'father's brother' have the same moral authority. The
difference is that some 'fathers' control scarce resources that their 'sons' desire.

One point must be mentioned. The intensity of adher-
ence to these norms varies with distance of social relationships. There is a similar pattern to Iteso incest
prohibitions. Technically it is incestuous to have sexual
relations with a member of one's own exogamous clan. Most
men say, however, that their first sexual experience is
with a 'sister' of the exogamous clan. Sexual relations
with a member of one's own lineage, however, is a genuinely horrifying act. The same principle operates in this
instance. A request that would automatically be complied
with if it came from a 'father' in one's own lineage would
be regarded as impertinent from a more distant 'father' in
one's exogamous clan.

Associated with this separation of adjacent generations
is a mild form of alliance between alternate generations.
Relations between ego and members of his grandparental or
grandchild's generation are not either reserved,

characterized by authority or hierarchial. The ritual
avoidance that characterizes relations between adjacent
generations is not found here. Instead the relationship
is one of warm affection and mild joking. A grandparent
often calls his grandchild of the opposite sex by the
appropriate term for spouse. I have even seen a grandparent and grandchild wrestle playfully. While in some
societies this alliance of alternate generations can be of
crucial importance for an understanding of residential
patterns or political alliance, this is not true for the
Iteso. It is probably for this reason that grandparents
are regarded with such positive affect and esteem. They
are removed from the conflict between personal desire and
kinship obligation.

The asymmetry of affinal relations has been discussed
in the preceding chapter. It was seen that with regard
to affinal relations avoidance patterns similar to those
found between adjacent generations also prevailed. Thus
a husband and wife cannot wear each other's clothes while
a brother and sister can wear the same clothes. The most
stringent avoidance is between affines in adjacent generations, but the avoidance is modified between affines of
the same generation. In ego's generation the vocative
term for affine, either ekameran or ejamu, is self-
reciprocal.

The most general statement that can be derived from a
discussion of the norms of kinship is that kinship relations which are characterized by hierarchy and authority
impose upon the persons who are involved in those relations a pattern of mutual avoidance. Further, it can be
stated that the closer the relationship in terms of genealogy the more strictly the norms are enforced, and that
avoidance is greater where relationships involve more than
one principle of hierarchy. Thus affines in adjacent
generations have relations characterized by the most
intense norms of avoidance because two hierarchical principles are involved. These are, first, the superiority
of wife-givers over wife-receivers and, second, the authority of the parental generation over children. This is
clearly seen in the rule of complete avoidance between a
male ego and his wife's mother. In this relationship the
avoidance is stricter than in any other for two reasons:
first, if the avoidance were not complete, a woman would
be in a position to exercise authority over a man and,
given the subordinate role of women in Iteso culture, this
could involve a serious contradiction; second, in contrast
to the relationship between a female ego and her husband's
father, co-residence does not require strict avoidance to
be modified.

In virtually all social relations into which Iteso enter, they will interact in terms of norms and identities which have as part of their make-up components derived from the kinship system. Two of these components, relative generation and sex, are to be found on all social occasions. A third component, type of genealogical connection, is related to the descent and kinship system and is relevant in those contexts where descent or cognatic or affinal kinship are defining characteristics of the situation. The objection may be raised that genealogical connection is the only 'true' kinship component among the three. The answer to this objection is that, in those situations where generation and sex are relevant and genealogical connection is not, the generation and sex components are expressed in an idiom derived from the kinship system. For example, males of the first ascending generation to ego are treated with 'fear' because they are assimilated to the identity of 'father', papa. On other occasions, persons may call someone whom they wish to flatter 'papa' even though he is not in the first ascending generation to ego. This is a tactical use of a term which is based on its moral significance (Bloch, 1971). Before we are able to understand both the tactical value of kinship terms and the relevance of components derived from the kinship system in other contexts, it is necessary to analyse the kinship system as a system of moral expectations in terms of which Iteso express judgments about themselves and others.

6 The developmental cycle in domestic groups

I

The preceding chapters have discussed two fields of social relations that are to be found in the political-jural domain of Iteso society. The first field of social relations is organized around the principle of territoriality. These relations have been subject to the most change. The second field of social relations is organized on kinship principles and as a system of meaning has remained relatively constant from the immediate precolonial period to the present. The focus of attention in the discussion of these two fields has been on the transition from a political system based on territorial sections to one based on neighbourhoods. In the discussion of both these fields political relations have been implicitly defined as social relations among household heads. At present these relations are egalitarian in some situations and hierarchical in others. An analysis of the kinship system helps to explain the ideology that governs the norms of hierarchical relations. It was also discovered that kinship values and norms operated both as constraints on the direction of choice and as incentives for the choice of political partners.

I have not yet provided any extended discussion of the goals that motivate political choices among the Iteso. In chapter 3, I did discuss a negative goal, the desire to flee from powerful enemies, but did not explain why Iteso flight took the form of the movement of households instead of individuals. I shall suggest in this chapter that the establishment of a viable household is the primary goal of all Iteso males. It is only after this goal has been obtained that men can consider other political goals, such as the exercise of power over other individuals. Furthermore, I shall demonstrate that persons become followers in

order to achieve the goal of household viability. Only
through an examination of the interplay of domestic con-
cerns and political relations can the particular pattern
taken by the developmental cycle in domestic groups among
the Iteso be understood. This chapter will also demonstrate that the politics of the developmental cycle con-
tribute to the particular form that groups take within the
political-jural domain. This chapter examines these problems through the explanation of two patterns of Iteso
behaviour that are related to the developmental cycle.
These are endemic conflict between brothers and the high
rate of household mobility.

II

Many essays on the developmental cycle are concerned with
understanding deviations from the culturally expected
pattern of development (see for example the essays in
Gulliver and Gray, 1964). The interest of this discussion
will be different. I am concerned to examine the relationship between the developmental cycle, the rules of
inheritance, and conflict over property.(1)
    Residence at marriage is neolocal for men and virilocal
for women. Each couple, within a short period after the
husband's first marriage, will establish a separate household. There is, as a result, an almost complete absence
of either patrilocal or joint family residence. Households are composed of husbands and wives and their offspring. They may be joined by temporary residents such as
an unmarried sibling, sister's child, wife's mother, a
workman or child of a friend. These persons are not regarded as members of the household when it is engaged in
ritual activities (except for husband's lineage mates).
If they should die while residing with the household head,
they must be buried outside the 'gate' of the household,
in the 'bush'. Other members of the household are buried
inside the 'gate'. Only the mother or a lineage mate of
the household head may be counted as a full member of a
household on ritual occasions.
    This pattern of residence does not mean that different
households founded by brothers or fathers and sons are
not found in a given area or neighbourhood. They often
are. I am discussing residence, however, entirely with
respect to the founding of a household. If other criteria
such as general area are introduced, then the residential
pattern becomes more confused. In that case almost one
third of residence choices would have been matrilocal in
the recent past and a classification of affinal-local

would have to be introduced.

In a sample of 250 households there were only 2 instances of patrilocal-extended family residence among the Iteso. In the first instance, the father's land was almost entirely seasonal swamp, and the houses of the father and his sons were built on a small hill that was the only part of the land that was not marshy for the entire year. The second case was of a man with four sons and about one half of a hectare of land. The man simply felt that he had too little to divide, and, since he possessed considerable outside income as a bone-healer, his sons did not wish to press the issue. The only ambiguous cases were several instances in which brothers possessed a joint holding, or where a father and an only son who is married held land together. In all of these cases the actual house complexes of the brothers and of the father and son instances were spatially separated.(2)

The term for household is *ere* (pl. *ireria*). This is a group that includes a man, his wives, their children, and any other people who happen to be living with that man. There is no separate term for 'family'. A group of full siblings, whether they are mature and married or not, is referred to as *etogo epe* (one house), or it is said that sometimes they come from *akok ape* (one stomach). The next kinship group which is larger in scale is the lineage, which is most frequently called ekek (see chapter 4). If a number of closely related agnates reside in the same area, the term ere will sometimes be extended to cover their households. Thus a father and his sons or a set of siblings might refer to their collection of households as an ere. This collective household would never be modified by a singular possessive adjective, e.g., *or'angi* (my home). It is instead always modified by a collective adjective as in *ore'kos* (our home). In the case of a married woman, when she says or'angi, she is referring to her husband's household; when she says ore'kos, she is referring to her father's and/or full brothers' households. When a man lives at some distance from his close agnates, he does not combine his household with theirs and refers to it by the term ore'kos.

The setting up of a separate household entitles a man to be called by the title of household head, *elop'ere*, 'owner of the home' (pl. *ikalopek ireria*). The position of household head is the only formal position of authority remaining in the political-jural domain (if externally imposed political office is discounted). After a man is married and has set up a separate household he is entitled to be called *ekiliokit*, a 'man' and 'husband'. Until such time he is referred to as *etelepat*, a 'boy'. As an

etelepat he can be ordered about in ways that would be in-
sulting to an adult male. Only after marriage is a female
called aberu, 'woman' or 'wife'. Until that time she is
called apese, 'girl'. It is through the process of marrying and setting up a separate household that people
achieve full adult status. In the case of men, the setting up of a separate household is particularly crucial.
Even if a man is married, until he has created an independent household, other people will refer to him as etelepat,
'boy'.

The process by which an independent household is established is relatively simple. A boy, with a number of
friends, seeks permission of the father and brother of a
girl for marriage. The girl is sent to the household of
the boy's father. The marriage ceremony is performed by
the wives of the men of the boy's lineage and the couple
occupy the boy's bachelor hut. For the first six months
the wife will work under the supervision of her husband's
mother while the boy and his wife prepare and cultivate
the fields that his father has transferred to the young
man.

During this time various demands for bridewealth will
be made by the girl's father and brothers. If they feel
the young man's father is reluctant to pay, they may bring
the girl back to her natal home. This period is crucial
for the establishment of amiable affinal relations and the
majority of separations will occur at this time. A father
is required to provide the cows of bridewealth for the
first marriage of a son. These cows can only come, however, from one of three places: the residual herd of the
father, the cows assigned to the mother of the young man,
or the bridewealth received from the marriages of the
full sisters of the boy. If the bridewealth is obtained
from the property of another matrisegment, as sometimes
happens, then permission of the co-wife must be granted.
This occurs only if the co-wife has no male children. The
bride then owes special services to her husband's mother's
co-wife, who calls the bride aberu angi (my wife).

After the young couple harvest their first crops, they
move to a separate household that the husband has built on
his own land. Ceremonies for the opening of a new hearth
will be performed and a special beer party held to commemorate the opening of a new home. The process of establishing a separate household usually takes from six months
to a year. Outraged opinion will be brought to bear if
considerable delay is involved. Also, the girl's father
and brothers will exert considerable pressure on the
couple to set up a separate household. Almost all the
cases in which the setting up of a household is delayed

involve men who are employed, as Iteso say, 'outside the
reserve', that is, as labour migrants who are unable to
direct their energies to the task of building a household
and farming. The cash income of these men gives them considerable independence from their wives' fathers and brothers. They often assuage the feelings of their affines
with gifts and the quick transfer of a large number of
the cows of bridewealth.

At the establishment of a household, the husband will
assign to his wife fields in which to grow food crops.
The woman's rights in these fields are entirely alienable.
The husband is required to prepare the fields for sowing,
while the wife does everything else. In practice a husband
often helps his wife with agricultural activities but
never with the more purely domestic activities of grinding,
threshing, cooking, gathering wood, etc. Cash crops are
each spouse's individual concern. A woman is often assigned a relatively worn-out and dug-over field if she wishes
to plant cotton. Although the labour is not obligatory,
women often help their husbands with the sowing, weeding
and harvesting of their cotton and maize which are the
primary cash crops.

Women earn additional income through the selling of
food crops at the market, planting small amounts of
cotton, and the brewing of various kinds of beer and
Nubian gin for sale. Whatever they earn cannot be approp-
riated by their husbands. They use the money for buying
meat for meals, cigarettes, some clothes, paying school
fees for their children and for small donations at church.
The primary responsibilities of the husband are to provide
a modicum of clothing, housing and granaries, and to prepare land for planting. If a man has the money, it is
felt that he should buy meat once a week. A woman is required to provide regular meals for her children and her
husband whenever he chooses to eat at her hearth, and
sexual services whenever he desires. It is also felt that
she should brew beer for the working parties which the
husband assembles for farming his cash crops. She is required to brew beer for domestic and ritual occasions.

If a man owns any livestock, he may assign some to his
wife for her use. The cows' milk is used by the wives.
Additional milk will be sold. This can provide some women
with considerable cash income. The husband may not appropriate the cash from milk sales without his wife's permission. However, a man may reassign these cows to other
wives or simply not assign them at all. If he does not
assign the cows to a wife, he usually loans them out to
another man who, in return for caring for them, receives
the use of the cows' milk and one or two calves if the

cow produces many healthy offspring while in his care.
Bulls and oxen are less frequently loaned out although
they are assigned to different matrisegments.   Stock
associateship, which involves the outright gift of cattle,
is of very little importance among the Iteso.   On the
other hand, the loaning of cows which is properly called
cattle trusteeship (Gulliver, 1956), is very frequent.
The choice of a cattle trustee partner involves considerations of his skill in keeping cows and friendship.

Often younger full siblings and, if she is old enough,
their mother, choose to live at the home of the eldest
married son of a matrisegment.   It is expected that ulti-
mately a mother will live with her youngest son.   Elder
brothers act as a kind of father to their younger siblings.
Once an elder brother has become a household head a mild
form of avoidance is set up.   In this instance an elder
brother has considerable authority over his younger brother, especially before the younger brother is married,
and particularly if the relationship is between full brothers.   When a younger brother marries, the relationship
between a younger brother's wife and his elder brother is,
in normative terms, similar to the relationship between
the woman and her husband's father, one of fairly severe
avoidance.   On the other hand, younger brothers traditionally had rights of sexual access to their elder brothers'
wives.   Many Iteso informants now deny this but there is
no jural sanction against a man having sexual relations
with an elder brother's wife.   As one informant put it,
'He can't be fined a cow, so it isn't adultery; he can't
be fined a ram, so it isn't incest.   It must be simple
theft!'   Thus elder brothers, because of their hierarchical authority roles, are treated as fathers in   some contexts.

After some time, when cordial relations have been
firmly established between a wife and the people of her
husband's lineage, beer will be brewed by the wife for the
ceremony of easing the ritual avoidance between herself
and her husband's father.   After this ceremony, the customary patterns associated with avoidance are less
strictly observed.   For example, a woman and her father-
in-law are allowed to have beer straws in a pot of beer
at the same time, which they could not do before.   The
father then gives his son's wife a cow which will form
the nucleus of the matrisegment's herd and cannot be ali-
enated by the husband without the wife's permission.   If
she has not borne children, special fertility ceremonies
will be performed.   After the birth of a number of children and on the occasion of an unexplained series of ill-
nesses, the final ceremony of incorporation into her

husband's clan will be performed by the wives of the husband's lineage mates. This may take anywhere from five to
twenty years after the first marriage ceremony.

As the husband becomes established, if he is at all
successful, he will begin to think about taking a second
and then a third wife. A powerful impetus to marrying a
second time is the first wife's failure to bear any male
children. If the husband's mother is dead or otherwise
not available, the first wife, now known as the senior
wife (*aberu nak' aparik*)(3) acts in the role of husband's
mother and the new wife spends six months or so helping
her at her hearth. Once again a separate hearth is established, livestock are assigned and fields allocated. Each
wife is a separate economic and social unit in the household and no necessary forms of co-operation are enforced.

Many wives approve of their husbands taking a second
wife. They say that this way they can be sure that he
will not get venereal disease and give it to them because,
after another marriage, he will confine his sexual activities to the home. They also add that a second woman in
the home will help in easing the burden of work. I do not
really see how this is possible, since each wife virtually
duplicates the work of the other. In two years in the
field I only observed one instance of co-wives who shared
a hearth together. Conflict between co-wives is fairly
frequent and includes numerous accusations of sorcery.
Iteso husbands say that a sensible man does not show
favouritism to any particular wife and visits each in
turn. Given the frequency of husband-wife conflicts over
alleged favouritism, I would suggest that sense, or sensi-
bility, is not an outstanding characteristic of Iteso
men.

As the children of a mother grow up they move from
their mother's house to a separate bachelor hut that the
elder son usually builds for himself about the time he
reaches the age of twelve. This hut often provides shel-
ter for his younger brothers and sisters. His first
sexual experiences will take place here. His sisters
often cook for him and provide domestic services. When
the boy first marries he and his wife will live in this
hut until he builds his own home.

After all his sons have become fully grown, it is customary for a man to enter a semi-retired stage of life.
His sons pressure him to divide his remaining land and the
residual herd among them. It is expected that his youngest wife will remain to take care of him while the older
ones go off, each to live at the home of one of their
sons. Until his death, however, a man may retain control
of both his residual herd and the cows assigned to each

house and brought in through the marriage of the daughters of that house. He may not, however, dispose of the cows, especially of bridewealth, of a given house without first informing his married sons of the action. A son can bring litigation against his father for failure either to provide land at marriage or to provide cows for bridewealth. Furthermore, if a married son feels his father is using cattle that ought to be reserved for the bridewealth of his younger brothers, he can also lodge a complaint. One difficulty for sons is that, if the household's total herd is large, they rarely have any certain idea of all the cows that belong to their matrisegment. It would violate the etiquette of kinship for a son to confront his father directly. Therefore, he must rely on gossip and the knowledge of neighbours and the elders of his lineage for his information. This leaves considerable ambiguity with respect to the claims of different matrisegments regarding the rights in cows. Different sets of full brothers can and do bring forward witnesses to claim that offspring of cow X or Y really belong to their house. Since the cows may have been acquired 20 to 30 years before and, in addition, have been dispersed and redispersed between different cattle-trustee partners, the possibility for differential claims and considerable conflict is real.

III

Though the Iteso practice a form of anticipatory inheritance, men often die before reaching the ideal stage of having completely distributed all their property. In this case the elder full brother acts as trustee for his younger brothers. If there is no elder full brother who is a jural major, the man who inherits the widow, or the husband's brother act as trustee and household head. It is expected that a brother, if available and willing, will inherit the widow.

Iteso believe that the eldest full son of a house should get a larger share of inheritance than his younger brothers. Frequently, however, younger brothers claim that their elder brother or brothers have taken a larger share of the inheritance than is just. Sometimes the property in cattle will have been used for the marriages of older full brothers, and nothing will remain for the younger ones. Then the elder brothers are under a moral obligation to provide bridewealth for their younger siblings. If there is considerable difference in age between younger and elder brother, the elder brother may be caught between the obligations of anticipatory inheritance of his

sons and the residual rights of his younger full brother.
Again the conflicting demands of the situation render the
relationship between full brother and younger brother a
focus for potential conflict.

In the case of inheritance given in Case 5 the division
of a household into separate matrisegments with respect to
heritable property is illustrated clearly.

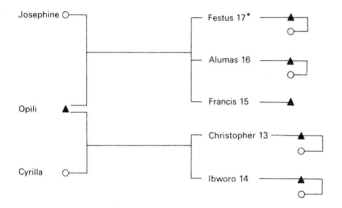

FIGURE 6   Opili's family
*Numbers refer to plots of households on map of Akudiet
neighbourhood, p. 121.

Case 5: Opili's estate

Opili was an older man with two wives and considerable
wealth in cows. He died in February 1965. In the
course of the following year his sons retrieved all the
cattle held in trusteeship. They were unable to agree
on the division of the estate and approached the chief
of the location to help them. The primary conflict was
between the two sets of brothers over the number of
cows belonging to each matrisegment.

Opili married two wives. The senior was named
Josephine and she had three sons, Festus, Alumas, and
Francis, born in that order. The junior wife, Cyrilla,
had two sons, Christopher and Ibworo. Only Francis was
unmarried.

The sub-chief assigned three elders of the area to
act as witnesses and to adjudicate the claims. They
were chosen on the basis of co-residence, common clan-

ship and presumed knowledge of Opili's affairs. They
were Puce, Aura and Opetoi, who also attended in his
capacity as headman of the locality.

From a total of 27 cows, 2 were found to belong to
the children of Cyrilla. Two more cows were added to
their share 'to assuage their feelings', to make a
total of four. As the only unmarried son in his house
Francis was given 11 cows for bridewealth. Alumas was
given 5 and Festus 4 in order for them to pay the remainder of their bridewealth. Of the remaining 4, 1
was given to the elders for their services and 1 cow
was reserved for a funeral sacrifice to Opili. The
remaining 2 cows were given over to the senior wife
Josephine. The first cow she claimed as the *akiteng
nak'ingorit,* the cow of the last born, which will
eventually belong to Francis. The last cow Josephine
claimed for her own use. As she lives in the household of Francis, this cow will also go to him.

Opili's bicycle went to Festus as the eldest son,
Josephine claimed that since Opili's plough was purchased from the sale of a cow from her house, she
should decide who was to receive it. The plough went
to Francis.

The residual land was divided among the children.
The eldest son, Festus, claimed the largest share, and
a piece of the land originally allotted to Alumas was
given to Festus.

Relations between the children of Josephine became
strained after this. Alumas felt that Francis had
received an undue share of inheritance and Festus had
received too much land. Francis and Festus are very
close and co-operate in ploughing. Francis contrib-
utes the plough and chains and three oxen, and Festus
two oxen.

About two years after the division of the inheritance, Alumas and Festus were drinking beer in a neighbour's home. Alumas is said to have started a fight
with Festus. Francis, when he heard about the fight,
attempted to waylay Alumas on his way home. Festus
then reported Alumas as a sorcerer to the chief of the
location. Friends of Alumas warned him of the chief's
impending inspection so that nothing suspicious was
found in his home.

Another time, Alumas' rooster wandered into Francis' land and Francis killed the rooster and buried
the evidence. Alumas' wife witnessed the act, however, and Francis was taken before the headman and
fined fourteen shillings, which was never paid.

Alumas has since moved his home to the other side of

his property in order to be as far away from Francis' household as possible, and Alumas no longer has any social intercourse with his two brothers.

While conflict is frequent between full brothers, this is rather an extreme case. Usually a living parent or parents' sibling, such as father's brother, exert moral influence on their children. As Iteso put it, 'children are ashamed to quarrel in front of their parents'. Informants suggested that in this case Josephine had lost her moral power by siding with her last born son, Francis, and trying to get an abnormally large inheritance for him. Before the division of the estate Francis and his brothers had presented a solidary front vis-à-vis their half-brothers and had demanded arbitration by the chief's representatives. They obviously had little to lose as it was clear that the great majority of the movable property belonged to their house. Relations with Cyrilla's children have been relatively distant ever since.

The case illustrates the two stages in which conflict often proceeds. First, there is conflict between matrisegments, especially over the residual herd. There is some suspicion that the chief's representatives may have been bribed since cows that Cyrilla's children claimed were not assigned to any house were claimed by Josephine's children. Thus matrisegments form a corporate unit with respect to rights in property before the division of an estate. Unlike the Jie (Gulliver, 1956), shares within a matrisegment are allotted individually at the division of the family estate, or after members mature. The ideal rule is that seniority in order of birth confers the largest share. This is modified by other factors, however, such as the pattern of anticipatory inheritance whereby the elders' sons have already received the greater part of their legacy. In the case of Opili's estate it was modified by the active intervention of Josephine on behalf of her last born son. Thus, the corporate solidarity of a matrisegment is nullified by the individual division of the family estate after the death of the household head. Conflict often divides the matrisegment because of the differential claims of persons to their share of the matrisegment's property, and the resulting resentment that people who regard themselves as having been cheated often feel.

The patterns of conflict between matrisegments and within matrisegments have been accelerated by the introduction of individual land tenure since 1956 and the increasing scarcity of arable land due to population pressure. An additional factor that may have served to increase the rate and intensity of conflict within house-

holds is the declining power and ability of senior
agnates to assert their will over junior agnates and, as
a consequence, to settle disputes.   Claims to corporate
rights in land on the basis of matrisegment membership are
often put forward but are not recognized.   If joint holdings become common, the kinship basis for these holdings
could be a set of full brothers and this would decrease
the frequency of open conflict within matrisegments.

There is also potential for conflict between fathers
and sons, both over the family estate, and as equal competitors within the political-jural domain.   It is, however,
restrained in two ways.   First, the norms of kinship pre-
scribe a pattern of ritual avoidance between a father and
son, once a son has become a household head, and so a
political equal of his father.   Second, conflict between a
father and son over their rights in the family estate is
muted by the pattern of anticipatory inheritance and the
jural sanctions a son can apply if his father refuses to
recognize the son's rights.   Furthermore, a son can utilize the superior position of his mother's brother, who is
a wife-giver to father, to bring the issue to public
notice, or be present to defend his sister's son's rights
as Karani did in the case of Ejakait's land (Case 2).   In
the past, when land was not scarce, the most important
factor tying a son residentially to his father and brothers was rights in moveable property (particularly
cattle), which composed the bulk and certainly the most
valuable part of the family estate.   A man with a poor
father, or one who was estranged from his full brothers,
was better off moving under the authority of a patron,
who would give him the economic and political help in
establishing a separate household that he was unable to
obtain from his own close agnates.   The norms of kinship,
and the lack of an extended or joint family residential
pattern, enabled a man to establish a household at a considerable distance from his agnates if he wished.

IV

Conflict has been shown to be related to the rules of inheritance and disputes over the family estate.   Because of
kinship norms and jural mechanisms the locus of open conflict is within rather than between generations.   Conflict
tends to occur in two stages: first, between sets of full
brothers and, second, within those sets of full brothers.
This conflict violates the 'axiom of amity' (Fortes, 1969)
that is supposed to characterize relations with siblings.
An open breach between any kind of sibling rarely occurs

before the death of the father who is the household head.
There are two reasons for this. First, mutual respect for
a father can be used to muffle conflict. As an example,
Ejakait thought his half-brother, Wasike, had taken a cow
that belonged to him. He asked Wasike to go with him to
see their father, Aura, on an entirely different matter.
Once there he had Aura adjudicate the matter and 'out of
respect' to Aura, Wasike acquiesced. In a different arena
he probably would not have given in so easily (see Case
2). Case and genealogical material indicate that in the
past, if an open breach occurred before the death of the
father, it was invariably accompanied by a residential
move. Conflict is certainly even more extreme and frequent now, because of the scarcity of land.

The desire to establish an independent household has
been the primary motivating factor for the pattern of conflict that I have discussed in this chapter. An independent household is normally established through marriage
and the partition of the family estate. The traditional
bulk of the family estate was wealth in cattle. Cattle
were utilized both as bridewealth and as political capital
that could be exchanged for followers. In terms of goals
and incentives, there were influences from two domains
which served to maintain the pattern of nuclear family
households which are characteristic of the developmental
cycle among the Iteso. First, conflicts within the domestic domain between sets of half brothers and, eventually,
within sets of full brothers provided a centripetal force
that made for residential mobility. Sets of brothers who
had quarrelled over the family estate found it very difficult to live together in the same place. Their animosity
was exacerbated by fears of sorcery. There was, in addition, a need for capital on the part of those brothers who
had failed to obtain enough cattle to marry and establish
a household. These capital-hungry men were forced to look
outside their families to find cattle. Second, they found
their capital in the surplus cattle of would-be political
leaders who were willing to finance the marriages and
establish the households of their followers. Thus, the
processes concerned with leader-follower relations in the
political-jural domain also served to maintain the high
rate of residential mobility by providing economic incentives for household moves.

There is a two-way relationship between the pattern of
household fission and the pattern of leader-following
relation in Iteso society. First, the high rate of residential mobility serves to maintain political relationships between persons who are distant agnates or non-
agnates. Second, leaders provide economic resources that

that are needed by followers as a result of conflict within domestic groups. A partial reason for this conflict is that leaders deny resources to their agnates in order to give them to their followers, thereby forcing the agnates to become followers of other leaders. The processes surrounding leader-follower relations in the political-jural domain and fission within domestic groups have a mutually reinforcing effect on each other.

There are, however, other factors which affect residential choice. An important one is the reliance of agnates upon each other in occasions of crisis. This often results in a kind of reverse residential move, as agnates resolve conflicts, in order to avail themselves of each other's services at a moral crisis such as death. This would help to account for the ping-pong pattern of the history of the residential choices of many Iteso households.

When the scale of Iteso political groups declined (as described in chapter 3), the rate of household mobility was drastically increased. The result of this increased rate was to decrease the forces that helped to keep agnates together, and thus to decrease the possible size of domestic groups. I believe this occurred without alteration of the norms of family life as they already provided a structural 'fit' with such a pattern. At present, a reverse process is taking place. The system that I have described could only be maintained under conditions in which land was a relatively free good. Today, with land becoming scarce, residential mobility has virtually ceased. The result, which has not yet appeared, will undoubtedly be transformations in kinship norms and familial relations because these will no longer 'fit' with the conditions of residential stability. Thus, future changes among the Iteso will most likely occur within the domestic domain.

7 Akudiet neighbourhood

This chapter contains an analysis of the development of
one neighbourhood, which I call Akudiet. There are two
reasons for undertaking such an analysis. The first is
to illustrate the actual operations of the fields of
social relations that were described in the preceding
chapters. The second is to determine in what way, other
than as a system of ideals and values, the neighbourhood
can be examined as a social grouping.

Akudiet is situated on the Malaba-Amukura road and
comprises a square of land bordering on the eastern side
of the road from Aturet market in the north to the ruins
of the District Officer's camp in the south (see Map 4).
Almost all of the homes are under the authority of the
..eadman, Gastory Opetoi. His locality is a much larger
area which includes Akudiet, and borders on the south side
of the Malaba-Amukura road. It extends about one-half to
three-quarters of a mile to the southeast of the road.
The parcels of land of some people are split by the road
itself. The neighbourhood which I am discussing composes
the northwest third of the locality.

Akudiet locality (ekitala) is part of Amukura sub-
location. The sub-location is a large area in the centre
of South Teso location. The most prominent physical feature of the centre of the location is a series of hills and
rocky outcroppings running in a north-south direction
parallel to and about two or three miles from the border
between Kenya and Uganda. The hills stop at Machakus
market about three miles south of Malaba, which is on the
boundary between North and South Teso locations. They
pick up again in North Teso location where they are known
as the Cherelemuk hills. In the north they blend into the
foothills of Mt Elgon. The whole series of hills is known

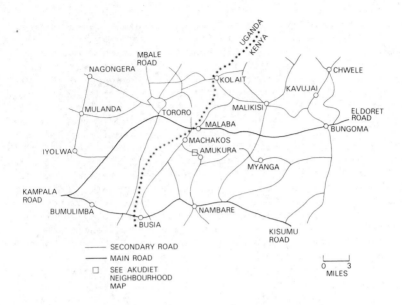

MAP 4 Northern Division Busia District

as the Teso hills. The tallest of the hills is known as
Cherelemuk Rock. A cave in the Rock is the starting point
for the ritual cycle of Babukusu circumcision ceremonies.
The second tallest hill is at Amukura and this was an important secondary ritual place. It may be because of
these ritual attachments that the hills were defended more
fiercely by the Babukusu and thus left as enclaves to be
captured later during the Iteso advance into Kenya. In
any case, the ruggedness of the terrain provided a better
means of defence than the savannah surrounding the hills.
The ruggedness may also have made the hills less attract-
ive as places to pioneer. This, at least, is what some of
my informants suggest. Genealogical information indicates
that parts of the Teso hills were the last area to be pioneered and settled by the Iteso even though they were in
the centre of the Iteso area in Kenya. At present the
administrative centres of both North and South Teso locations are in these hills.

The dominant geographical feature of the locality is
the Malaba-Amukura road. The locality is most frequently
known as Akudiet, which means 'sharp corner', because it
forms a part of a very sharp curve in the road. The more
southerly portions of the locality blend into the Amukura
school-mission-market complex and are generally known as
part of Amukura. There are 98 households under the authority of the headman. I am concerned here with some 70
contiguous households whose heads assert that they interact more with each other than with other households in
the locality or in nearby localities.

The headman, Gastory Opetoi, lives on the southern edge
of this somewhat arbitrarily defined neighbourhood. He
says his locality is divided into four neighbourhoods.
These he calls Akudiet, Aterait, Obur and Kolemunyang.
Aura, who is a prominent elder of long standing in the
locality, regards it as divided into three neighbourhoods.
These are Asinge, Obur and Komolo. Augustino Inapa, a
middle-aged household head who is not socially active,
sees the locality as divided into two neighbourhoods:
Komolo and Okatekok. Festo Ekasiba, a young household
head, says that Akudiet is divided into three neighbourhoods which are called Asinge, Okatekok and Obur. Mark
Odera is a middle-aged elder who aspires to be an influential person and has a wide range of social contacts and
an active social life. He sees the locality as divided
into three neighbourhoods: Akudiet, Asinge and Obur.
Elunga'at is a very knowledgeable elder who lives next
door to Aura. He regards the locality as being divided
into four neighbourhoods. These are Obur, Aterait,
Akoret, and Amakada. Peter Osera is another elder of

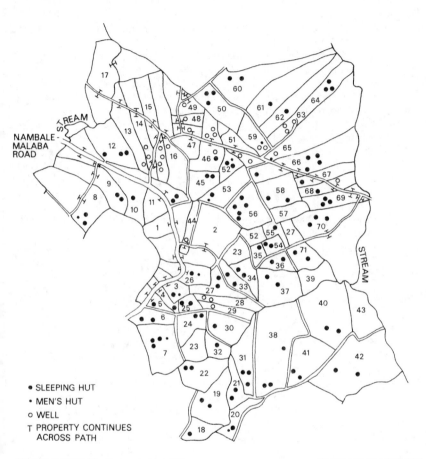

● SLEEPING HUT
• MEN'S HUT
○ WELL
T PROPERTY CONTINUES
  ACROSS PATH

SOURCE: SURVEY OF KENYA MARCH, 1971   SCALE 1:5000 (APPROX.)

MAP 5 Akudiet neighbourhood

Elunga'at's lineage and clan. He sees the locality as
divided into the following four neighbourhoods: Akoret,
Komolo, Kuruk and Obur. This material is summarized in
Table 5. The numbers following their names can be used
to locate their plot in the map of Akudiet in Figure 11.

All the household heads of the neighbourhood could be
listed in similar fashion. The six in Table 5 were chosen
because they represent the range of social types to be
found in the neighbourhood, and they all agree that each
of them belongs in the same neighbourhood.

Table 5 indicates that, while there is some agreement
about the names that should be applied to the set of
neighbourhoods in the locality, there is considerable lack
of consensus about the members of the groups signified by
these names.(1) It is important to point out the complete
absence of any semblance of consensus. It may be reasonable to assume that even if there is a general lack of
agreement on the names of other neighbourhoods in the locality, household heads might agree as to the name given
to the neighbourhood where each person regards himself as
residing. This is not the case. Their own neighbourhood
names are distributed unevenly throughout the list and
only two out of the total of seven common names are not
listed by any person as being the name for his own neighbourhood.

This lack of agreement is most startling if we examine
the four households of one lineage, Palinyang of clan
Ikomolo luk'Anyoutiang. These four households are all
contiguous to each other and occupy a block of land
shaped somewhat like an axe (see Figure 7 and Table 6).

If Table 6 is read across from left to right each
household head's placement of himself and his lineage
mates will appear in the appropriate box under the person's name. Thus Ejakait lists himself as living in
Asinge; for Aura and Ijaja he does not know the name of
their neighbourhood. He also regards his half-brother
Wasike as living in Asinge. Aura and Ijaja list everyone
as living in Asinge and Wasike lists everyone as living in
Aterait.

There is even an absence of agreement among the four
household heads of one lineage who are living contigu-
ously. The disagreement becomes even more apparent if the
entire lists of neighbourhood household heads given by
each of the four were to be examined. Aura and Ijaja
regard their neighbourhood as proceeding primarily to the
north and including a few households to the south of
Ejakait and Wasike's land. Ejakait and Wasike, on the
other hand, regard their neighbourhoods as proceeding
primarily to the south. The major difference is that

TABLE 5 Different names for neighbourhoods in Akudiet locality

Household heads	#	Akudiet	Aterait	Obur	Komolo	Okatekok	Asinge	Kolemunyang	Amakada	Akoret
Cornel Ijaja	51			✓	✓		×	✓		
Gastory Opetoi	26	×	✓	✓				✓		
Aura	65			✓	✓		×			
Augustino Inapa	50				×	✓				
Festo Ekasiba	33	×		✓		✓	✓			
Mark Odera	63	×		✓			✓			
Elunga'at	66		✓	✓					✓	×
Peter Osera	58			✓	✓					×
Wasike	56		×	✓			✓			
Ejakait	53		✓	✓	✓		×			

× indicates neighbourhood of informant's residence
✓ indicates other neighbourhoods in the locality
numbers refer to plots on map of Akudiet neighbourhood (Map 5)

TABLE 6   Neighbourhood placement by members of lineage
Palinyang

Who placed	Where placed			
	Ejakait	Aura	Ijaja	Wasike
Ejakait	Asinge	?	?	Asinge
Aura	Asinge	Asinge	Asinge	Asinge
Ijaja	Asinge	Asinge	Asinge	Asinge
Wasike	Aterait	Aterait	Aterait	Aterait

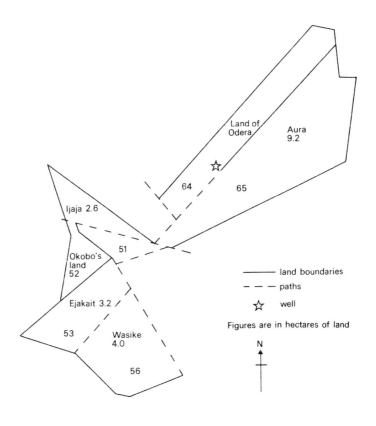

FIGURE 7   Land of lineage Palinyang

Ejakait views the power line as the marker between neighbourhoods and Wasike does not. It is important to note
that Aura and Ijaja have far more contemporaries to the
north of their homes than to the south. The opposite
holds for Wasike and Ejakait. Hence we can conclude that
the criterion of similar age is an implicit principle used
in the choice of neighbours.

It is interesting, however, to note that the contemporaries Ejakait and Wasike do not agree on neighbourhood
names. They both agree that there is a neighbourhood
called Aterait but Wasike thinks that he, Aura, Ejakait
and Ijaja all live in it, and Ejakait thinks that he and
Wasike live in Asinge. Ejakait and Wasike have different
personal situations. Wasike has political ambitions. He
aspires to be an influential person and, as a consequence,
often has a number of young men lounging about his home
who Ejakait says come from Aterait, but who Wasike says
are the young men of the neighbourhood. Wasike earns a
steady income as a cattle trader and in July of 1971
opened a *hoteli* (restaurant) in Amukura market. Ejakait,
in contrast to Wasike, is an ambitious young man who is
looking outside his neighbourhood for a reliable source of
steady income and capital accumulation. He resists the
demands on his time and resources from the co-residents of
his neighbourhood. Two of the most demanding of those co-
residents, incidentally, are his father and father's brother, Aura and Ijaja, respectively. Shortly after I left

FIGURE 8   Relations within lineage Palinyang

the field, I heard that Ejakait went into business as a
maize dealer with his wife's brother, who lives about six
miles away. Thus Ejakait is interested in limiting the
extent of his neighbourhood because of economic ambitions
while Wasike is interested in extending his neighbourhood
because of local-level political ambitions. Ejakait lists
thirteen households as being in his neighbourhood and
Wasike lists thirty-seven. The best opportunity for Wasike's ambitions to be realized lies in the group of younger household heads that Ejakait agrees should be called
Aterait - only Wasike now regards himself as part of that
group. Ejakait, on the other hand, has no interests and
very little interaction with that group and, furthermore,
wishes he could minimize his interaction with some of the

households that border on his own. This accounts for his
confusion as to where to place Aura and Ijaja.

The disagreement over neighbourhood name and membership
is due to a variety of personal reasons which are related
to perception of social relations. This can be seen if we
return to Table 5 (p. 123). Elunga'at and Peter Osera
list their neighbourhood name as Akoret. The name means a
place where food is distributed according to shares. If a
clan or lineage segments, the place where a sacrifice is
made to sanctify the division is called Akoret after the
sharing out of the sacrificed animal according to the new
social units. Elunga'at's and Osera's clan, Ikatekok
luk'epikisit, had such a division near their houses and
that division is memorialized in the name. When I brought
this difference of opinion to the attention of the headman, Opetoi, he advised me to ignore ·Elunga'at who, he
said, was only displaying his usual ignorance.

There is general agreement that there is a neighbourhood called Obur (the place of the stream) in which none
of the informants lives. The people of Obur also express
a complete consensus over their neighbourhood membership
and name. Obur is a triangular area surrounded on two
sides by streams and on the third by a swamp. It is a
rather unhealthy place and the land is not desirable. The
people living there (households 31, 38, 41, 40, 43 in Map
5) are classified as sorcerers and worse. They were
assigned land in the area because of their unappetizing
characteristics so 'they could kill each other off'. Most
people of the locality have as little to do with the
people of Obur as possible. The consensus in Table 5 reflects general agreement about the presumed characteristics of the people of that area.

Komolo is another frequently listed name. This reflects the overwhelming predominance of clan Ikomolo in
the southernly two-thirds of the locality. Komolo is 'the
place of the Ikomolo'. Many of the people of the middle
segment of the locality refer to it not as Komolo but
rather as Aterait, 'the place of the *Atera* trees'. Only
Ejakait uses both Aterait and Komolo as neighbourhood
names. This is probably a result of his having heard both
names used in the course of the interviews that we conducted together. But only Inapa placed himself as living in
Komolo. This reflects his view of himself as the member
of a minority clan, Ikaruok, living among the Ikomolo.

Similar reasons could be deduced for all the lists of
names given in Table 5. The data given above, however, is
sufficient to demonstrate that the system of names for
neighbourhoods contains a kind of implicit analytical
scheme that encodes an individual's perception of where

the different foci of social interactions occur in a locality and also the social causes that determine these foci.
A number of factors are associated with patterns of names
found in the list. They include clanship, political affiliation, economic demands, and similarity of age. In
accordance with the Iteso unilineal ideology discussed in
chapter 5, clanship is a very common presumed cause.

I chose the name Akudiet because it seemed the most
neutral and amenable to agreement and also encompassed the
largest number of households. This is a reflection of my
own form of participation in the neighbourhood as a kind
of quasi-resident. My own particular interests as a
social researcher were in maintaining the largest number
and widest ranging net of social ties. In order to do
this I had to be perceived as not being so closely affiliated to any segment so that I would push that segment's
interests at the expense of another segment. I was thus
interested in obtaining the confidence and support of as
many people as possible without seeming to offend any. In
this my strategy was not too different from the influential persons of the neighbourhood. The two most influential persons in the list, Opetoi and Odera, both list Akudiet as their neighbourhood of residence, even though they
live on opposite sides of the neighbourhood. Interestingly enough, however, their lists of household heads of
the neighbourhood do not include each other. They are
competing influentials. They were also two of my very
best informants. Not too surprisingly, therefore, the
neighbourhood as I perceive it is bounded by Odera's
household on the north and Opetoi's on the south. Thus,
in true Lévi-Straussian fashion, the anthropologist's
version of neighbourhood organization must be regarded as
simply another version of a myth (1963).

This analysis serves to reconcile the paradox of some
agreement as to names associated with disagreement over
the persons to whom these names ought to be applied.
Neighbourhood names are a kind of culturally agreed upon
shorthand for social alignments. Given a lack of localized corporate groups in Iteso social structure, these
alignments vary from day to day. Each person's list of
names is his personal assessment of neighbourhood composition. The assessment is based partly on one person's
limited social experience and partly on his personal
desires and ambitions. This causes the assessment to be
relatively unpredictable. As the analysis has demonstrated, each list tells us more about a single person than a
whole neighbourhood.

So far I have described some notions about the social
composition of a locality that are held by a group of

co-residents who generally agree that they all belong to
the same social unit. The evidence has been enough to
demonstrate that the commonsense procedure that is utilized by most social anthropologists in defining local
units will not work. Most anthropologists operate at the
level of: people called X live here and people called Y
live there. Even in some societies, such as the Tallensi,
where boundaries are diffuse and vague the problem of
local unit classification is not insuperable, because
there is no confusion except on the boundaries between
two groups (Fortes, 1945, p. 16). Fortes' problem was to
discover the relationship between patterns of social
action and the indigenous classification of those patterns. His solution was relatively simple because there
was a large degree of coincidence between residential
patterns and culturally recognized divisions. Among the
Iteso the general coincidence of ideology of local group
composition and terminology for naming or distinguishing
between local groups does not exist. This raises a whole
series of questions that have not, to my knowledge, been
asked about local groups in an African rural society.
The first and probably the most important of these questions is that, given a lack of any reliable indigenous
system of classification, what criteria, if any, can be
utilized to distinguish local units? Put another way,
the question can be asked: We know the Iteso have the *idea*
of neighbourhoods (see chapter 3); what evidence demon-
strates that they have the actual neighbourhoods themselves if they cannot even agree on a name for one?
   The lack of discussion of this issue by most anthropologists is predicated on the simple (but usually accurate) assumption that the system of names for local groups
has a direct functional relationship with the local groups
themselves. The names provide a social classification of
regularities within groups and differences between groups.
The functional assumption is that this provides persons
with a predictable basis for interaction. Thus a Karimojong expects the Karimojong of a different territorial
section to recognize rights and duties within that section
to pray at a common ritual ground and to organize war
parties together. The Iteso system of neighbourhood
classification does not operate in this way because it
does not provide the regularity and predictability that
is based on social consensus. If a functional relationship does exist between local group classification and
some characteristic of neighbourhood organization, the
relationship will be more complex than the simple one
that may usually be assumed.

II

As a result of this problem of classification, we are
forced to examine the relationship between the abstract
ideas and values about social relations within neighbourhoods that were examined in chapter 3 and the actual form
of neighbourhood organization itself. To some degree this
question has already been answered. A full answer depends
on the analysis of the development of actual neighbourhoods, a task to which I shall now proceed.

The description of Akudiet neighbourhood will deal with
two dimensions, the history of the development of the
neighbourhood and ongoing patterns of social relations.

Akudiet neighbourhood and locality is on the northeast
side of Amukura hill which is the second largest hill in
Northern Division, Busia. It is an area of relatively
recent settlement. Iteso began to move into this area
just prior to the onset of colonial rule, perhaps around
1895. The general pattern of settlement was described by
the older informants of the area as being similar to the
pioneering of an area under the section (etem) system.
The people of sub-clan Ikomolo luk'anyoutiang settled the
northeast-southeast side of the hill, Ikuruk the northeast
to northwest side, and Ikaijoro in the southeast quadrant.
The rest was inhabited, but I am concerned here with the
area settled by the Ikomolo.

The Ikomolo pioneers had previously lived in what is
now Lupida sub-location of Bukhayo location, about seven
miles away at Myanga (see Map 4, p. 119). There they
formed the core of a sub-section. Their area was part of
an unprotected flat plain and, as a result of Babukusu
military success and the contraction of the Iteso frontier, they became vulnerable to attack. The clan members
dispersed to other places for protection. A leading
elder, Acakai, organized the members of his clan and led
them to settle in the relative safety of Amukura hill,
which was an area easy to defend from attack. Shortly
after this time colonial rule was established. Therefore,
the section system did not become established on Amukura
hill. There is no evidence that Acakai ever acted as a
section or sub-section head (lok'etem). He was, however,
recognized as the most effective leader in his area and
the general spokesman for the people there. When better
communications were established, the most important figure
of clan Ikomolo in Asinge sub-location wished to reaffirm
the ties of exogamous clanship with the people of Amukura.
He decided to do this by sacrificing a bull with Acakai
because he was the most eminent figure of the clan in the
area, the 'patron' par excellence.

Among the agnates who accompanied Acakai were Palinyang, Oskol, Oduyot, Aline, Orute and Inapa. Palinyang
and Aine were in the same lineage. The others may have
formed part of another effective lineage. The genealogical material I gathered is often so contradictory on this
point that I am unable to form an opinion. I give below
two lists that are typical of the differences found in
genealogies.

1 Laurent Inapa lists all of the following as the
children of Anyou who moved into the Akudiet area
together: Irario, Palinyang, Oteba, Odeke, Omariakol,
Onapa, Oudi, Omorut, Ekworo, Orute, Isikol. According
to Inapa these are children of one man, Anyou, by two
different wives whose names are not known. The leader
of the group was Onapa and they all split into different lineages about 1912. Inapa is the son of Oteba.
All the names given in Inapa's genealogy represent
names memorialized in existing effective lineages.
Inapa's direct genealogy is as follows:

Δ— Ekabelet

*Δ— Anyou

Δ— Oteba

Δ— Laurent Inapa

2 Wencelaus Ikemer is an elder of lineage Orute.
According to his account Akudiet was settled by Orute,
Ekwaro, Onapa, Odiyot, Acakai and Palinyang, who were
all at least half-brothers and the son of Emopus.
After the original lineage fission, the descendants of
Onapa and Orute remained together as one lineage until
about 1940 when they split. Ikemer's genealogy is as
follows:

Δ— Alum

Δ— Emopus

*Δ— Orute

Δ— Okwenyi

Δ— Wencelaus Ikemer

*Represents highest level of reliability

We can note that with the exception of the generation
where the various lineage founders are located, there is
no genealogical agreement.(2)

Thus far it has been established that a number of agnates of one exogamous clan, Ikomolo luk'anyoutiang, pioneered the entire Akudiet area sometime between 1895 and
1905. Their descendants form the majority of the residents in the locality today in addition to many of them
living on the outer edges of the locality. Besides the
Ikomolo, a group of unrelated members of the clan Ikatekok
luk'epikisit entered the area a little later. They are

represented in Table 5 (p. 123) by numbers 66 and 58.
Their first homes were in the present centre of Akudiet
neighbourhoods and their second homes in the locality to
the southeast, Kodedema. The leader of this group was a
man called Kamara, who entered the area with five or six
clanmates. They apparently came directly from the Uganda
side of the border. Kamara had ten living children and
the descendants of this group are dispersed in over fifteen different areas. Consequently, they refer to Akudiet
as Akoret (see p. 126). It is possible that if the normal
political development of the precolonial period had been
allowed to proceed, Ikomolo and Ikatekok would have provided agnatic cores for two different sub-units of one
section.

III

While some members of the various emergent lineages remained in the general area, others dispersed to a large
number of places. Many people settled in land schemes in
Busoga in Uganda and on the Uasin Gishu plateau in Western
Kenya.
   In order to demonstrate the complexity of household
movements that was characteristic of the people who ulti-
mately chose to remain in Akudiet, I shall give below the
history of one such group of houses which is represented
by lineage Palinyang of Ikomolo luk'anyoutiang, and then
examine the means by which representatives of other clans
came to reside in the area.

Case 6: History of lineage Palinyang

   Palinyang was born in Lupida, which is near Myanga in
Bukhayo location and to the west of Amukura. His probable date of birth was around 1860. He was born into a
sub-section named after the Ikomolo luk'anyoutiang clan
clan, of which he was a member. Because of extensive
raiding by the Babukusu, the Iteso of Lupida were
forced to abandon the area. Acakai, the most prominent leader, fled to Amukura to an area occupied by
the Igara clan; and Palinyang fled to Malaba on the
Kenya-Uganda border, where he lived with his mother's
brother. After some time Acakai called his fellow
clansmen together, and they established themselves in
present-day Akudiet.
   By this time Palinyang had married two wives. The
first, Icaot, came from the Kotur area, and by 1914
Palinyang had six surviving children by her, four boys

and two daughters. The second wife, Maasai, was of
clan Ilooka and came from near the area where Palinyang
was born. Palinyang had only one son by her, called
Aura.

One day in 1915 Palinyang went to a beer-party at
the home of a nearby clansman. On his way home he was
speared and killed by a man called Emu. Emu had hidden
in the bushes near a path in the hope of killing someone else who had been at the same beer-party and was
also a member of Palinyang's clan. That person was
called Omaria. It seems that Omaria's brother, Esaire,
had been killed fighting the Babukusu. Omaria accused
Emu, 'who had a reputation', of killing Esaire through
sorcery. Omaria swore that he would kill Emu for vengeance. Emu tried to kill Omaria for protection. Unfortunately, he killed Palinyang by mistake. Before he
died Palinyang was able to name his killer.

The people of Palinyang's locality organized a vengeance party and killed a person of Emu's locality and
clan. A truce was arranged and six of Palinyang's cows
were given as compensation to the survivors of the man
they killed. Emu gave ten cows and his daughter in
marriage as compensation for his mistaken murder. The
girl was married by Palinyang's eldest son, Ekiring.

Palinyang's first wife was inherited by Irario, a
lineage mate, and his second wife, Maasai, was inherited by Kitui, Palinyang's father's brother's son.
Maasai was the first, and only, wife of Kitui. At this
time, Aura, who was Palinyang's only child by Maasai,
was about ten.

The children of Palinyang by the first wife moved to
live with Irario, whose home was in Kodedema. Shortly
afterwards Kitui, along with his new wife and her
child, also moved to Kodedema. While he remained there
Kitui, however, was 'a man who liked to roam from home
to home'. The era of labour migration that was opening
up was suited for his temperament, and he took to dis-
appearing from home for long periods.

By 1929 Aura had found employment as a 'soldier'
(askari) of the local chief, Enyusat. Shortly after
that he became a court messenger. Relations between
him and his half-brothers were severely strained and,
at one time, Aura claims they attempted to kill him.
Therefore, on the advice of the chief, he determined to
move. Around 1930 he returned to Akudiet to claim his
father's original land. Aura was shown where to build
his home by Imweno, who had been a lineage mate of
Palinyang's when the two of them first moved to
Akudiet. Since then the lineage has split.

Aura took with him Ijaja and Atyang, his siblings, as Iteso say, 'of one mother but two fathers'. These three regarded themselves as full siblings and have allowed the maternal tie to override their different paternal ties. Genealogies are in the process of being changed so that Kitui is now becoming a full brother of Palinyang rather than a simple lineage mate. Aura used the bridewealth received from his half-sister Atyang's marriage to take a second wife. Afterwards he provided the bridewealth for Ijaja's marriage.

Between fifteen and twenty years after the move friendly relations were again established between Aura and his half-brothers, who had remained in Kodedema. In early 1970 Ekiring died. He was the last surviving member of Aura's generation in Kodedema. At Aura's death, the lineage called Palinyang will split in two with one segment localized in Akudiet and another localized in Kodedema. At present there is considerable tension between the two segments. I have seen this tension expressed during the performance of various lineage rituals. The people of lineage Palinyang who are localized in Akudiet assert that the members who live in Kodedema are sorcerers.

When household heads were forced to plant boundaries in 1956, Aura was in a very good position. He instituted a series of cases against his neighbours and was able to claim a very large portion of land, over nineteen hectares, if his brother Ijaja's piece of land is included. His land came primarily at the expense of the descendants of Imweno, the man who had welcomed Aura back to Akudiet in 1930. The daughter of Imweno had married Okobo of Ikuruk clan, who also lived in Kodedema. He was having some trouble where he lived. An unknown person continually put human feces on his doorstep at night and aroused considerable fear of sorcery. Okobo's wife's brother forced him to move to live with them. In a land case Aura claimed all of Okobo's five hectares of land and received about four and a half. Odera, the paternal grandson of Imweno, brough a countercase against Aura in which he claimed that Aura had no right to live in Akudiet at all, and that all of the land had originally belonged to Imweno. With the support of members of the Ikatekok clan, Elunga'at and Imuju, who lived nearby (Elunga'at is number 7 in Table 5, p. 123) Aura won the case (see Figure 8, p. 125). Aura then tried to sue Yoronimo, whose land bordered to the southeast of Aura's. Yoronimo is very powerful and rich and Aura eventually decided to drop the case.

Within the group of homes represented by lineage Palinyang, considerable animosity has developed. Tensions between the matrisegments represented by Ejakait and Wasike have already been examined (see Case 2). In addition there is considerable tension between Aura and Ijaja. Ijaja and Ejakait support and aid each other. Aura is continually after Ejakait to forego his intimacy with Ijaja. Aura claims that Ijaja is a sorcerer and would even kill his own kin. Except for the necessary lineage rituals, Aura and Ijaja avoid each other as much as they can. This conflict does not extend to their wives who are very close. Wasike supports his father Aura and also avoids Ijaja. Ijaja claims that Aura has stolen bridewealth that actually belongs to him; that is, the cows that came from Ijaja's full sister's bridewealth. Aura asserts that he repaid the debt when he provided bridewealth for Ijaja. The latter is complicated by Ijaja's first marriage, which ended in divorce fifteen years ago. The bridewealth, however, has not been repaid.

I might add here that Kitui finally returned to Akudiet in 1957 to live out his final years near his son Ijaja. He died in 1964.

Case 7: Clan Ikaruok

Ogwanei of clan Ikaruok luk'oriama moved from Uganda to settle in Kocek to the west of Amukura hill sometime during the Iteso penetration of the Kenya side of the border. He had five sons. They were Ajelo, Emunyot, Maguria, Omoit and Inapa. Emunyot and Maguria died without issue. The descendants of Ajelo split off to form a separate lineage shortly after the First World War. Omoit married two wives. The first wife, Akojot, was the sister of Imweno, one of the first Ikomolo to settle in Akudiet. The second came from Aturet, which is nearby. Omoit died at a relatively young age, probably in 1920. At the time he was living with his second wife's brother in Aturet. Since he died of leprosy his wives were not remarriageable or inheritable. The son of his second wife remained with his mother's brother. The children of his first wife went with their mother to live with her brother Imweno at Akudiet. The stigma of leprosy is rumoured to have caused the descendants of Ajelot to split off and form a separate lineage. In any case Omoit and Inapa were only half-brothers to Ajelot.

Omoit had five sons by his first wife. They were (in order of birth) Opuriai, Iriama, Mainya, Onya and

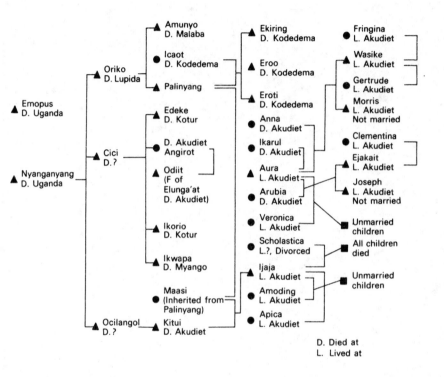

FIGURE 9   Genealogy collected from Aura and Ijaja, clan
Ikomolo

Imo. As a young man Mainya went to Nairobi. He was
never heard from again. Iriama married a girl from
Aturet and after some time migrated to a settlement
scheme at Bugiri in Uganda where he died in the mid-
1960s. His children remain there. The oldest son
Opuriai is a man of about sixty-five. He has remained
in Akudiet. He married three wives. The first died
without issue. Two sons of the second have married and
live in Akudiet. The third wife has had three sons, all
all of whom are minors. The youngest married son of
Opuriai is called Chrisanthus Panyako. He is a primary
school teacher and is buying land in his father's
neighbourhood for himself. Chrisanthus and Ejakait
(see Case 6) were friends until Chrisanthus purchased a
piece of land from Ejakait's father's brother, Ijaja,
and then defaulted on his payments.

So far only Omoit and his children have been discussed. Remaining is Inapa, the younger brother of Omoit.
Inapa was born around 1885 and remained in Kocek until
about 1914 or so. He went off about this time to work
in Kisumu. While he was in Kisumu he got into a fight
with a man from the dominant clan in his natal area and
killed that man. Inapa's children say that the man was
a government agent and Inapa was resisting being draf-
ted into the army. He did not return home because he
feared the dead man's relatives would take vengeance.
Instead he took his wife to live with his mother's
brother at Buyofu in Bukhayo location probably in 1917.
Around 1925, after his first male child was born, Inapa
moved to Akudiet to live with his wife's father Emongoluk, the father of the Opili in Case 5. It seems that
Emongoluk had cursed the child and thus caused it to
refuse to suckle the breast of its mother. It is said
that Emongoluk did this because he had not received any
bridewealth. The mother and child returned to Akudiet
for the ceremony in which a curse is removed, and Emongoluk refused to let them return home. Inapa then decided to move to Akudiet. There is no doubt that a considerable element in his decision to move was the presence of the wife and children of his brother Omoit.
Also, by this time, he no longer had to fear vengeance
at the hands of the relatives of the man he killed.
This was probably due to the increasing effectiveness
of colonial authorities.

Inapa married a second wife but none of her children
lived. He had two sons by the first wife, Augustino
Inapa and Emanyala. Emanyala is something of a profli-
gate and has had three divorces. He has no wife or
children at present. Both brothers' land is registered

in Augustino's name. Emanyala eats at Augustino's
wife's hearth but keeps his sleeping hut at some distance.

At present there is some tension between the descendants of Omoit and those of Inapa. It seems that, at
one time, a domestic ritual was performed for Opuriai's
wife, and Inapa, as Opuriai's father's brother, claimed
a large share of the sacrificed cow. Iriama, who is
Opuriai's brother, opposed the division and actually
fought physically with Inapa. He hit Inapa on the head
with a stick and seriously injured him. By fighting
with Inapa, his father's brother, Iriama violated the
most significant norm of Iteso kinship, the separation
of adjacent generations. As a consequence of this act,
he opened himself to ritual retaliation. Shortly after
this dispute Iriama moved to Uganda. Inapa went to a
professional curser and had the 'people of Iriama'
cursed. Since then several deaths have occurred in
Opuriai's home and both Iriama and his wife have died.
In 1970 Opuriai ordered his eldest son to take a cow
to the curser to eliminate ('pay') the cursing. There
must have been considerable prior strain between Inapa
and Omoit's children for a dispute of such violence to
have occurred.

Case 8: Clan Ikuruk

Otuco and Idenyi were two brothers in clan Ikuruk Luki-
dere who migrated from Uganda over the Kenya side of
the border to Asinge sub-location. Idenyi later moved
to the area near Nambale where he died. Otuco died in
Asinge. Itela was the son of Otuco. He married the
elder sister of Odiyot, one of the Ikomolo pioneers of
Akudiet locality. Some time after he married Odiyot's
sister, Itela moved to Akudiet. Later on after he had
established himself he brought his younger lineage
mates to live with him in Akudiet. These were Kwanga,
Otiengi and Epero - all sons of Idenyi, Itela's
father's brother. They were among the first people to
settle in Akudiet after the first Ikomolo and Ikatikok
pioneers. Odiyot, the sponsor of Itela, was an exceptionally rich and powerful man who was renowned as a
fighter. He was often described as a good example of a
successful patron.

Itela had six sons. Two were labour migrants who
died outside the Iteso area. Three died in Akudiet,
and one is alive. Of the two that died in Akudiet the
oldest was Opili. He had one son who has since migrated to Eldoret. The second, Oroni, had two sons who

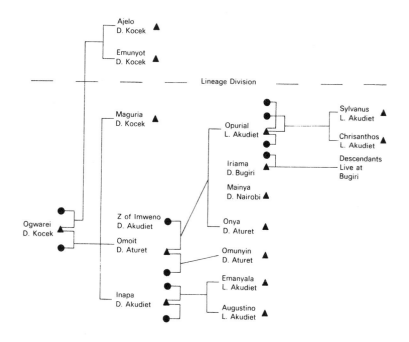

FIGURE 10   Genealogy of clan Ikaruok

are household heads in Akudiet. The third, Obwaku, left
two young sons who are cared for by the only living
brother, Itela.

Of the three lineage mates that Itela brought to live
with him in Akudiet one, Kwanga, died as a labourer in
Nairobi. He left four sons, however. The eldest, Papa,
is employed and lives in Kampala. The next, Okobo,
lives in Akudiet but at the other side of the neighbourhood. He married the sister of Odera and lost most of
the land his wife's agnates had given him in a case with
Aura (see Case 6). His lineage mates pooled their resources to give Okobo another small piece from their
own. His registered land, therefore, is in two separate
pieces. The third son of Kwanga, Okello, died in Nairobi. The fourth son, Babu, died in Akudiet. Babu inherited his wife, Toto, from his father's brother. Toto
is a sister of one of the household heads of the Ikatikok pioneers.

Otiengi, the lineage mate of Itela, died in Akudiet.
He had three sons. Only one, Odinga has remained in
Akudiet.

The fourth brother, Epero, also died in Akudiet. His
wife was inherited by Babu. Epero had one son.

In addition to bringing his father's brother's sons
to live with him, Itela brought his widowed sister to
live at Akudiet in 1940. She was accompanied by her
daughter and her husband Marko. Itela's sister had no
sons and after her husband died she refused to be inherited and moved to live with her married daughter.
There were a number of deaths in the home, however, and
sorcery was suspected. Therefore, the whole family
moved to live with the old woman's brother. It is a
somewhat unusual residence choice, wife's mother's
brother, but perfectly permissible in terms of the
norms of kinship. The household head, Marko, died in
1956 and his only son Omuse occupies a small piece of
land.

Case 9: Clan Ikajoro

Okude was the eldest son of Otwane of clan Ikajoro Luki-
doko. He was born in Komolo locality, which is to the
southeast of Akudiet. He was one of four brothers.
His younger brother Pascal moved to the west of Amukura
hill in order to live with affines. The other two brothers remained in Komolo. Okude married a daughter of
Odiyot, an Ikomolo pioneer in Akudiet (see Case 8).
When his wife became sick she returned to her father's
home for ceremonies to be performed in order to cure

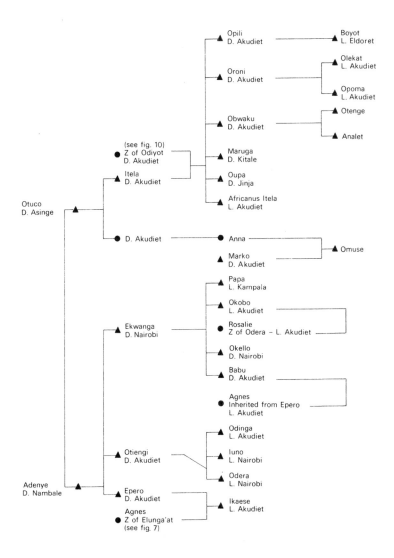

FIGURE 11   Genealogy of clan Ikuruk

her. Her father refused to let her return to her husband's home, which was notorious for its sorcery.
Therefore, Okude was forced to migrate to his wife's
home. After some time he married a second wife who
bore him one son. The first wife had two sons. Okude
died in 1950. He moved to Akudiet in 1930. Because of
their minority status and short length of residence,
the sons of Okude were given a very small piece of land,
about 2.5 hectares. Omukaga, of lineage Acakai of clan
Ikomolo, decided to sue the sons of Okude. He claimed
that they were residing on land that was originally
used by Acakai and not Odiyot. Therefore, they had no
right to be there. Omukaga later admitted to me that
his claim was false. He felt, however, that there was
a good chance of the claim being settled in his favour
because the sons of Okude were rather young and had no
basis of local support. Odiyot's sons, who might have
been expected to support their sister's children were
all dead, and all his grandsons happened to be in jail
or living away. Omukaga was eventually given 0.7 hectares of land. This leaves three potential households
with 1.8 hectares, or 0.6 hectares apiece. This is one
of the smallest holdings that I have recorded for any
Etesot. Recently one of the three brothers moved to
live with his father's brother in Amukura. The father's brother, Pascal, has daughters only, and the young
man, Opoma, will inherit from Pascal. Opoma's mother
was Okude's second wife, so Opoma had not maternal
relatives in Akudiet - unlike the other two men who did
and remained there.

Although members of two clans, Ikomolo and Ikatikok,
were the first neighbourhood residents, a number of households belonging to other clans are now represented in the
neighbourhood. These households were all connected in one
way or another with the pioneer families that were the
first to move into Akudiet. (My use of the word 'pioneer'
is analogous to Vincent's (1971) use of 'core family'.)
These households were (except in one case) related through
affinal or matrifilial ties to pioneering Ikomolo households. Given the Iteso pattern of laterally extending
ties of kinship, this has meant that these kinship ties
have provided a normative structure and social idiom
within which social relations could take place. I should
point out that affinal ties and ties based on matrifiliation frequently have more importance than ties of common
lineage when it comes to residence choice. At the very
least they must be accorded an equal status with lineage-
based affiliation. Cases 7, 8 and 9 illustrate the kinds
of affinal relations that preceded residence changes.

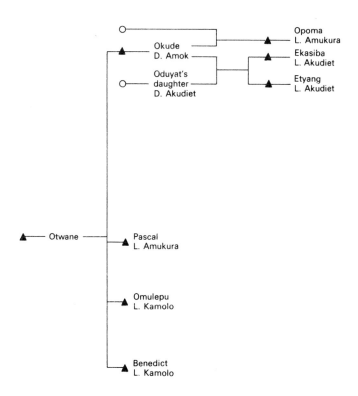

FIGURE 12   Genealogy of clan Ikajoro

Case 7 is especially relevant. Although Omoit and Inapa
were full brothers they or their children moved to Akudiet, not because of common lineage membership, but because of different affinal ties to members of the same
exogamous sub-clan resident in that area. In Case 7 we
first see members of one clan, Ikuruk, who are residing
in the locality because of affinal ties, bringing in their
own affines. Thus the members of clan Ikajoro residing
there are affines of the affines of the pioneers. This is
not a particularly enviable position when it comes to conflict. Their structural weakness was demonstrated by the

land case in which they were involved.

IV

These cases document the development of Akudiet neighbourhood, and the manner by which the present inhabitants came
to reside there. The data presented above illustrate the
assertions about neighbourhood, kinship and leadership
patterns presented in the preceding chapters. Three aspects of neighbourhood development emerge from the complex of cases. First, in the absence of functionally significant corporate lineage organization, the norms of kinship form a structure which both influences and imposes
limitations on the pattern of residence choices. Second,
conflicts originating in the domestic domain were very
often the impetus both for the transfer of political
allegiance and changes in residence pattern. Third, the
patterns of leadership by which local followings were established no longer exist. These will all be further
examined within the context of the history of Akudiet.

The rate of spatial mobility among the Iteso has slowed
considerably until it has come almost to a full stop in
recent years. The most important, and obvious, factor in
this change has been the changing relation of the Iteso to
the land. Three factors have been important in changing
Iteso attitudes and rules regarding land. The first is
the rapidly increasing population. Such recent outlets as
permanent labour migration and moving to settlement
schemes in the Uasin Gishu area and Uganda are no longer
open. Parcels of land that were formerly disdained as
being too poor or uncomfortable are now being farmed and
fought over.

The second factor in changing attitudes has been
increased per capita requirements for land. Cash cropping
is the sole way for most Iteso to earn substantial cash
income. The increasing involvement of the Iteso in the
cash economy and the consequent demand for goods and services has meant that larger acreages of land are coming
under cultivation for maize and cotton. Yet the per capita amount of land under cultivation for subsistence has
remained constant. At present all but the poorest households maintain a 50-50 mix of labour and capital devoted
to cash and subsistence farming. There is a little not-
iced characteristic of societies such as the Iteso, which
maintain a subsistence plus cash economy. This is that
per capita land requirements are relatively high because
the people involved are trying to maintain two different
economies.

Third, the Kenya government instituted a programme of individual land registration in 1969. This has increased the rate of already ongoing changes in a number of ways. First, land had already come to be regarded as a scarce good. Boundaries were planted as the result of official pressure in 1956. After this, land began to be exchanged for cash considerations. This meant that people were no longer willing to exchange what was now a valuable commodity, land, for intangible goods like power and prestige. The transitional political system that I described in chapter 3 was based on a low valuation placed on land. People were willing to move only because they could easily exchange rights in land in their original place of residence for rights in the second place. It was the limited value of land that allowed it to be the basis for building up a local following. The incentive still exists for people to become followers in the special sense of moving to live under the aegis of another person. It is simply that, because land is scarce and valuable, the opportunity only rarely occurs. In almost all the cases the patron who brings in a client has no sons to act as heirs. In Case 9 Opoma moved to live with his father's brother under such circumstances.

By registering land and providing a forum in which conflicting claims can be argued, the National government has forced the issue of the increasing value of land to become a paramount concern. This was because conflict between claimants over the same piece of land was played out in a public arena. In addition, the rules of land registration were such that after three hearings the claims were settled irrevocably. This required people to consider the option of either foregoing a claim to a piece of land or publicly disputing with kinsmen and neighbours. The latter alternative is distasteful to many Iteso. Yet it was frequently chosen, simply necause the loss of a basic resource was at stake.

This conflict over land has had two consequences for neighbourhood organization. The first is that the process of building up local followings has been disrupted because of the scarcity of a basic resource, land. In the early colonial period leaders could build up a following by luring people to move to their area in exchange for capital and political protection only because land was readily available. In a situation where land is a scarce good, local followings cannot be built up on the basis of residential changes.

The second consequence was that local groups which were based on ties of co-residence which are overlain by ties of kinship were fundamentally disrupted. This can be seen

in Case 6. Palinyang and Imweno were pioneers together.
Imweno welcomed Palinyang's son Aura, when Aura returned
to Akudiet. Now there is considerable bitterness between
Aura and Imweno's grandsons because of land cases. However, the remarkable ability of Iteso to neglect disputes
without resolving them is illustrated in this case and in
Case 2. As a result of conflict over land in Aura's
family, Ejakait, Aura's son, and Odera, Imweno's grandson,
have become firm allies.

V

Present conditions have also had serious consequences for
the pattern of political leadership. In chapter 3 I described a change in the type of leadership at the local
level as being from a kind of patron to a broker. This
occurred for two reasons. First, the consolidation of
colonial rule imposed a political structure external to
Iteso society which served as a source of authority, prestige and economic input in the form of cash income and
development resources. Consequently, a series of brokers
who could mediate between the officials and local level
people developed. These brokers did not compete with
local level patrons because the processes by which patrons
were able to build up followings were stopped.

Patrons depended upon the availability of land in order
to build up their following. The ideal way in which a
patron established himself was to pioneer an area with
some followers and to bring in others at a later period.
In order to do this he utilized previously existing affinal and cognatic ties in addition to social ties of common
clanship. A supplementary way in which one became a patron was to take the place of an ineffective or dead
patron. Overt conflict between patrons was rare (except
for the feud) because there was no fixed resource to be in
conflict over. The conflict was expressed instead in
mutual competition for the same potential followers. The
most important social process that allowed patrons to
build followings was the developmental cycle of domestic
groups. Conflicts over the family estate provided some
Iteso with motives for moving to another place where there
was the promise of greater input of capital for the establishment of an economically viable household.

As household moves became less frequent, potential patrons found it impossible to build followings. In addition, two factors undermined their political significance: (a) The 'Pax Britannica' and its successor the 'Pax
Kenya' lessened the need for protection from feud and

external marauding. (b) The entry of the Iteso into the
cash economy has provided the Iteso with a whole new set
of economic motives. School fees, medical fees, taxes,
clothing, ploughs and oxen, prestige, goods, etc., all
compete for capital and income with gifts to followers.
Thus, the economic means by which followers are rewarded
appears extravagant in the present context. The consequence of all this has been that from about 1930 few
people attempted to become patrons and instead, if they
had local level political ambitions, put their energies
into becoming brokers. An example of such a person is
Ejakait's brother Wasike. The men who were patrons either
became government officials, if they were powerful enough,
or became increasingly powerless. They did, however,
command considerable prestige because of the status they
once had.

With the passing away of patrons, neighbourhood boundaries became blurred and ego-oriented. Instead of multiple ties to a focal ego defining the neighbourhood, a
series of overlapping ties based on kinship, friendship,
and co-operations have become the essential characteristics which separate one neighbourhood from another. In
addition another vaguely defined territorial group has
assumed increasing importance in Iteso life. It is what
I choose to call (following Evans-Pritchard, 1940) a
'district'. This is not explicitly recognized by the
Iteso but is a vaguely bounded area in which the majority
of a person's total social relations take place. These
social relations include marriage choice, active kinship
ties, friendship ties, and other relationships. Iteso of
Akudiet recognize a district in a vague way when they
speak of 'Amukura' as a local group of people in whose
homes they can feel comfortable and where they are
'known'. Brokers tend to regard the district rather than
the neighbourhood as the basis of their political activity. The importance of a district has meant that, even
though the neighbourhood has remained as a unit, its
boundaries have become even more vague, since people often
equate district ties with neighbourhood ties. I find it
surprising that the term Ekitala has not been applied to
the district as an emergent social unit. Perhaps this is
because it is associated with an official government
group, the headman's area.

VI

In the preceding sections I have attempted to define a
vaguely bounded social unit, an actual neighbourhood

called Akudiet, in two ways. The first was in terms of
the social perceptions of a group of people who chose each
other as being members of the same neighbourhood. In
chapter 3 it was shown that the social concept of a neighbourhood did exist. In this chapter it was shown that
there was a tendency for some people to choose each other
as neighbourhood co-residents rather than other groups of
people. However, perceptions of the name and composition
of the neighbourhood did vary considerably from household
head to household head. This was seen to be due to a combination of individual life-experience and personal ambitions.

The synchronic approach that I utilized in the first
portion of the chapter was adequate for defining the
emergent boundaries and composition of neighbourhoods. It
is inadequate, however, if one wishes to understand the
social processes through which neighbourhoods originate
and develop and the ways in which neighbourhood organization is maintained. In order to understand these aspects
of neighbourhoods I had to take a diachronic approach.
This was done through a social history of Akudiet neighbourhood. I demonstrated that empty land was pioneered
by men of Ikomolo and Ikatikok clans. Followers were
brought into the area first by relatively distant ties of
agnation and then through the selective utilization of
ties of cognatic and affinal kinship. In other words,
non-agnates increased in importance after the original
group of Ikomolo agnates established themselves. The
significance of these non-agnatic ties increased in an
atmosphere of competition among several agnatically related patrons.

It is at this point in the social history of Akudiet
that two names of patrons stand out. These are Acakai and
Odiyot. As patrons they seem to have pursued two different strategies. Acakai maximized ties of clanship. He
was known as the pre-eminent member of his clan in the
locality. The history of the lineage that bears his name
is interesting in this regard. It is represented by 27
households dwelling locally and has collateral lines that
were attached to it two generations back from senior living household heads. In other words, there are living
household heads of lineage Acakai who are related as
father's father's brother's son's sons (second cousins) to
each other. I recorded no other example of a lineage of
such breadth and depth among the Iteso.

The average number of households found in any given
lineage in a survey of 200 households was 12.5 and the
number of households ranged from 2 to 28. It should be
pointed out here that the enormous size of lineage Acakai

makes it subject to tensions, some of which have been
recorded in Case 1. It may be on the verge of fission.
Informants in Akudiet stated that if it had not been for
Acakai's fame and successes as a leader, his prolific
output of children, and his longevity, the lineage bearing
his name would have divided long ago. I would suggest,
however, that an important factor in the delayed fission
of lineage Acakai has been the remarkable lack of residential mobility that has characterized the lineage. Unlike
almost all Iteso lineages of similar or even younger age
(see Palinyang, Case 6 as an example), Acakai has remained
residentially stable. This is because a large portion of
Acakai's following was composed of his lineage. The
length of his term as a leader prevented residential mobility of his followers, and when he finally died, there
were external factors such as government rules and lack of
land which constrained lineage members from moving in the
face of conflict.

The strategy that Acakai followed – maximizing clan and
lineage ties - was not the usual one. He was successful
in this because he possessed relative seniority and wealth
before he moved to Akudiet and he had few competitors
among his lineage and clan mates. Odiyot, on the other
hand, followed the more usual strategy of maximizing non-
agnatic ties. He was a younger man that Acakai although
their periods of patronship overlapped. They seem to have
been regarded as competitors, but the sentiments of common
lineage-clanship probably restrained them from engaging in
open conflict. The descendants of Odiyot's non-agnatic
kin remain in Akudiet. The circumstances under which they
moved there are discussed in Cases 7, 8 and 9. Some of
them even brought in non-agnates of their own. The descendants of the pioneers can be said to have primary ties
to each other, and to have acted as patrons. The patrons'
non-agnates were connected to the pioneers by a set of
what I call secondary ties. Finally, a few households
were connected to the pioneers by tertiary ties; that is,
they were the non-agnates of non-agnates. Over time these
ties became modified by the establishment of new sets of
affinal relations between households in Akudiet. This was
done through the marriages of the sisters and daughters of
households having secondary and tertiary ties with other
pioneer households and with each other. The consequence
of this was that the original patron-client kinship ties
became only one set of possible ties that people could
utilize in given social situations. Over time, these
patron-client ties lost their political significance as
old patrons died or retired and new ones did not replace
them. Thus the neighbourhood lost a focal ego for its

orientation and instead became characterized by a dense
network of multiple overlapping ties. In other words, we
have returned to Gulliver's notion of the 'cluster' (see
chapter 3). This accounts for the exceptionally fuzzy
conceptions of boundaries, names, and membership that
characterize the response of members of Akudiet neighbourhood. Without a patron-client relationship to lend stability to local group membership, other factors became
important in decisions about neighbourhood name and composition. As we have seen, these factors are both complex
and changing. These other factors were always present in
Iteso neighbourhoods. The difference was that a single
type of relationship - between the patron and his clients
- overrode other factors in the situation. As the external political situation changed, the importance of the
patron declined. His protection no longer meant the difference between survival and death. Therefore, the
relationship with a patron was no longer more important
than a relationship with other neighbours. The other factors assumed greater importance and we find the complex
and shifting situation that exists today.

VII

The major difficulty in dealing with Iteso neighbourhoods
is not their amorphous composition or the vagueness of the
Iteso when they describe them. The difficulty is at the
analytical rather than the descriptive level. The Iteso
neighbourhood is a constantly changing phenomenon. Because different neighbourhoods are in different stages of
development, it is not possible to describe a 'normal'
neighbourhood in a static or synchronic fashion. This is
the same problem that has been experienced with regard to
the description and analysis of domestic groups (Fortes,
1958). The solution has been to describe the developmental cycle of these groups because it is realized that the
'normal' structure of these groups is different at different phases of development. This mode of description is
relatively easy when the developmental processes to be
described are repetitive, and not directional.(3) In the
case of the Iteso neighbourhood, we are dealing with a
system which has undergone, and is undergoing, rapid
change. The result of this change has been that the
repetitive cycles have been interrupted, and new cycles
have been introduced. At present, these new cycles are
being interrupted in their own turn. The end product is
a succession of seemingly stable territorial phenomena
which disappear rapidly. This is the stuff of which

social history is made.

Akudiet neighbourhood exhibits the characteristics that are described above. It emerged out of the disintegration of a territorial section. Its founders may have desired to re-establish their sub-section, but were unable to do so because of external political factors. In the chaotic conditions of the early 1900s patron-client relations structured territorial organization. If conditions had remained stable, we might assume that the high rate of household mobility, coupled with the patron-client system, would have led to the decline of some neighbourhoods as they approached a fissile stage in their developmental cycle and, associated with this, the emergence of new neighbourhoods which would be oriented to different and younger focal egos who were patrons. Once again, however, external political conditions prevented this situation from occurring. Instead, the patron role became politically irrelevant and the neighbourhood shifted to a more egalitarian form of organization. This is the situation that we find today. However, the high rate of household mobility that has prevented local organization from developing corporate attributes has been eliminated, again by external factors. Thus significant changes in the form of neighbourhood organization are to be expected. The developmental cycle of neighbourhoods has once again been interrupted, and it is highly likely that neighbourhood organization will once again undergo structural alterations.

8 Conclusion

In this chapter I wish to return to the problem that I
raised in the introduction; that is, the difficulty in
defining and discovering patterns of social change. The
primary assumption underlying the descriptive dimension
of this analysis has been that societies are not undiff-
erentiated wholes and, as a consequence, the factors that
influence persons to alter the manner in which they get
things done will have an uneven effect on different
aspects of society. Social change can be discovered by
comparing different aspects of society over time to see
whether these aspects have altered at different rates. In
order to be able to analyse social change in this manner,
social anthropologists need a descriptive framework which
allows them to discriminate among different parts or
spheres of a single social system.

This monograph has used the concepts of 'field' and
'domain' in order to distinguish the different parts of
the Iteso social system. These are only two of a variety
of other labels available to social anthropologists to
denote the systems of social relationships that they describe. 'System', 'sub-system', 'structure' and 'organization' are only a few that come readily to mind. Given
that there are choices, the label an anthropologist uses
frequently tells the reader something about the image of
society that the anthropologist holds and the direction of
his analysis. That is my intention in choosing the concepts of 'field' and 'domain'.

The concept of a social field was first advanced as a
corrective to the notion that a social system was composed
of discrete parts integrated in a harmonious whole. As
Fortes used the concept of field in 'Dynamics of Clanship'
(1945), the field of clanship of any maximal lineage

overlaps but does not coincide with the field of clanship
of another maximal lineage of the same clan (p. 89).   In
other words, two lineages of the same clan do not agree on
what constitutes the other lineages of the same clan.
Thus clanship in its actual operation among the Tallensi
is a contradictory phenomenon, and Fortes uses the notion
of field as a means of describing not only consistency but
conflict in its operation.   In the Tallensi case, the consequence of different lineages having overlapping fields
of clanship is that specific lineages can play intercalary
roles between clans.   Fortes used the concept of a field
because he was interested not only in the internal operation of fields but in the consequences that result from
the feature that fields are overlapping phenomena.   Hence
he was, and is, concerned with what Dorothy Emmet calls
the 'operative effect' of fields - how far an actor's
behaviour (in one field) is affected by his social relationships in another field, and vice versa (1972, p. xvii).
In another place in 'Dynamics' (1945, p. xi) Fortes defines a 'field of social relations' as having extension in
space or time.   Once again we see a concern with defining
parts of social systems not only as structures but as
having to take account of situational factors.   This definition of a field has been taken up by Turner (1957) and
Bailey (1960) among others.   The problem with this usage
is that a field then becomes reduced to a series of situations or an arena in which social dramas are played out,
and the systematic normative and ideological aspects of
fields of social relations become lost.   As a consequence
the constraining influences of norms, values and prior
commitments, in fact, the interrelationship of one field
with other fields, is neglected.

  This much is clear in Fortes.   Over the years he has
applied the notion of a field to a variety of different
phenomena (Barnes, 1971, p. 218).   Yet, he has consist-
ently been concerned with describing a social system as
composed of overlapping fields and discovering the operative effects of fields on each other.   The use of the concept of field, pioneered by Fortes, is a means whereby
social systems can be described without the assumption
that they have a tendency towards stability.   A difficulty
lies, however, in the different ways in which the concept
has been used.

  At this point it may be useful to define a field as a
system of social relationships, and their associated
activities in time and space, which overlap with other
such systems.   This definition agrees with one of Bailey's
uses of the concept in 'Tribe, Caste and Nation' (1960),
where he describes the political field as encompassing a

variety of situations which are defined in terms of different normative structures he characterizes as 'tribe',
'caste' and 'nation'. The merit of this definition is
that it combines for analysis not only the normative aspects of social relationships and activities, but also the
'processes by which individuals choose between alternative
courses of action and manipulate various norms and values
in order to justify them' (Long, 1968, p. 9). The concept
of a social field then seeks to describe in one framework
both institutionalized forms of actions and the strategies
that actors pursue.

One consequence of this definition is that an action
can be defined as part of any number of different fields
- given the problem in which the anthropologist is interested. This returns again to the overlapping aspect of
the concept of a field. In order to explain a given pattern of behaviour, it is necessary to discover the different fields of which it can be seen as being part. Thus,
in this study, choice of a place in which to found an
independent household is seen as an activity in the
fields of kinship, politics (in the sense of leader-
follower relations), domestic life and territoriality.
The different patterns of action that people follow when
they do found an independent household can then be explained in terms of their pattern of social relationships
in the fields of kinship, politics and so on.

The concept of field, however, is useful for more than
just describing the factors that influence the pursuit of
different strategies. By conceiving of a field as composed of different levels or aspects of behaviour, the
pattern of relationships among fields can be described in
a precise manner. Since systems of social relationships
lie at the centre of the concept of a social field, the
same distinctions that can be applied to levels of the
analysis of systems of social relationships can be dis-
cerned in social fields. Hence, fields can be described
in terms of their ideological, normative and behavioural
aspects as can any system of social relationships (Moore,
1969). Two fields may overlap at any level. In the
example given above I was primarily concerned with expli-
cating action at the behavioural level. In another kind
of example, in Evans-Pritchard's analysis of the feud
among the Nuer, descent is described as a field (system in
Evans-Pritchard's terms) which overlaps with the territorial field at the level of ideology rather than behaviour (1940).

A major problem remains with the use of the concept of
the social field. Rather like the concept of 'context',
it can be defined in as narrow or wide a manner as the

analyst wishes (Gellner, 1970), and there is no way of
telling whether the arbitrary definition of the anthropologist obscures or advances our understanding of a particular society. In practice, however, anthropologists frequently base their definition of a social field on criteria derived from the society being investigated. They
do this by taking the system of social identities in terms
of which people define situations as the starting point
for the definition of a field. Thus, Norman Long, in
investigating social change among the Lala of Zambia,
examines changes occurring within three fields; the economic, the residential, and that involving the evaluation
of social status (1968, p. 10). These are defined as
fields because Long can isolate coherent systems of social
relations which form the centre of the field. The implication of this practice is that fields have a structure,
and that the structure is a model derived from the shared
meanings in terms of which persons in a society define
their social life. Thus the point of view I am taking
asserts that shared beliefs and values are important for
the definition of social fields as well as social roles
and processes. This is an element that is implicit but
not stressed in Fortes's latest formulation, as when he
describes the concept of domain as reflecting 'the experience people have of their social life' (1969, p. 99).

   Once the fields of a social system have been defined,
the second step is to examine the pattern of relationships
among fields. One way this can be done is through the
concept of social identity. When two persons interact,
they frequently do so through a composite of social
identities, which Goodenough calls a 'social persona'
(1965). For example, when two Iteso interact as neighbours, their normative behaviour is also governed by rules
derived from their relative positions within the fields of
kinship, religion and politics.

   In some circumstances actors must satisfy the requirements of certain of the identities that they wish to
assume before they can combine them with other identities
into a persona. These identities are situationally but
not temporally prior. For example, among the Iteso,
women must be married adults before they can act as the
initiators of rituals. The identity 'wife' is a requirement for a person to assume the identity 'ritual initia-
tor'. In our own society a person must be legally of age
before he can buy and sell stocks without his guardian's
consent. Hence the identity 'adult' is prior to the identity of stock market actor. Associated with identities
are what Goodenough calls 'statuses', which are the right
and duty bearing components of social action. Fortes

tends to emphasize the right and duty bearing aspect
whereas I am as concerned with identities as with statuses.

An example that Fortes uses may illustrate the distinctions that I am trying to describe here. Among the
Ashanti an adult man may occupy two identities in the
field of kinship. As a household head he has a distinctive set of rights and duties towards his family, especially his sons. As a mother's brother he has another set
of duties toward the children of his sister. This second
set of rights and duties are unlike his domestic (household) rights and duties. Instead they are related to the
man's civic status and are part of the field that includes
his position in his lineage, chiefdom and so on. Fortes
concludes that 'if we take such a person's total field of
kinship relations, we find that its management involves
compliance with norms that emanate from two distinct and
in some ways opposed domains of social structure' (1969,
p. 98).

These distinctive 'domains' are fields that generate
identities and associated rights and duties that are
mutually exclusive for actors. If a person is acting as
a member of a household vis-à-vis another member of that
household, he is not defined as a political actor, even
though he may have to take into consideration situations
where and when he will act in what Fortes would call his
civic capacity. Thus domains are fields that structure
the identities and rights and duties in terms of which
people interact with each other. A person cannot act in
terms of more than one domain at any given time. Fields,
however, are not domains, because they are distributed
between domains. In the Ashanti example given above,
kinship is a field because it is distributed between the
political-jural and domestic domains of Ashanti social
structure. It is not a domain because identities derived
from the field of kinship operate as part of the definition of the situation in both domains. In social relationships a persona may be composed of identities derived
from a number of fields but only one domain. Put another
way, we may say that domains do not overlap with other
domains. Fields overlap with each other and also with
domains. Structurally differentiated societies may have
many domains. Those that are not structurally differentiated are characterized by multiplex role relations
and may have only two domains, the political-jural and the
domestic domains. The importance of the fields of kinship, age and religion is that they provide structural
links between these two domains (Fortes, 1958, p. 6). The
description of the inter-relationships among fields allows

the anthropologist to discover the location and source of
conflict and contradiction, a very important aspect of
social systems for the study of social change.

This elaboration of the concepts of field and domain
may seem to do little more than provide a taxonomic frame
in which to locate observations. I would agree. The
major course of strength of modern social anthropology has
been the development of an adequate analytical theory that
facilitates the description of social patterns. In Falding's terms (1971, p. 501), social anthropology is in
possession of a conceptual apparatus for sorting out the
pieces of the social world before getting on to the task
of explaining it. (This is somewhat similar to Fortes's
(1970) distinction between analysis and description.)
Fortes points out that his elaboration of the concept of
domain has only heuristic value. By this I take him to
mean that the concepts of 'field' and 'domain' are useful
for describing the parts of a social system and isolating
the interrelationships among those parts. The concepts
do not predicate the conditions under which the phenomena
being described occur. That is a task for explanatory
theory rather than descriptive or analytical theory.

Describing the interrelationships among the parts of a
social system is a first and necessary task in social
analysis. It is particularly important for the study of
social change. Since Marx we have been aware that the
explanation of change is tied to the discovery of patterns
of tension and conflict. The concepts of field and domain
were developed in order to discover these aspects of
social systems as well as harmony and integration.

The twin concepts of field and domain can help to describe and explain patterns of social change. There are
two ways in which they aid in the investigation of social
change. The first is that the concept of a field allows
for the examination of social processes in addition to
role systems. In this way the analyst is constrained to
describe the cumulative results of individuals' multiple
reinterpretations of their social roles. The results of
these multiple reinterpretations is, as Dorothy Emmet
(1958) has demonstrated, what we call 'social change'. By
focusing on the patterns of the reinterpretations and not
on separate reinterpretations themselves (as, for example,
Barnett's (1953) innovation theory does), the effect of
external factors that constrain actors to alter their
roles in particular fields may be considered.

The second way in which the concept of field facilitates the analysis of change follows from the first.
After the effects of change on one field or domain have
been described, the influence of other parts of a social

system on the direction of change can be analysed. This
influence is discovered by examining the manner in which
actions in different social fields have consequences for
each other. By investigating the relations between different fields, hypotheses regarding the consequences of
change in one aspect of society for other aspects of a
society can be tested, and the reciprocal influences that
a social field exerts on change in other fields can be
described. Thus, an examination of the interrelationships
among different fields allows for the separation of the
factors influencing the rate of change from the factors
influencing the direction of change. The first set is
often to be found in external influences on particular
fields. (At least this is true for the recent history of
the Iteso.) The second set of factors is usually to be
found in the reciprocal relations between fields.

   In this way the concepts of field and domain are analytical tools that can be used to discover different rates
of change (within specific fields), and the direction of
change (in the reciprocal relations between fields).
Fortes's concept of the domain as a particular kind of
field provides a beginning for organizing data regarding
social change in terms of the structure of social systems.
The factors influencing change in the political-jural
domain, and the influence of the relationship between the
political-jural and domestic domains on the direction of
change have been the subjects of this analysis. In the
next section of this chapter I shall describe these con-
clusions in terms of the conceptual apparatus elaborated
in this section.

II

Among the Iteso the structure of political-jural domain of
social relations has undergone extensive change since the
late 1890s. Activities in the political-jural domain have
always been concerned with two goals. The first of these
goals is to assure the protection and integrity of Iteso
social groups. The second goal has been to order social
relations within these groups. In the precolonial period,
the largest of these groups was the territorial section.

   The territorial section was a political and ritual
corporation. It was composed of persons who were under an
obligation to come to their common defence, to settle disputes between members of the same section, and to perform
rituals under the leadership of the elders of the section.
Ritual sanctions and the use of force could be applied to
members of a section who failed to honour these

obligations. Section membership was organized in terms of
rules and regulations that were in Fortes's sense part of
the jural dimension of Iteso society (1969, p. 87-8).
Failure to honour the obligations of section membership
brought upon the offender the sanctions that had the back-
ing of the whole society, or at least the largest groups
of it. The most striking forms of sanction, and in Iteso
thought the most severe, were the curse of the ritual
elders and banishment from the section. The section was
led by an office holder or head who co-ordinated the
actions of the members of a section in warfare and served
as a jural official who could decide the outcome of disputes between section members. There is also some evidence that he could represent the interests of his section
in dealing with other sections.

Sections were usually composed of three or four smaller
groups that were headed by an official with responsibilities and privileges similar to those of the section head.
This official I call the sub-section head, and the group
the sub-section. The Iteso words for section and sub-
section are the same. This indicates that in some sense
Iteso regarded sections and sub-sections as functionally
equivalent units. Sub-sections were composed of a group
of residentially contiguous households united to each
other through an ideology of common descent and by obligations to settle disputes among themselves under the
leadership of the sub-section lead. In Iteso ideology a
sub-section was founded by a group of agnates of the same
generation and exogamous clan. Eventually these agnates
and their descendants would form the nucleus of a new
exogamous clan. This group of agnates, as a result of
common clanship, formed a pool of persons able to participate in mortuary ritual, conduct and defend each other
in the operation of the feud, and control rights over the
most scarce goods in the precolonial Iteso polity, cattle
and women.

In actuality sub-sections were composed of both a core
of persons related by common ties of exogamous clanship
and many of their clients, who were related to their
patrons by a variety of cognatic and affinal ties.
Clients were important resources in political competitions
because they were tied to their patrons and unable to
switch allegiance to other members of the sub-section,
although they were able to move to live with patrons in
other sub-sections. Persons with political ambitions
either remained within their own sub-sections or pioneered
new sub-sections. They also, by virtue of their control
of wealth, exercised considerable power of their junior
agnates. These junior agnates had the choices of becoming

a client in a section controlled by another exogamous clan
or remaining under the authority of their senior agnates.
Successful participation in warfare and the founding of a
new territorial sub-section provided an alternative to
these options.

The options of founding a new sub-section and expanding
at the expense of other ethnic groups were frequently
exercised by the Iteso in pre-colonial Kenya. Political
and economic factors such as the desire to obtain the
resources to found households and the ambition to become
political leaders were part of the factors predisposing
the Iteso to expand rapidly. The inability of the
surrounding tribes to protect themselves when measured
against the ability of the Iteso to retaliate against
aggression was another factor predisposing the Iteso to
predatory expansion. There may have been moral injunc-
tions against Iteso attacking other Iteso, but evidence
on this point is uncertain. Some sections did co-operate
with each other, however, in warfare and possibly in
defence.

Ecology is a factor in this expansion in the sense that
the ability to move households rapidly and flexibly is
adaptive under conditions of uncertain rainfall. A pattern of expansionary movement, however, is not necessarily
entailed by the rainfall pattern. There is no evidence to
indicate that the Iteso either exhausted or overcrowded
their precolonial environment. Population densities indicate that the land that the Iteso occupied was underuti-
lized, as was true of most societies in the Western Kenya-
Eastern Uganda area. The dynamics of Iteso expansion are
explained by examining the interrelationships of ecology,
access to scarce resources, patterns and choices of
leader-follower relationships, and external politics.

Sub-sections were composed, as I have said, of a number
of residentially contiguous households. Relations within
households were not ordered by the same norms as social
relations between households. The household head, who was
and is always a male, represented his household in deal-
ings with other households or in section and sub-section
activities. Women were and remain jural minors in all
political activities. At marriage they are transferred
from a household headed by and under the authority of
their father or father's successor to a household headed
by and under the authority of their husband. As a consequence of the distinction that Iteso make between inter-
and intra-household social relations, we can discriminate
between distinct and separate political-jural and domestic
domains of Iteso social structure.

The preceding paragraphs have described the structure

of the political-jural domain of precolonial Iteso social
structure. Within the political-jural domain identities
and membership in sections, sub-sections and age groups
were situationally related to territorial activities.
Sections and sub-sections were defined primarily in territorial terms. In order to participate in social relations
within the territorial field, a person had to obtain the
status of household head. The activities which were relevant to this field were organized around warfare, defence
and the adjudication of disputes. The social identities
in terms of which these activities took place were defined
in terms of section and sub-section membership, and
leader-follower relations.

On some of these occasions when sections performed
rituals, social identities were also defined in terms of
the field of religion and organized according to the principle of stratification by age. Stratification by age
provided for the orderly transmission of political authority. Since religious authority had its social expression
in ceremonies performed by groups defined in terms of
relative position within the age system, the allocation
of roles in public ritual was determined on the basis of
the principle of stratification by age. The aspect of
the religious field that operated in the political-jural
domain largely coincides with groups organized on an age
basis. The situations in which identities in these various fields became relevant was determined by processes in
the territorial field. By this I mean that almost all the
occasions when persons' identities as members of the age
and religious groups were relevant were occasions when
they were acting in their capacities as members of territorial sections. Social relations within the political-
jural domain of precolonial Iteso society can be summed
up as follows: territorial groups provided for the external independence and internal order, especially through
the offices of the section and sub-section leaders. Age
groups provided for the orderly transmission of authority,
which itself was sanctioned in super-natural terms through
the operation of public ritual.

The field of kinship was distributed between both the
political-jural and the domestic domains of precolonial
Iteso society. Its political-jural significance was two-
fold. First, the ideology and normative structure of
relations among agnates provided organizing principles on
which sub-sections were based. Second, kinship-based
identities embodied a set of norms in terms of which relations of power could operate and be justified. As a
result of the intersection of kinship and leader-follower
relations, the choices of leaders and followers were and

are limited for each other. Within the domestic domain,
conflicts among kinsmen over the family estate were associated with the motives that induced persons to move away
from previous residences.

Kinship also provides an important bridge between the
political-jural and domestic domains. Social roles within
households are derived from and link persons to roles
within the larger system of kinship identities. Familial
social relations form the basis of identities within the
household. Members of households are usually linked to
each other by ties of filiation and marriage. These link-
ages also tie persons to other persons with whom they
interact in the political-jural domain. Thus ties of
cumulative patrifiliation tie a person to the system of
patrilineal descent groups. On the other hand ties of
matrifiliation tie a person to maternal kin with whom he
may choose to have significant political relationships.
These ties, and the necessity for a person to maintain
them as options, have consequences for how he conducts his
activities in the domestic domain. This is particularly
true for men since they represent their household in the
political-jural domain. On the other hand, a person's
complex of agnatic, cognatic and affinal ties provide him
with options for evading unpleasant or unwanted social
relationships in his capacities as a political-jural and
a domestic actor.

The most important institution of the domestic domain
is the household. Recruitment to this group is based on
kinship principles. The household is the most significant economic institution among the Iteso since it is
within households that most consumption and production
occurs. In addition, the household has rights over the
most important forms of capital goods among the Iteso,
cattle and land. While not all labour inputs for a household come from within it, a person's household is the only
sure source of labour in Iteso society. Household partition is strongly influenced by factors within the field of
kinship which are external to households, and thus outside
the domestic domain. These factors include the limited
range of kinsmen who are defined as appropriate for helping a person to found his own household, and the other
obligations on scarce resources with which these kinsmen,
such as mother's brothers, are faced.

Even though kinship structures are not the basis of
political structures (although descent provided the ideology for sub-section activities), an understanding of the
kinship system is crucial. The relations of the different
levels of the field of kinship to the political-jural
domain has already been discussed. In the domestic

domain, kinship as a field impinges on the operation of
domestic groups. The authority of a wife-giver who becomes a mother's brother allows him to intervene in domestic relations. Also lineage solidarity, which operates
through the ritual process, has a stabilizing effect on
domestic relations. This is because the married women of
a lineage form a ritual corporation whose focus is, among
other things, the fertility and well being of domestic
groups of which the women are members.

Since 1890 the most far-reaching changes have occurred
in the territorial field of the political-jural domain.
As a result of the process the incorporation of the
Iteso into the colonial polity, the local basis of leader-
follower relations changed drastically. Instead of politically corporate territorial sections, there emerged at
first territorially based political coalitions that were
organized for defence and oriented to a common leader.
As the process of incorporation continued, the need to
organize for defence decreased. The orientation of the
neighbourhood to a common leader was transferred into the
personal, ego-orientation of neighbourhoods that exists
today. Because of the primacy of the territorial field in
the political-jural domain, these changes had significant
consequences for the social field concerned with age and
religion. Public religion and the age-set system disappeared rapidly. The internal structure of the field of
kinship remained relatively unaffected because it was
associated more with political processes such as the
recruitment of a following than with the maintenance of
territorial structures, except for the relationship of
descent as an ideological justification for sub-section
actions. Accompanying these changes in the structure of
the relationships among fields was a rapid increase in the
frequency of household movements. The reasons for these
movements were political in the sense that household
heads were seeking safety in a highly uncertain situation
in which large-scale political action was ineffective and
dangerous. On the other hand, because large-scale political action no longer worked, the means of control and the
incentives that senior agnates could use in order to maintain large political followings were no longer operative.
Hence, there were fewer sanctions against attempting to
use a wider range of social relations in order to achieve
the goal of household viability and also more reasons for
followers to try to maintain as wide a range of options
as possible. The intermediate period of 1900-30 of social
change can be described as one of increased subordination
in wider political relations and increased autonomy in
narrower political relations.

The pattern of political domination and the means
whereby the Iteso were incorporated into the colonial state
explain the causes for and the impetus to rapid change in
the political-jural domain of Iteso social structure.
These events can even serve to explain why Iteso either
did not exercise some political options that would have
influenced the direction of change. At the very least,
the examination of these historical factors can explain
why some options were not adaptive and consequently would
have failed if tried. This does not constitute, however,
an explanation of the direction of social change. In
order to discover the reasons for particular patterns of
change having been chosen, factors that are both internal
and external to Iteso society must be examined. Only then
will it be possible to discover why some dimensions of
Iteso society changed more than others and what influenced
the directions of these changes.

Hence the transition from a territorial section system
to a neighbourhood system must be explained as partly the
result of the political history of the Iteso and partly
the result of the interaction between the political-jural
and domestic domains. The high rate of spatial mobility
that appears to have always been characteristic of Iteso
history enforced limits on the possible directions that
changes in territorial organization could take. The Iteso
were unable to achieve stability of personnel in local
groups because the impetus to household movements was very
great for many persons. There were also the further limitations on choice imposed by the pattern of colonial domination. This factor created circumstances in which political organizations that were small in scale, flexible in
make-up, and ephemeral in nature were adaptive. The
neighbourhood as a form of organization fits this description for three reasons: (a) It was successful as a form of
political organization because it adapted Iteso political
relationships to the external events with which they had
to come to terms. (b) The neighbourhood utilized leader-
follower relationships that were already existing in the
political-jural domain. (c) It was a form of organization
that fit with processes in the domestic domain which had
not altered radically under colonial domination.

First, the neighbourhood as a form of organization was
flexible and small enough in scale that Iteso were able to
hide their political actions from the Wanga agents of the
British. Second, the social relationships among leaders
and followers that formed the core of neighbourhoods remained the same as they were, in both content and often in
personnel, in the precolonial period. Finally, the flexibility of neighbourhoods was well adapted to the pattern

of household partition and the high rate of household
mobility that existed in the precolonial period. In addition, patterns of conflict in households over the family
estate and the resolutions of these conflicts by spatial
separation provide Iteso with incentives to enter into
relationships with patrons for protection and to obtain
the resources necessary to establish an independent household. Thus conflicts in domestic groups both reinforced
and were reinforced by the politics at the neighbourhood
level.

The next changes to occur were alterations in the pattern of leader-follower relations in neighbourhoods. Once
again these changes were instigated by events over which
the Iteso had no control, the establishment of colonial
administration over the Iteso. The integration of the
Iteso into colonial Kenya resulted in Iteso being able to
obtain income from local government positions, cash crops
and labour migration. They were able to use these new
forms of resources to achieve old goals, particularly the
establishment of independent households. Iteso were also
subjected to different patterns of social control in the
form of taxes, the enforcement of laws, labour levies and
so on. The traditional patrons were not able to protect
Iteso from the capricious exercise of administrative authority. At the same time Iteso no longer needed their
patrons to organize for defence and help to establish new
households. Hence the patron-client relationship disappeared and neighbourhoods became even more vaguely
bounded. At the same time they were integrated into
larger scale administrative units.

With the requirement for protection from maurauders
eliminated, the high rate of household mobility decreased.
A factor that served to further decrease the rate of
household mobility was the ability of Iteso to obtain the
means of establishing an independent household through
the non-traditional channel of cash income. This has
meant that conflicts over moveable resources such as
cattle do not have to be conducted as intensely as they
once were. However, population growth and the land requirements for cash cropping have created new problems.
With land becoming a scarce good household mobility, which
was based on unlimited access to land, has almost completely disappeared. Patterns of social relations within
the domestic domain will no doubt be altered as a result
of these changes based on events external to Iteso society. The direction of change that Iteso choose will be
adaptations to processes internal to Iteso society as well
as caused by factors external to it. The perspective that
helped to explain social change among the Iteso in the
past will also serve to explain it in the future.

Notes

CHAPTER 1 INTRODUCTION

1 The Northern Iteso are described in Gulliver and
   Gulliver (1968), Lawrance (1957), and Wright (1942);
   in addition to various small articles of dubious reliability on various aspects of Iteso history and social
   organization in the 'Uganda Journal'. Vincent's (1971)
   account of a polyethnic community in Teso District,
   Uganda, provides the most analytical description of
   Northern Iteso society that is available. She is more
   concerned, however, with political processes relating
   to polyethnicity than with changing patterns of indigenous social organization. Of the Southern Iteso the
   Gullivers tell us: 'There is little or no information
   available on the Iworopom or the Kenya Itesio' (p. 17).
2 Hogbin's lectures on social change (1958) illustrate
   the difficulties of attempting to describe social
   change in the abstract.
3 The most recent work on Nilotic languages is Ehret
   (1971) and he accepts Greenberg's classification of
   Ateso, the language of the Iteso (p. 10).
4 Unless I refer specifically to events or people on the
   Uganda side of the border my analysis should not be
   regarded as reliable for the situation there. The information that I do have suggests that there is little
   difference between the Iteso living on the two sides of
   the border. What differences that do exist can be
   traced to different policies followed by the Uganda
   Protectorate and the Kenya Colony.
5 These figures were obtained from the office of the
   District Clerk, Busia District, Kenya.

CHAPTER 2 THE PRECOLONIAL POLITICAL SYSTEM

1 Any thorough examination of the problems which arise
from this heterogeneity must await the completion of
research that is presently contemplated or being undertaken. I shall give two examples here of the problems
which can be encountered if the historical context is
not taken into account.

First, the Jo Padhola and the Bagweri (societies to
the west and northwest of the Iteso - see ethnic map,
chapter 1) possessed age systems of the Iteso type.
They are respectively Nilotic- and Bantu-speaking
peoples. The Jo Padhola adopted the Iteso age system
as part of the process of political centralization that
they underwent in the late nineteenth century, probably
in response to pressure from the Iteso and the Baganda
(Southall, 1957). The Bagweri have an Iteso type age
system in some clans (of probable Iteso origin) as they
absorbed large numbers of Iteso in the late nineteenth
century.

Second, traditional techniques of ritual slaughtering for the Kenya Iteso have all been abandoned in
favour of cutting the throat of any animal to be
slaughtered. No Etesot can give a reasonable explanation for this change in ritual technique. One clue is
that throat cutting is an Islamic practice, but there
are no Moslems among the Iteso. However, for a large
part of the colonial period, the Kenya Iteso were under
the political domination of the Wanga kingdom, whose
ruling house was Moslem and who insisted that Islamic
rules of slaughter were practised wherever they ruled.

2 There is a brief history of the Northern Iteso in Lawrance (1957). More elaborate is Webster et al. (1973).

3 The Iteso penetration of Teso District of Uganda is a
confused subject and not really germane to this discussion. Only one topic requires comment here. A number
of clans which claim to be of Iworopom origin are found
throughout the tribes of the Karamojong cluster. The
Iworopom may have been a tribe occupying Southern Karamoja. The story collected by Turpin (1948) suggests
that the descendants of the Iworopom are the Iteso of
Tororo and Kenya. This suggestion has also been advanced by the Gullivers (1968), Lawrance (1957), Webster
(1973), and the foremost expert on the Iworopom, John
Wilson (1970). I do know from Iteso informants that
the Karamojong call the Southern Iteso 'Iworopom'.
Further, some clan names of Iworopom origin are found
among the Iteso, and Ogot's dates for the second wave
of Iteso migrations into Bukedi (1967) might coincide

with the expulsion of the Iworopom from Karamoja. The
only difficulty in solving this ethnographic mystery
is that the name Iworopom is completely unknown among
the Southern Iteso and no traditions which could be
associated with them are to be found. This was an issue
to which I devoted a considerable amount of energy, but
I cannot say that it was in any way rewarding.
4   See Were's account of Iteso-Babukusu warfare (1967a,
    pp. 134-7).
5   'Mangati' is also a vernacular term for the Barabaig or
    Tatog of Tanzania. I believe it is the Maasai word for
    'savage'.
6   The major criteria that Dyson-Hudson uses in order to
    define a section is that it is the largest scale terri-
    torial group which is 'able to act independently and
    repeatedly in pursuit of political policy' (1966, p.
    250). This definition also applies to the group which
    the Southern Iteso call an etem. The Turkana provide
    an interesting contrast because their nomadism prevents
    them from uniting into sub-groups on the basis of ter-
    ritorial affiliation (see Gulliver, 1955).
7   The Ground Hornbill is a slow and clumsy bird on the
    ground. In flight, however, it is a majestic sight.
8   I have avoided a comparative analysis of the Iteso age
    systems with other societies of the Teso-Karimajong
    cluster or even other East African societies because
    my own data is slight, and I may be confusing organi-
    zational patterns with structural principles.

CHAPTER 3   THE EMERGENCE OF NEIGHBOURHOODS

1   Were (1967a) has demonstrated that Abaluyia "sub-
    tribes" were composed of groups migrating from many
    disparate areas and subject to sudden fragmentation.
2   The material given after this point refers only to
    events occurring east of the Malaba River in what
    eventually became Kenya. I do not think that the his-
    tory of the Iteso to the west of the Malaba was signi-
    ficantly different. However, I do not have reliable or
    extensive information for the area.
3   B.E.A. is the abbreviation for British East Africa, the
    earlier name for what was to become Kenya colony. The
    Western Region of Kenya was transferred to British East
    Africa in 1902. Lugumi is a mistaken version of El
    Gumi, the Uasin Gishu Maasai name for the Iteso, and
    the Ketosh (properly spelled Kitosh) are presently
    known as Babukusu.
4   The Northern Iteso had a very different administrative

history. They were conquered for the British by
Baganda troops under the leadership of Semei Kakungulu,
who immediately set up an administrative system along
Baganda lines (Lawrance, 1957). As a consequence the
political development of Teso District, Uganda, has
taken a different path.

5   I must add here that although agnation was not directly
related to the composition of neighbourhood groups,
there was a tendency for there to be a fairly large
number of agnatically related people living in any one
area. This would be especially true if two neighbouring patrons were members of the same sub-clan. The
consequence of large numbers of agnates living close by
would be to provide a large number of people available
for ritual, and aid in the event of a feud. Also,
exogamous sub-clans tended to be localized in four or
five distinct areas with some members randomly distributed over the rest of the Iteso area.

This pattern of agnatic clustering is the probable
result of the influence of two factors. First, Iteso
waver between maximizing one of two opposing kinship
options: (a) living with agnates who are jurally bound
to ego but among whom there is an atmosphere of mutual
antagonism; (b) living with non-agnates to whom ego is
bound by ties of sentiment but who are unreliable in
situations of crisis because they are not jurally
obliged to help a person when he is in difficulties.
Many therefore preferred to live among agnates. The
second factor was the attempt of members of one sub-
section to re-establish their section in a different
area sometime after an initial dispersal. Although
genealogical evidence clearly indicates that such
attempts were made in a number of instances, they
always failed because of the external political situation discussed in section II of this chapter. These
attempts did result in some agnates living together in
the same general area.

6   Because of Boissevain's strictures against the use of
the term, I do not choose to call this form of political organization a 'quasi-group' (Mayer, 1966). However, it then becomes necessary to distinguish between
two types of coalitions with different structural
features. The first is an ego-oriented coalition,
which I shall simply term 'coalition'. The second is
Gulliver's 'cluster' (1971), which does not have an ego
orientation. See the discussion in the remainder of
the chapter.

7   Some of these patterns of choice and their meaning for
household heads are described in chapter 7.

8   Among the Karamojong the word ekitala refers to a
    ridge of land where homes are to be found. The term
    also means a section (Dyson-Hudson, 1966, p. 126).
9   Rice has been recently introduced as a cash crop and
    planted in these seasonal swamps.
10 A third way in which a neighbourhood can be described
    is by examining the development of patterns of social
    relations between people who regard themselves as
    neighbours. I propose to do this by giving the social
    history of one neighbourhood, or set of neighbour
    hoods, depending upon how one looks at it, in some
    detail in chapter 7.
11 After the completion of agricultural chores women
    become involved in a whole set of domestic duties that
    married men may not undertake. They are not allowed
    to play elee because it is thought that they will not
    be able to brew good beer. There is a symbolic associ-
    ation of beer making with the domestic duties of
    women against beer consumption associated with the
    married men of a neighbourhood.
        Elee is a game that is played all over Africa. In
    Uganda it is known as *Mweso*. It is a competitive game
    of lightning calculation in which stones or seeds are
    moved around in holes on a board. There are many
    variations and a complicated set of rules.
12 See the discussion of the concept in Barbara Ward
    (1966).
13 As a result of conditions relating to the scarcity of
    land, the neighbourhood system is presently under-
    going considerable change. This is not, however, my
    concern here.

CHAPTER 4   CHANGING PATTERNS OF KINSHIP AND DESCENT

1   This statement is similar to a conclusion that
    Schneider has arrived at in 'American Kinship' (1968).
    I am not interested in analysing Iteso kinship culture
    at the same level of depth as Schneider. I think that
    Schneider's 'enduring diffuse solidarity' is a prop-
    erty of all identity relationships and, therefore, not
    very useful for a sociological analysis. The discus-
    sion of unilineal kinship in the succeeding chapters
    will indicate that two Iteso who are related on the
    basis of nominal clanship do not actually believe that
    they share common substance. This certainly brings
    into question the extentionist hypothesis that under-
    lies much work in kinship. I do not intend to become
    mired in that particular debate in a discussion of a

single kinship system. My own position, which I think
fits Iteso kinship facts, is that familial relations
in the domestic domain provide a 'moral model' (to use
Southwold's phrase) for kinship relations within the
political-jural domain (see Southwold, 1971, for a
clear statement of this position).

2 Evans-Pritchard (1951) describes a situation in Nuer
villages whereby affines are transformed into cognates
after the birth of children. This would seem to be the
social correlate of the cultural situation that I am
describing here.

3 A reason that I choose to call these unilineal groups
'clans' is that structurally similar groups with the
same names are found throughout the other tribes of the
Karamojong cluster (Gulliver, 1952) and, in order to
facilitate comparisons, I have kept a term used by
Gulliver (1953, 1956) and Dyson-Hudson (1966).

4 Given the lack of corporate activities associated with
nominal clans it is legitimate then to ask why these
unilineal categories have persisted in Iteso society.
In other African societies which are characterized by
a high rate of spatial mobility and a fragmentary basis
for local organization, clanship has disappeared. The
Ndembu are a good example of this phenomenon (Turner,
1957). The best answer I can give for the Iteso is
that while nominal clanship does not provide much of a
basis for the establishment of a relationship it does
provide some basis, and with nominal clanship are
associated kinship norms into which that relationship
can be fit.

I will give one example here. One man who was
trying to curry favour with me prior to asking for a
loan told me that he was closely related to an elderly
female informant of mine. The informant denied any
relationship at all. An examination of the situation
showed that the mother of my informant belonged to the
same nominal clan as the mother of the man, and that
the two mothers stood in the relationship of FZ - BD of
the nominal clan to each other. Thus the man was related to my informant as a classificatory MFZD whom he
called eja (see chapter 5 for an analysis of the system
of kinship terminology). This was a rather tenuous
basis for a relationship and, as far as my female informant was concerned, no relationship at all. Yet I
am sure that if there were some good reason for her to
be related to the claimant she would seize a nominal
clanship as a pretext as readily as he did. However,
as far as she was concerned 'Mam ong k'ajeni nesi'
(lit. I don't know him). A derived sense of the verb

akijen, 'to know', is 'to be related'.
5 This is a list of the most commonly mentioned nominal
   clans:

*Ikariwok	Ikomolo	Ilooka
Ikuruk	Irarak	Ikatanya
*Itengor	Isama	Isidelewa
Ipasam	Igoria	Ikajoro
Igara	Ikatelemu	Ipalam
Ikinom	Ikodai	Ibasere
Ibatai	Ilogir	Idoko
Ibekai	*Ikatekok	Imudei
Icegen	Ikamarinyang	Ikewata
Ikapenyu		

*These are found throughout the Karamojong cluster.
   Some clans are clearly not of Nilo-Hamitic origin.
Ikomolo is an Ateso version of Omolo, a very common
Lwoo speaking clan and Ibasere is clearly not Nilo-
Hamitic and may refer to the Sewe or Sere, a mysterious
'Maasai' type people who were said to have raided the
inhabitants of Bukedi district before the coming of the
Iteso (Ogot, 1967, p. 66). Unlike some expanding societies, however, the Iteso did not take on numbers of
people.
6 Thus under the criterion that Murdoch (1949) uses for
   defining clans, exogamous clans are not clans at all.
7 Mitchell's use of the term 'category' is meant to refer
   to a social category and not a cultural category. Cultural categories, which I discuss in the first sections
   of this chapter, are a related series of cognitive and
   symbolic discriminations. A social category is a class
   of objects which arouse expectations or elicit behaviour. In order to understand differences between different social categories, their relations to cultural
   categories must be examined.
8 I have not discussed affinal relations between or with
   women. This is really a separate topic in itself.
   It is complicated by the dual status women have as
   members of both their natal and their husband's agnatic
   groups.
9 The other maternal kinsman MZ and her husband really
   assume a secondary role, not unlike that of FZ and
   her husband. The term for MZ and FZ is the same.
   It is interesting to note in this connection that a
   woman has no special term for either her brother's
   or sister's children. They are all idwe ('children')
   although her brother's and sister's children call her
   eja.
10 This figure excludes all marriages of less than one
   year duration, whether ended in divorce or not. If

these marriages are included, the figure rises to 20 per cent.

CHAPTER 5   KINSHIP TERMS AND NORMS

1   See Evans-Pritchard's (1940) description of the situational significance of Nuer categories of *buth* and *mar* for a similar pattern.
2   I note here that women do not distinguish between own and brother's children, on the one hand, and sister's children on the other. Because their dual status as members of both their natal and husband's agnatic kin categories lets them view all children as descendants. This view of kinsmen is associated with a cultural emphasis on women as producers of children and guardians of clan and lineage fertility and continuity.
3   It is customary to analyse the referential system of terminology and not the vocative system. As the discussion of the two systems makes clear, the referential system is rather underdeveloped.
4   The respect and fear that characterises relations between adjacent generations is somewhat modified in the case of maternal kin. The 'brothers' of ego's father are to be treated in the same manner as father. Situational factors, such as were described in chapter 4 for mother's brothers, often modify the relationship between ego and particular father's brothers.

CHAPTER 6   THE DEVELOPMENTAL CYCLE IN DOMESTIC GROUPS

1   Among the Iteso almost all households conform to the ideal pattern.
2   In almost all of these cases the causal factor influencing a joint residence pattern is lack of land. This is because the option of moving to an area where land is plentiful and free no longer exists. In the father-only son case, there could be no dispute over inheritance, so the land was registered in both their names. Difficulties due to lack of land are a very recent phenomenon. Land was not even sold until 1950.
3   Aparik is the adjectival form of *aparas,* a plant that symbolizes the orderly transfer of fertility from one group or person to another.

CHAPTER 7 AKUDIET NEIGHBOURHOOD

1 The persons listed in Table 5 are drawn from a survey
of all the households under the authority of headman
Gastory Opetoi. The ten were chosen for three reasons. First, they represent all the major descent
groups found in the neighbourhood. Second, all ten
agreed that at least six of the other nine of them
belonged to the same neighbourhood. Third, a represen-
tative sample of persons of diverse age, economic
status, and political ambition is included.
2 There are essentially two difficulties that impede
genealogical reconstruction. First, Iteso genealogical
memory is short, often not going back more than two
generations from ego. The effective reliable length of
genealogies only spans the lineage. Second, breadth of
genealogy is frequently transferred to depth. Often an
informant lists a set of siblings as fathers and sons.
It may very well be that a political influence is at
work here. As I indicated in chapter 1, Iteso express
considerable anxiety over the legitimacy of their
tribal land tenure. One means of establishing legitimacy is by a long genealogy of ancestors who have died
on the Kenya side of the border. This often led, I
believe, to the kind of manipulation I describe above.
The Iteso kinship system, in any case, is one in which
lateral spread is as important as lineal depth. Accu-
racy can be arrived at only by correlating genealogies
collected from segments of unilineal groups localized
in different areas. For the purposes of analysing
local level organization, however, genealogical accur-
acy is not absolutely necessary.
3 See Vogt (1960) for a discussion of repetitive versus
directional processes.

Bibliography

BAILEY, F.G. (1960), 'Tribe, Caste and Nation', London: Oxford University Press.

BARNES, J.A. (1967), The Frequency of Divorce, in A.L. Epstein (ed.), 'The Craft of Social Anthropology', London: Tavistock.

BARNES, J.A. (1971), 'Three Styles in the Study of Kinship', London: Tavistock.

BARNES, J.A. (1972), Social Networks, Addison-Wesley Module in Anthropology No. 26, Reading, Mass.: Addison-Wesley.

BARNETT, H.B. (1953), 'Innovation: The Basis of Cultural Change', New York: McGraw-Hill.

BERNARDI, B. (1951), The Age-System of Nilo-Hamitic Peoples: A Critical Evaluation, 'Africa', XXI, pp. 316-33.

BLOCH, MAURICE (1971), The Moral and Tactical Meaning of Kinship Terms, 'Man', vol. 6, no. 1, pp. 79-88.

BOISSEVAIN, J. (1971), Second Thoughts on Quasi-groups, Categories and Coalitions, 'Man', vol. 6, no. 3, pp. 468-73.

COHEN, PERCY (1968), 'Modern Social Theory', New York: Basic Books.

COLSON, ELIZABETH (1962), 'The Plateau Tonga of Northern Rhodesia', Manchester: Manchester University Press.

DYSON-HUDSON, NEVILLE (1966), 'Karimojong Politics', London: Oxford University Press.

EHRET, CHRISTOPHER (1971), 'Southern Nilotic History', Evanston, Ill.: Northwestern University Press.

EMMET, DOROTHY (1972), 'Function, Purpose, and Powers', London: Macmillan.

ERAPU, L. (1969), 'Restless Feet', Nairobi: East African Publishing Bureau.

EVANS-PRITCHARD, E.E. (1940), 'The Nuer', London: Oxford University Press.

EVANS-PRITCHARD, E.E. (1951), 'Kinship and Marriage among

the Nuer', London: Oxford University Press.
FALDING, HARALD (1971), Explanatory Theory, Analytical
Theory, and the Ideal Type, in Kenneth Thompson and Jeremy
Tunstall (eds), 'Sociological Perspectives', London:
Penguin.
FALLERS, L.A. (1959), Some Determinants of Marriage Sta-
bility in Busoga: A Reformulation of Gluckman's Hypothe-
sis, 'Africa', vol. xxvii, pp. 106-23.
FORTES, MEYER (1945), 'The Dynamics of Clanship Among the
Tallensi', London: Oxford University Press.
FORTES, MEYER (1953), The Structure of Unilineal Descent
Groups, 'American Anthropologist', vol. 55, pp. 17-41.
FORTES, MEYER (1958), Introduction, in J. Goody (ed.),
'The Developmental Cycle in Domestic Groups', Cambridge:
Cambridge University Press.
FORTES, MEYER (1969), 'Kinship and the Social Order',
Chicago: Aldine.
FORTES, MEYER (1970), 'Time and Social Structure and Other
Essays', London: Athlone Press.
GELLNER, ERNEST (1970), Concepts and Society, in B. Wilson
(ed.), 'Rationality', Oxford: Basil Blackwell.
GLUCKMAN, M. (1950), Kinship and Marriage Among the Lozi
of Northern Rhodesia and the Zulu of Natal, in A.R.
Radcliffe-Brown and C.D. Forde (eds), 'African Systems of
Kinship and Marriage', London: Oxford University Press.
GLUCKMAN, M. (1965), 'Politics, Law and Ritual in Tribal
Society', Chicago: Aldine.
GOFFMAN, ERVING (1961), 'Encounters: Two Studies in the
Sociology of Interaction', Indianapolis: Bobbs-Merrill
Company.
GOODENOUGH, WARD H. (1965), Rethinking 'Status' and
'Role': Toward a General Model of the Cultural Organiza-
tion of Social Relationship, in M. Banton (ed.), 'The
Relevance of Models for Social Anthropology', A.S.A. Mono-
graphs I, London: Tavistock Publications.
GREENBERG, J.H. (1957), 'Nilo-Hamitic' and 'Hamito-
Semitic': A Reply, 'Africa', vol. xxvii, pp. 364-78.
GREENBERG, J.H. (1963), 'The Languages of Africa', Bloom-
ington: Indiana University Press.
GULLIVER, PAMELA and GULLIVER, P.H. (1968), 'The Central
Nilo-Hamites', London: International African Institute.
GULLIVER, P.H. (1952), The Karimojong Cluster, 'Africa',
vol. xxii, pp. 1-21.
GULLIVER, P.H. (1953), The Age Organization of the Jie
Tribe, 'Journal of the Royal Anthropological Institute',
vol. lxxxiii, 2, pp. 147-68.
GULLIVER, P.H. (1957), 'The Family Herds', London: Rout-
ledge & Kegan Paul.
GULLIVER, P.H. (1971), 'Neighbors and Networks', Berkeley:

University of California Press.
GULLIVER, P.H. and GRAY, R.F. (eds) (1964), 'The Family
Estate in East Africa', London: Routledge & Kegan Paul.
HOGBIN, H. IAN (1958), 'Social Change', London: E.A.
Watts.
JOHNSTON, SIR HARRY (1902), 'The Uganda Protectorate',
vol. II, London: Hutchinson.
KEESING, ROGER (1971), Descent, Residence and Cultural
Codes, in C. Jayawardena and L. Hiatt (eds), 'Essays in
Oceanic Anthropology', Sydney: Angus & Robertson.
KENYA NATIONAL ARCHIVES, DC/NN/.S/1, 'Character of Chiefs'.
KENYA NATIONAL ARCHIVES, NN/23, Political Record Books.
KIGGEN, REV. FATHER J. (1953a), 'Ateso-English Dictionary',
Ngora: Mill Hill Mission.
KOGGEN, REV. FATHER J. (1953b), 'English-Ateso Dictionary',
Ngora: Mill Hill Mission.
LAWRANCE, J.C.D. (1957), 'The Iteso', London: Oxford
University Press.
LEACH, E.R. (1966), Concerning Trobriand Clans and the Kin
Category 'Tabu', in Jack Goody (ed.), 'The Developmental
Cycle in Domestic Groups', Cambridge: Cambridge University
Press.
LÉVI-STRAUSS, CLAUDE (1953), Social Structure, in A.L.
Kroeber (ed.), 'Anthropology Today', Chicago: University
of Chicago Press.
LÉVI-STRAUSS, CLAUDE (1963), The Structural Study of Myth,
in 'Structural Anthropology', New York: Basic Books.
LONG, NORMAN (1968), 'Social Change and the Individual',
Manchester: Manchester University Press.
MAYER, A.C. (1966), The Significance of Quasi-Groups in
Complex Society, in M. Banton (ed.), 'The Social Anthropo-
logy of Complex Societies', A.S.A. Monographs IV, London,
Tavistock Publications.
MITCHELL, J. CLYDE (1966), Theoretical Orientations in
African Urban Studies, in M. Banton (ed.), 'The Social
Anthropology of Complex Societies', A.S.A. Monographs IV,
London: Tavistock Publications.
MOORE, SALLY FALK (1969), Descent and Legal Position, in
L. Nader (ed.), 'Law in Culture and Society', Chicago:
Aldine.
MOORE, WILBERT (1963), 'Social Change', New York:
Prentice-Hall.
MUNGEAM, G.H. (1966), 'British Rule in Kenya', London:
Oxford University Press.
MURDOCH, J.P. (1949), 'Social Structure', New York:
Macmillan.
NAGASHIMA, N. (1968/9), Historical Relations Among the
Central Nilo-Hamites, 'Sociology Papers', University of
East Africa Social Science Council Conference, Kampala:

Makerere Institute of Social Research.
OGOT, B.A. (1963), British Administration in the Central
Nyanza District of Kenya, 1900-60, 'Journal of African
History', vol. IV, 2, pp. 249-73.
OGOT, B.A. (1967), History of the Southern Luo', Nairobi:
Eastern African Publishing House.
PACKARD, R.S. (unpublished MS), A History of Dispersal
Centers in Eastern Uganda and Western Kenya.
PETERS, CARL (1891), 'New Light on Dark Africa', London:
Ward Lock.
RUEL, M.J. (n.d.), 'Kuria Generation Sets', Kampala: East
African Institute of Social Research.
SAHLINS, MARSHALL (1969), The Segmentary Lineage: An
Organization of Predatory Expansion, in Ronald Cohen and
John Middleton (eds), 'Comparative Political Systems',
New York: Natural History Press.
SCHAPERA, ISAAC (1967), 'Government and Politics in Tribal
Societies', New York: Schocken Books.
SCHNEIDER, DAVID M. (1956),'American Kinship: A Cultural
Account', Englewood Cliffs: Prentice-Hall.
SCOTT, R.M. (1969), Soils, in W.T. Morgan (ed.), 'East
Africa: Its Peoples and Resources', Nairobi: Oxford Uni-
versity Press.
SHUT, REV. FATHER A. (unpublished MS), Ateso-English Word
List.
SOUTHALL, A. (1952), 'Lineage Formation Among the Luo',
Memorandum of the International African Institute.
SOUTHALL, A. (1957), 'Padhola: Comparative Social Struc-
ture', East African Institute of Social Research.
SOUTHWOLD, MARTIN (1971), Meanings of Kinship, in Rodney
Needham (ed.), 'Rethinking Kinship and Marriage', A.S.A.
Monographs XI, London: Tavistock Publications.
SUTTON, JOHN A. (1970), Some Reflections on the Early
History of Kenya, in B.A. Ogot (ed.), 'Hadith 2', Nairobi:
East African Publishing House.
THOMSON, J. (1885), 'Through Masailand', London: Sampson,
Low, Marston, Searle & Rivington.
TURNER, V.W. (1957), 'Schism and Continuity in an African
Society', Manchester: Manchester University Press.
TURPIN, C.A. (1948), The Occupation of the Turkwel River
Area by the Karamojong Tribe, 'Uganda Journal', vol. 12,
pp. 161-5.
VINCENT, J. (1971), 'An African Elite', New York: Columbia
University Press.
VOGT, E.Z. (1960), On the Concepts of Structure and Pro-
cess in Cultural Anthropology, 'American Anthropologist',
vol. LXII, pp. 18-32.
WARD, BARBARA E. (1966), Varieties of the Conscious
Model: The Fishermen of South China, in M. Banton (ed.),

'The Relevance of Models for Social Anthropology', A.S.A. Monographs I, London: Tavistock Publications.

WEBSTER, J.B. et al. (1973), 'The Iteso during the Asonya', Nairobi: East African Publishing House.

WERE, GIDEON (1967a), 'A History of the Abaluyia of Western Kenya', Nairobi: East African Publishing House.

WERE, GIDEON (1967b), 'Western Kenya Historical Texts', Nairobi: East African Literature Bureau.

WILSON, JOHN (1970), Preliminary Observations on the Oropom People of Karamoja, 'Uganda Journal', vol. 34, part 2, pp. 125-47.

WINTER, E.H. (n.d.), 'Bwamba Economy', Kampala: East African Institute of Social Research.

WINTER, E.H. (1956), 'Bwamba: A Structural-Functional Analysis of a Patrilineal Society', Cambridge: Heffer & Sons.

WRIGHT, A.C.A. (1942), Notes on Iteso Social Organization, 'Uganda Journal', vol. 9, pp. 57-80.

WRIGHT, A.C.A. (1958), A Review of J.C.D. Lawrance's 'The Iteso', 'Uganda Journal', vol. 22, pp. 89-91.

Index

Routledge Social Science Series

Routledge & Kegan Paul London, Henley and Boston

39 Store Street, London WC1E 7DD
Broadway House, Newtown Road, Henley-on-Thames,
Oxon RG9 1EN
9 Park Street, Boston, Mass. 02108

Contents

*Authors wishing to submit manuscripts for any series in
this catalogue should send them to the Social Science Editor,
Routledge & Kegan Paul Ltd, 39 Store Street,
London WC1E 7DD*

● *Books so marked are available in paperback
All books are in Metric Demy 8vo format (216 × 138mm approx.)*

International Library of Sociology

General Editor John Rex

GENERAL SOCIOLOGY

Barnsley, J. H. The Social Reality of Ethics. *464 pp.*

Belshaw, Cyril. The Conditions of Social Performance. *An Exploratory Theory. 144 pp.*

Brown, Robert. Explanation in Social Science. *208 pp.*

● Rules and Laws in Sociology. *192 pp.*

Bruford, W. H. Chekhov and His Russia. *A Sociological Study. 244 pp.*

Cain, Maureen E. Society and the Policeman's Role. *326 pp.*

●**Fletcher, Colin.** Beneath the Surface. *An Account of Three Styles of Sociological Research. 221 pp.*

Gibson, Quentin. The Logic of Social Enquiry. *240 pp.*

Glucksmann, M. Structuralist Analysis in Contemporary Social Thought. *212 pp.*

Gurvitch, Georges. Sociology of Law. *Preface by Roscoe Pound. 264 pp.*

Hodge, H. A. Wilhelm Dilthey. *An Introduction. 184 pp.*

Homans, George C. Sentiments and Activities. *336 pp.*

Johnson, Harry M. Sociology: *a Systematic Introduction. Foreword by Robert K. Merton. 710 pp.*

●**Keat, Russell,** and **Urry, John.** Social Theory as Science. *278 pp.*

Mannheim, Karl. Essays on Sociology and Social Psychology. *Edited by Paul Keckskemeti. With Editorial Note by Adolph Lowe. 344 pp.*

Systematic Sociology: *An Introduction to the Study of Society. Edited by J. S. Erös and Professor W. A. C. Stewart. 220 pp.*

Martindale, Don. The Nature and Types of Sociological Theory. *292 pp.*

●**Maus, Heinz.** A Short History of Sociology. *234 pp.*

Mey, Harald. Field-Theory. *A Study of its Application in the Social Sciences. 352 pp.*

Myrdal, Gunnar. Value in Social Theory: *A Collection of Essays on Methodology. Edited by Paul Streeten. 332 pp.*

Ogburn, William F., and **Nimkoff, Meyer F.** A Handbook of Sociology. *Preface by Karl Mannheim. 656 pp. 46 figures. 35 tables.*

Parsons, Talcott, and **Smelser, Neil J.** Economy and Society: *A Study in the Integration of Economic and Social Theory. 362 pp.*

Podgórecki, Adam. Practical Social Sciences. *About 200 pp.*

●**Rex, John.** Key Problems of Sociological Theory. *220 pp.*

Sociology and the Demystification of the Modern World. *282 pp.*

●**Rex, John** (Ed.) Approaches to Sociology. *Contributions by Peter Abell, Frank Bechhofer, Basil Bernstein, Ronald Fletcher, David Frisby, Miriam Glucksmann, Peter Lassman, Herminio Martins, John Rex, Roland Robertson, John Westergaard and Jock Young. 302 pp.*

Rigby, A. Alternative Realities. *352 pp.*

Roche, M. Phenomenology, Language and the Social Sciences. *374 pp.*

Sahay, A. Sociological Analysis. *220 pp.*
Simirenko, Alex (Ed.) Soviet Sociology. *Historical Antecedents and Current Appraisals. Introduction by Alex Simirenko. 376 pp.*
Strasser, Hermann. The Normative Structure of Sociology. *Conservative and Emancipatory Themes in Social Thought. About 340 pp.*
Urry, John. Reference Groups and the Theory of Revolution. *244 pp.*
Weinberg, E. Development of Sociology in the Soviet Union. *173 pp.*

FOREIGN CLASSICS OF SOCIOLOGY

●**Durkheim, Emile.** Suicide. *A Study in Sociology. Edited and with an Introduction by George Simpson. 404 pp.*
●**Gerth, H. H.,** and **Mills, C. Wright.** From Max Weber: *Essays in Sociology. 502 pp.*
●**Tönnies, Ferdinand.** Community and Association. (*Gemeinschaft und Gesellschaft.*) *Translated and Supplemented by Charles P. Loomis. Foreword by Pitirim A. Sorokin. 334 pp.*

SOCIAL STRUCTURE

Andreski, Stanislav. Military Organization and Society. *Foreword by Professor A. R. Radcliffe-Brown. 226 pp. 1 folder.*
Carlton, Eric. Ideology and Social Order. *Preface by Professor Philip Abrahams. About 320 pp.*
Coontz, Sydney H. Population Theories and the Economic Interpretation. *202 pp.*
Coser, Lewis. The Functions of Social Conflict. *204 pp.*
Dickie-Clark, H. F. Marginal Situation: *A Sociological Study of a Coloured Group. 240 pp. 11 tables.*
Glaser, Barney, and **Strauss, Anselm L.** Status Passage. *A Formal Theory. 208 pp.*
Glass, D. V. (Ed.) Social Mobility in Britain. *Contributions by J. Berent, T. Bottomore, R. C. Chambers, J. Floud, D. V. Glass, J. R. Hall, H. T. Himmelweit, R. K. Kelsall, F. M. Martin, C. A. Moser, R. Mukherjee, and W. Ziegel. 420 pp.*
Johnstone, Frederick A. Class, Race and Gold. *A Study of Class Relations and Racial Discrimination in South Africa. 312 pp.*
Jones, Garth N. Planned Organizational Change: *An Exploratory Study Using an Empirical Approach. 268 pp.*
Kelsall, R. K. Higher Civil Servants in Britain: *From 1870 to the Present Day. 268 pp. 31 tables.*
König, René. The Community. *232 pp. Illustrated.*
●**Lawton, Denis.** Social Class, Language and Education. *192 pp.*
McLeish, John. The Theory of Social Change: *Four Views Considered. 128 pp.*
Marsh, David C. The Changing Social Structure of England and Wales, 1871-1961. *288 pp.*
Menzies, Ken. Talcott Parsons and the Social Image of Man. *About 208 pp.*

●**Mouzelis, Nicos.** Organization and Bureaucracy. *An Analysis of Modern Theories. 240 pp.*

Mulkay, M. J. Functionalism, Exchange and Theoretical Strategy. *272 pp.*

Ossowski, Stanislaw. Class Structure in the Social Consciousness. *210 pp.*

●**Podgórecki, Adam.** Law and Society. *302 pp.*

Renner, Karl. Institutions of Private Law and Their Social Functions. *Edited, with an Introduction and Notes, by O. Kahn-Freud. Translated by Agnes Schwarzschild. 316 pp.*

SOCIOLOGY AND POLITICS

Acton, T. A. Gypsy Politics and Social Change. *316 pp.*

Clegg, Stuart. Power, Rule and Domination. *A Critical and Empirical Understanding of Power in Sociological Theory and Organisational Life. About 300 pp.*

Hechter, Michael. Internal Colonialism. *The Celtic Fringe in British National Development, 1536–1966. 361 pp.*

Hertz, Frederick. Nationality in History and Politics: *A Psychology and Sociology of National Sentiment and Nationalism. 432 pp.*

Kornhauser, William. The Politics of Mass Society. *272 pp. 20 tables.*

●**Kroes, R.** Soldiers and Students. *A Study of Right- and Left-wing Students. 174 pp.*

Laidler, Harry W. History of Socialism. *Social-Economic Movements: An Historical and Comparative Survey of Socialism, Communism, Co-operation, Utopianism; and other Systems of Reform and Reconstruction. 992 pp.*

Lasswell, H. D. Analysis of Political Behaviour. *324 pp.*

Martin, David A. Pacifism: *an Historical and Sociological Study. 262 pp.*

Martin, Roderick. Sociology of Power. *About 272 pp.*

Myrdal, Gunnar. The Political Element in the Development of Economic Theory. *Translated from the German by Paul Streeten. 282 pp.*

Wilson, H. T. The American Ideology. *Science, Technology and Organization of Modes of Rationality. About 280 pp.*

Wootton, Graham. Workers, Unions and the State. *188 pp.*

CRIMINOLOGY

Ancel, Marc. Social Defence: *A Modern Approach to Criminal Problems. Foreword by Leon Radzinowicz. 240 pp.*

Cain, Maureen E. Society and the Policeman's Role. *326 pp.*

Cloward, Richard A., and **Ohlin, Lloyd E.** Delinquency and Opportunity: *A Theory of Delinquent Gangs. 248 pp.*

Downes, David M. The Delinquent Solution. *A Study in Subcultural Theory. 296 pp.*

Dunlop, A. B., and **McCabe, S.** Young Men in Detention Centres. *192 pp.*

Friedlander, Kate. The Psycho-Analytical Approach to Juvenile Delinquency: *Theory, Case Studies, Treatment. 320 pp.*

Glueck, Sheldon, and **Eleanor.** Family Environment and Delinquency. *With the statistical assistance of Rose W. Kneznek. 340 pp.*

Lopez-Rey, Manuel. Crime. *An Analytical Appraisal. 288 pp.*

Mannheim, Hermann. Comparative Criminology: *a Text Book. Two volumes. 442 pp. and 380 pp.*

Morris, Terence. The Criminal Area: *A Study in Social Ecology. Foreword by Hermann Mannheim. 232 pp. 25 tables. 4 maps.*

Rock, Paul. Making People Pay. *338 pp.*

● **Taylor, Ian, Walton, Paul,** and **Young, Jock.** The New Criminology. *For a Social Theory of Deviance. 325 pp.*

● **Taylor, Ian, Walton, Paul,** and **Young, Jock** (Eds). Critical Criminology. *268 pp.*

SOCIAL PSYCHOLOGY

Bagley, Christopher. The Social Psychology of the Epileptic Child. *320 pp.*

Barbu, Zevedei. Problems of Historical Psychology. *248 pp.*

Blackburn, Julian. Psychology and the Social Pattern. *184 pp.*

● **Brittan, Arthur.** Meanings and Situations. *224 pp.*

Carroll, J. Break-Out from the Crystal Palace. *200 pp.*

● **Fleming, C. M.** Adolescence: Its Social Psychology. *With an Introduction to recent findings from the fields of Anthropology, Physiology, Medicine, Psychometrics and Sociometry. 288 pp.*

● The Social Psychology of Education: *An Introduction and Guide to Its Study. 136 pp.*

● **Homans, George C.** The Human Group. *Foreword by Bernard DeVoto. Introduction by Robert K. Merton. 526 pp.*

● Social Behaviour: *its Elementary Forms. 416 pp.*

● **Klein, Josephine.** The Study of Groups. *226 pp. 31 figures. 5 tables.*

Linton, Ralph. The Cultural Background of Personality. *132 pp.*

● **Mayo, Elton.** The Social Problems of an Industrial Civilization. *With an appendix on the Political Problem. 180 pp.*

Ottaway, A. K. C. Learning Through Group Experience. *176 pp.*

Plummer, Ken. Sexual Stigma. *An Interactionist Account. 254 pp.*

● **Rose, Arnold M.** (Ed.) Human Behaviour and Social Processes: *an Interactionist Approach. Contributions by Arnold M. Rose, Ralph H. Turner, Anselm Strauss, Everett C. Hughes, E. Franklin Frazier, Howard S. Becker, et al. 696 pp.*

Smelser, Neil J. Theory of Collective Behaviour. *448 pp.*

Stephenson, Geoffrey M. The Development of Conscience. *128 pp.*

Young, Kimball. Handbook of Social Psychology. *658 pp. 16 figures. 10 tables.*

SOCIOLOGY OF THE FAMILY

Banks, J. A. Prosperity and Parenthood: *A Study of Family Planning among The Victorian Middle Classes. 262 pp.*

Bell, Colin R. Middle Class Families: *Social and Geographical Mobility. 224 pp.*

Burton, Lindy. Vulnerable Children. *272 pp.*

Gavron, Hannah. The Captive Wife: *Conflicts of Household Mothers.* *190 pp.*

George, Victor, and **Wilding, Paul.** Motherless Families. *248 pp.*

Klein, Josephine. Samples from English Cultures.
　1. Three Preliminary Studies and Aspects of Adult Life in England. *447 pp.*
　2. Child-Rearing Practices and Index. *247 pp.*

Klein, Viola. The Feminine Character. *History of an Ideology. 244 pp.*

McWhinnie, Alexina M. Adopted Children. *How They Grow Up. 304 pp.*

Morgan, D. H. J. Social Theory and the Family. *About 320 pp.*

Myrdal, Alva, and **Klein, Viola.** Women's Two Roles: *Home and Work.* *238 pp. 27 tables.*

Parsons, Talcott, and **Bales, Robert F.** Family: Socialization and Inter-action Process. *In collaboration with James Olds, Morris Zelditch and Philip E. Slater. 456 pp. 50 figures and tables.*

SOCIAL SERVICES

Bastide, Roger. The Sociology of Mental Disorder. *Translated from the French by Jean McNeil. 260 pp.*

Carlebach, Julius. Caring For Children in Trouble. *266 pp.*

George, Victor. Foster Care. *Theory and Practice. 234 pp.*
　Social Security: *Beveridge and After. 258 pp.*

George, V., and **Wilding, P.** Motherless Families. *248 pp.*

● **Goetschius, George W.** Working with Community Groups. *256 pp.*

Goetschius, George W., and **Tash, Joan.** Working with Unattached Youth. *416 pp.*

Hall, M. P., and **Howes, I. V.** The Church in Social Work. *A Study of Moral Welfare Work undertaken by the Church of England. 320 pp.*

Heywood, Jean S. Children in Care: *the Development of the Service for the Deprived Child. 264 pp.*

Hoenig, J., and **Hamilton, Marian W.** The De-Segregation of the Mentally Ill. *284 pp.*

Jones, Kathleen. Mental Health and Social Policy, 1845-1959. *264 pp.*

King, Roy D., Raynes, Norma V., and **Tizard, Jack.** Patterns of Residential Care. *356 pp.*

Leigh, John. Young People and Leisure. *256 pp.*

● **Mays, John.** (Ed.) Penelope Hall's Social Services of England and Wales. *About 324 pp.*

Morris, Mary. Voluntary Work and the Welfare State. *300 pp.*

Nokes, P. L. The Professional Task in Welfare Practice. *152 pp.*

Timms, Noel. Psychiatric Social Work in Great Britain (1939-1962). *280 pp.*
　Social Casework: *Principles and Practice. 256 pp.*

Young, A. F. Social Services in British Industry. *272 pp.*

SOCIOLOGY OF EDUCATION

Banks, Olive. Parity and Prestige in English Secondary Education: a Study in Educational Sociology. *272 pp.*

Bentwich, Joseph. Education in Israel. *224 pp. 8 pp. plates.*

●**Blyth, W. A. L.** English Primary Education. *A Sociological Description.*
1. Schools. *232 pp.*
2. Background. *168 pp.*

Collier, K. G. The Social Purposes of Education: *Personal and Social Values in Education. 268 pp.*

Dale, R. R., and **Griffith, S.** Down Stream: *Failure in the Grammar School. 108 pp.*

Evans, K. M. Sociometry and Education. *158 pp.*

●**Ford, Julienne.** Social Class and the Comprehensive School. *192 pp.*

Foster, P. J. Education and Social Change in Ghana. *336 pp. 3 maps.*

Fraser, W. R. Education and Society in Modern France. *150 pp.*

Grace, Gerald R. Role Conflict and the Teacher. *150 pp.*

Hans, Nicholas. New Trends in Education in the Eighteenth Century. *278 pp. 19 tables.*

● Comparative Education: *A Study of Educational Factors and Traditions. 360 pp.*

●**Hargreaves, David.** Interpersonal Relations and Education. *432 pp.*

● Social Relations in a Secondary School. *240 pp.*

Holmes, Brian. Problems in Education. *A Comparative Approach. 336 pp.*

King, Ronald. Values and Involvement in a Grammar School. *164 pp.*

School Organization and Pupil Involvement. *A Study of Secondary Schools.*

●**Mannheim, Karl,** and **Stewart, W. A. C.** An Introduction to the Sociology of Education. *206 pp.*

Morris, Raymond N. The Sixth Form and College Entrance. *231 pp.*

●**Musgrove, F.** Youth and the Social Order. *176 pp.*

●**Ottaway, A. K. C.** Education and Society: An Introduction to the Sociology of Education. *With an Introduction by W. O. Lester Smith. 212 pp.*

Peers, Robert. Adult Education: *A Comparative Study. 398 pp.*

Pritchard, D. G. Education and the Handicapped: *1760 to 1960. 258 pp.*

Stratta, Erica. The Education of Borstal Boys. *A Study of their Educational Experiences prior to, and during, Borstal Training. 256 pp.*

Taylor, P. H., Reid, W. A., and **Holley, B. J.** The English Sixth Form. *A Case Study in Curriculum Research. 200 pp.*

SOCIOLOGY OF CULTURE

Eppel, E. M., and **M.** Adolescents and Morality: *A Study of some Moral Values and Dilemmas of Working Adolescents in the Context of a changing Climate of Opinion. Foreword by W. J. H. Sprott. 268 pp. 39 tables.*

●**Fromm, Erich.** The Fear of Freedom. *286 pp.*

● The Sane Society. *400 pp.*

Mannheim, Karl. Essays on the Sociology of Culture. *Edited by Ernst Mannheim in co-operation with Paul Kecskemeti. Editorial Note by Adolph Lowe. 280 pp.*

Weber, Alfred. Farewell to European History: *or The Conquest of Nihilism. Translated from the German by R. F. C. Hull. 224 pp.*

SOCIOLOGY OF RELIGION

Argyle, Michael and Beit-Hallahmi, Benjamin. The Social Psychology of Religion. *About 256 pp.*

Glasner, Peter E. The Sociology of Secularisation. *A Critique of a Concept. About 180 pp.*

Nelson, G. K. Spiritualism and Society. *313 pp.*

Stark, Werner. The Sociology of Religion. *A Study of Christendom.*
  Volume I. *Established Religion. 248 pp.*
  Volume II. *Sectarian Religion. 368 pp.*
  Volume III. *The Universal Church. 464 pp.*
  Volume IV. *Types of Religious Man. 352 pp.*
  Volume V. *Types of Religious Culture. 464 pp.*

Turner, B. S. Weber and Islam. *216 pp.*

Watt, W. Montgomery. Islam and the Integration of Society. *320 pp.*

SOCIOLOGY OF ART AND LITERATURE

Jarvie, Ian C. Towards a Sociology of the Cinema. *A Comparative Essay on the Structure and Functioning of a Major Entertainment Industry. 405 pp.*

Rust, Frances S. Dance in Society. *An Analysis of the Relationships between the Social Dance and Society in England from the Middle Ages to the Present Day. 256 pp. 8 pp. of plates.*

Schücking, L. L. The Sociology of Literary Taste. *112 pp.*

Wolff, Janet. Hermeneutic Philosophy and the Sociology of Art. *150 pp.*

SOCIOLOGY OF KNOWLEDGE

Diesing, P. Patterns of Discovery in the Social Sciences. *262 pp.*

●Douglas, J. D. (Ed.) Understanding Everyday Life. *370 pp.*

●Hamilton, P. Knowledge and Social Structure. *174 pp.*

Jarvie, I. C. Concepts and Society. *232 pp.*

Mannheim, Karl. Essays on the Sociology of Knowledge. *Edited by Paul Kecskemeti. Editorial Note by Adolph Lowe. 353 pp.*

Remmling, Gunter W. The Sociology cf Karl Mannheim. *With a Bibliographical Guide to the Sociology of Knowledge, Ideological Analysis, and Social Planning. 255 pp.*

Remmling, Gunter W. (Ed.) Towards the Sociology of Knowledge. *Origin and Development of a Sociological Thought Style. 463 pp.*

Stark, Werner. The Sociology of Knowledge: *An Essay in Aid of a Deeper Understanding of the History of Ideas. 384 pp.*

URBAN SOCIOLOGY

Ashworth, William. The Genesis of Modern British Town Planning: *A Study in Economic and Social History of the Nineteenth and Twentieth Centuries. 288 pp.*

Cullingworth, J. B. Housing Needs and Planning Policy: *A Restatement of the Problems of Housing Need and 'Overspill' in England and Wales. 232 pp. 44 tables. 8 maps.*

Dickinson, Robert E. City and Region: *A Geographical Interpretation 608 pp. 125 figures.*

The West European City: *A Geographical Interpretation. 600 pp. 129 maps. 29 plates.*

● The City Region in Western Europe. *320 pp. Maps.*

Humphreys, Alexander J. New Dubliners: *Urbanization and the Irish Family. Foreword by George C. Homans. 304 pp.*

Jackson, Brian. Working Class Community: *Some General Notions raised by a Series of Studies in Northern England. 192 pp.*

Jennings, Hilda. Societies in the Making: *a Study of Development and Redevelopment within a County Borough. Foreword by D. A. Clark. 286 pp.*

●**Mann, P. H.** An Approach to Urban Sociology. *240 pp.*

Morris, R. N., and **Mogey, J.** The Sociology of Housing. *Studies at Berinsfield. 232 pp. 4 pp. plates.*

Rosser, C., and **Harris, C.** The Family and Social Change. *A Study of Family and Kinship in a South Wales Town. 352 pp. 8 maps.*

●**Stacey, Margaret, Batsone, Eric, Bell, Colin,** and **Thurcott, Anne.** Power, Persistence and Change. *A Second Study of Banbury. 196 pp.*

RURAL SOCIOLOGY

Haswell, M. R. The Economics of Development in Village India. *120 pp.*

Littlejohn, James. Westrigg: *the Sociology of a Cheviot Parish. 172 pp. 5 figures.*

Mayer, Adrian C. Peasants in the Pacific. *A Study of Fiji Indian Rural Society. 248 pp. 20 plates.*

Williams, W. M. The Sociology of an English Village: *Gosforth. 272 pp. 12 figures. 13 tables.*

SOCIOLOGY OF INDUSTRY AND DISTRIBUTION

Anderson, Nels. Work and Leisure. *280 pp.*

●Blau, Peter M., and Scott, W. Richard. Formal Organizations: *a Comparative approach. Introduction and Additional Bibliography by J. H. Smith.* 326 pp.

Dunkerley, David. The Foreman. *Aspects of Task and Structure. 192 pp.*

Eldridge, J. E. T. Industrial Disputes. *Essays in the Sociology of Industrial Relations. 288 pp.*

Hetzler, Stanley. Applied Measures for Promoting Technological Growth. *352 pp.*

Technological Growth and Social Change. *Achieving Modernization. 269 pp.*

Hollowell, Peter G. The Lorry Driver. *272 pp.*

●Oxaal, I., Barnett, T., and Booth, D. (Eds). Beyond the Sociology of Development. *Economy and Society in Latin America and Africa.* 295 pp.

Smelser, Neil J. Social Change in the Industrial Revolution: *An Application of Theory to the Lancashire Cotton Industry, 1770–1840. 468 pp. 12 figures. 14 tables.*

ANTHROPOLOGY

Ammar, Hamed. Growing up in an Egyptian Village: *Silwa, Province of Aswan. 336 pp.*

Brandel-Syrier, Mia. Reeftown Elite. *A Study of Social Mobility in a Modern African Community on the Reef. 376 pp.*

Dickie-Clark, H. F. The Marginal Situation. *A Sociological Study of a Coloured Group. 236 pp.*

Dube, S. C. Indian Village. *Foreword by Morris Edward Opler. 276 pp. 4 plates.*

India's Changing Villages: *Human Factors in Community Development. 260 pp. 8 plates. 1 map.*

Firth, Raymond. Malay Fishermen. *Their Peasant Economy. 420 pp. 17 pp. plates.*

Gulliver, P. H. Social Control in an African Society: a Study of the Arusha, Agricultural Masai of Northern Tanganyika. *320 pp. 8 plates. 10 figures.*

Family Herds. *288 pp.*

Ishwaran, K. Tradition and Economy in Village India: *An Interactionist Approach.*
Foreword by Conrad Arensburg. 176 pp.

Jarvie, Ian C. The Revolution in Anthropology. *268 pp.*

Little, Kenneth L. Mende of Sierra Leone. *308 pp. and folder.*

Negroes in Britain. *With a New Introduction and Contemporary Study by Leonard Bloom. 320 pp.*

Lowie, Robert H. Social Organization. *494 pp.*

Mayer, A. C. Peasants in the Pacific. *A Study of Fiji Indian Rural Society.* 248 pp.

Meer, Fatima. Race and Suicide in South Africa. *325 pp.*

Smith, Raymond T. The Negro Family in British Guiana: *Family Structure and Social Status in the Villages. With a Foreword by Meyer Fortes. 314 pp. 8 plates. 1 figure. 4 maps.*

Smooha, Sammy. Israel: Pluralism and Conflict. *About 320 pp.*

SOCIOLOGY AND PHILOSOPHY

Barnsley, John H. The Social Reality of Ethics. *A Comparative Analysis of Moral Codes. 448 pp.*

Diesing, Paul. Patterns of Discovery in the Social Sciences. *362 pp.*

●**Douglas, Jack D.** (Ed.) Understanding Everyday Life. *Toward the Reconstruction of Sociological Knowledge. Contributions by Alan F. Blum, Aaron W. Cicourel, Norman K. Denzin, Jack D. Douglas, John Heeren, Peter McHugh, Peter K. Manning, Melvin Power, Matthew Speier, Roy Turner, D. Lawrence Wieder, Thomas P. Wilson and Don H. Zimmerman. 370 pp.*

Gorman, Robert A. The Dual Vision. *Alfred Schutz and the Myth of Phenomenological Social Science. About 300 pp.*

Jarvie, Ian C. Concepts and Society. *216 pp.*

●**Pelz, Werner.** The Scope of Understanding in Sociology. *Towards a more radical reorientation in the social humanistic sciences. 283 pp.*

Roche, Maurice. Phenomenology, Language and the Social Sciences. *371 pp.*

Sahay, Arun. Sociological Analysis. *212 pp.*

Sklair, Leslie. The Sociology of Progress. *320 pp.*

Slater, P. Origin and Significance of the Frankfurt School. *A Marxist Perspective. About 192 pp.*

Smart, Barry. Sociology, Phenomenology and Marxian Analysis. *A Critical Discussion of the Theory and Practice of a Science of Society. 220 pp.*

International Library of Anthropology

General Editor Adam Kuper

Ahmed, A. S. Millenium and Charisma Among Pathans. *A Critical Essay in Social Anthropology. 192 pp.*

Brown, Paula. The Chimbu. *A Study of Change in the New Guinea Highlands. 151 pp.*

Gudeman, Stephen. Relationships, Residence and the Individual. *A Rural Panamanian Community. 288 pp. 11 Plates, 5 Figures, 2 Maps, 10 Tables.*

Hamnett, Ian. Chieftainship and Legitimacy. *An Anthropological Study of Executive Law in Lesotho. 163 pp.*

Hanson, F. Allan. Meaning in Culture. *127 pp.*

Lloyd, P. C. Power and Independence. *Urban Africans' Perception of Social Inequality. 264 pp.*

Pettigrew, Joyce. Robber Noblemen. *A Study of the Political System of the Sikh Jats. 284 pp.*

Street, Brian V. The Savage in Literature. *Representations of 'Primitive' Society in English Fiction, 1858–1920. 207 pp.*

Van Den Berghe, Pierre L. Power and Privilege at an African University. *278 pp.*

International Library of Social Policy

General Editor Kathleen Jones

Bayley, M. Mental Handicap and Community Care. *426 pp.*

Bottoms, A. E., and **McClean, J. D.** Defendants in the Criminal Process. *284 pp.*

Butler, J. R. Family Doctors and Public Policy. *208 pp.*

Davies, Martin. Prisoners of Society. *Attitudes and Aftercare. 204 pp.*

Gittus, Elizabeth. Flats, Families and the Under-Fives. *285 pp.*

Holman, Robert. Trading in Children. *A Study of Private Fostering. 355 pp.*

Jones, Howard, and **Cornes, Paul.** Open Prisons. *About 248 pp.*

Jones, Kathleen. History of the Mental Health Service. *428 pp.*

Jones, Kathleen, with **Brown, John, Cunningham, W. J., Roberts, Julian,** and **Williams, Peter.** Opening the Door. *A Study of New Policies for the Mentally Handicapped. 278 pp.*

Karn, Valerie. Retiring to the Seaside. *About 280 pp. 2 maps. Numerous tables.*

Thomas, J. E. The English Prison Officer since 1850: *A Study in Conflict. 258 pp.*

Walton, R. G. Women in Social Work. *303 pp.*

Woodward, J. To Do the Sick No Harm. *A Study of the British Voluntary Hospital System to 1875. 221 pp.*

International Library of Welfare and Philosophy

General Editors Noel Timms and David Watson

● **Plant, Raymond.** Community and Ideology. *104 pp.*

● **McDermott, F. E.** (Ed.) Self-Determination in Social Work. *A Collection of Essays on Self-determination and Related Concepts by Philosophers and Social Work Theorists. Contributors: F. P. Biestek, S. Bernstein, A. Keith-Lucas, D. Sayer, H. H. Perelman, C. Whittington, R. F. Stalley, F. E. McDermott, I. Berlin, H. J. McCloskey, H. L. A. Hart, J. Wilson, A. I. Melden, S. I. Benn. 254 pp.*

Ragg, Nicholas M. People Not Cases. *A Philosophical Approach to Social Work. About 250 pp.*

● **Timms, Noel,** and **Watson, David** (Eds). Talking About Welfare. *Readings in Philosophy and Social Policy. Contributors: T. H. Marshall, R. B. Brandt, G. H. von Wright, K. Nielsen, M. Cranston, R. M. Titmuss, R. S. Downie, E. Telfer, D. Donnison, J. Benson, P. Leonard, A. Keith-Lucas, D. Walsh, I. T. Ramsey. 320 pp.*

Primary Socialization, Language and Education

General Editor Basil Bernstein

Adlam, Diana S., *with the assistance of Geoffrey Turner and Lesley Lineker.* Code in Context. *About 272 pp.*

Bernstein, Basil. Class, Codes and Control. *3 volumes.*
   1. *Theoretical Studies Towards a Sociology of Language. 254 pp.*
   2. *Applied Studies Towards a Sociology of Language. 377 pp.*
● 3. *Towards a Theory of Educatiomal Transmission. 167 pp.*

Brandis, W., and **Bernstein, B.** Selection and Control. *176 pp.*

Brandis, Walter, and **Henderson, Dorothy.** Social Class, Language and Communication. *288 pp.*

Cook-Gumperz, Jenny. Social Control and Socialization. *A Study of Class Differences in the Language of Maternal Control. 290 pp.*

● **Gahagan, D. M.**, and **G. A.** Talk Reform. *Exploration in Language for Infant School Children. 160 pp.*

Hawkins, P. R. Social Class, the Nominal Group and Verbal Strategies. *About 220 pp.*

Robinson, W. P., and **Rackstraw, Susan D. A.** A Question of Answers. *2 volumes. 192 pp. and 180 pp.*

Turner, Geoffrey J., and **Mohan, Bernard A.** A Linguistic Description and Computer Programme for Children's Speech. *208 pp.*

Reports of the Institute of Community Studies

● **Cartwright, Ann.** Parents and Family Planning Services. *306 pp.*
   Patients and their Doctors. *A Study of General Practice. 304 pp.*

Dench, Geoff. Maltese in London. *A Case-study in the Erosion of Ethnic Consciousness. 302 pp.*

● **Jackson, Brian.** Streaming: *an Education System in Miniature. 168 pp.*

Jackson, Brian, and **Marsden, Dennis.** Education and the Working Class: *Some General Themes raised by a Study of 88 Working-class Children in a Northern Industrial City. 268 pp. 2 folders.*

Marris, Peter. The Experience of Higher Education. *232 pp. 27 tables.*
   Loss and Change. *192 pp.*

Marris, Peter, and **Rein, Martin.** Dilemmas of Social Reform. *Poverty and Community Action in the United States. 256 pp.*

Marris, Peter, and Somerset, Anthony. African Businessmen. *A Study of Entrepreneurship and Development in Kenya. 256 pp.*

Mills, Richard. Young Outsiders: *a Study in Alternative Communities. 216 pp.*

Runciman, W. G. Relative Deprivation and Social Justice. *A Study of Attitudes to Social Inequality in Twentieth-Century England. 352 pp.*

Willmott, Peter. Adolescent Boys in East London. *230 pp.*

Willmott, Peter, and Young, Michael. Family and Class in a London Suburb. *202 pp. 47 tables.*

Young, Michael. Innovation and Research in Education. *192 pp.*

●Young, Michael, and McGeeney, Patrick. Learning Begins at Home. *A Study of a Junior School and its Parents. 128 pp.*

Young, Michael, and Willmott, Peter. Family and Kinship in East London. *Foreword by Richard M. Titmuss. 252 pp. 39 tables.*

The Symmetrical Family. *410 pp.*

Reports of the Institute for Social Studies in Medical Care

Cartwright, Ann, Hockey, Lisbeth, and Anderson, John L. Life Before Death. *310 pp.*

Dunnell, Karen, and Cartwright, Ann. Medicine Takers, Prescribers and Hoarders. *190 pp.*

Medicine, Illness and Society

General Editor W. M. Williams

Robinson, David. The Process of Becoming Ill. *142 pp.*

Stacey, Margaret, *et al.* Hospitals, Children and Their Families. *The Report of a Pilot Study. 202 pp.*

Stimson, G. V., and Webb, B. Going to See the Doctor. *The Consultation Process in General Practice. 155 pp.*

Monographs in Social Theory

General Editor Arthur Brittan

●Barnes, B. Scientific Knowledge and Sociological Theory. *192 pp.*

Bauman, Zygmunt. Culture as Praxis. *204 pp.*

●Dixon, Keith. Sociological Theory. *Pretence and Possibility. 142 pp.*

Meltzer, B. N., Petras, J. W., and Reynolds, L. T. Symbolic Interactionism. *Genesis, Varieties and Criticisms. 144 pp.*

●Smith, Anthony D. The Concept of Social Change. *A Critique of the Functionalist Theory of Social Change. 208 pp.*

Routledge Social Science Journals

The British Journal of Sociology. *Editor – Angus Stewart; Associate Editor – Leslie Sklair. Vol. 1, No. 1 – March 1950 and Quarterly. Roy. 8vo. All back issues available. An international journal publishing original papers in the field of sociology and related areas.*
Community Work. *Edited by David Jones and Marjorie Mayo. 1973. Published annually.*
Economy and Society. *Vol. 1, No. 1. February 1972 and Quarterly. Metric Roy. 8vo. A journal for all social scientists covering sociology, philosophy, anthropology, economics and history. All back numbers available.*
Religion. Journal of Religion and Religions. *Chairman of Editorial Board, Ninian Smart. Vol. 1, No. 1, Spring 1971. A journal with an inter-disciplinary approach to the study of the phenomena of religion. All back numbers available.*
Year Book of Social Policy in Britain, The. *Edited by Kathleen Jones. 1971. Published annually.*

Social and Psychological Aspects of Medical Practice

Editor Trevor Silverstone

Lader, Malcolm. Psychophysiology of Mental Illness. *280 pp.*
● **Silverstone, Trevor,** and **Turner, Paul.** Drug Treatment in Psychiatry. *232 pp.*

Printed in Great Britain by
Lowe & Brydone Printers Limited, Thetford, Norfolk